THE PASSION AND RESURRECTION OF JESUS CHRIST

THE PASSION
AND RESURRECTION
OF JESUS CHRIST

PIERRE BENOIT, O.P.

Director of the Ecole Biblique et Archéologique Française,
Jerusalem

Translated by
BENET WEATHERHEAD

———◦◦◦———

New York
Herder and Herder
London
Darton, Longman and Todd

DARTON, LONGMAN & TODD LTD
64 Chiswick High Road, London W.4

HERDER & HERDER INC.
232 Madison Avenue, New York 10016

A Translation of
PASSION ET RESURRECTION DU SEIGNEUR
published by Les Editions du Cerf, Paris

Library of Congress Catalog Card No. 75-87748
SBN 232 48110 5

Printed in Great Britain by Western Printing
Services Ltd, Bristol. Nihil obstat: Nicholas
Tranter, S.T.L. Imprimatur: ✠ Patrick Casey,
Vic. Gen., Westminster, 14th May 1969. The
Nihil obstat and Imprimatur are a declaration
that a book or pamphlet is considered to be
free from doctrinal or moral error. It is not
implied that those who have granted the Nihil
obstat and the Imprimatur agree with the
contents, opinions or statements expressed.

CONTENTS

Note In the tables of parallel passages preceding each chapter, vertical
lines alongside certain passages indicate that they are displaced, i.e.,
that they do not, like the rest, follow the normal sequence of the
gospel; horizontal lines indicate that a portion of the text has been
omitted. The English version of the scriptures used is that of the
Jerusalem Bible; any exceptions to this, either in the synopses or in
the text, are noted by an asterisk.

INTRODUCTION

This work is the outcome of addresses given on several occasions to various audiences. I have intentionally retained the direct, and even intimate, style of an exposition that was originally improvised in simple and straightforward language. I have also avoided all technical language so that it may be easily understood by non-specialist readers. At the same time, this is not a devotional work. From time to time I have allowed myself to develop a spiritual point, but the main purpose is to provide an exegesis of the biblical text. This exegesis is thorough and based on careful study and research, even though this may not always be apparent; the few notes are meant merely to throw light on the text, and I have deliberately forgone the idea of giving even a summary bibliography of the subject, which would be vast.[1] It is also a theological exegesis, which does not stop at explaining literally the meaning of the text, but attempts to go deeper and, behind the words of men, to hear the word of God. Indeed, it is on these two levels, that of literary and historical criticism on the one hand and of theological teaching on the other, that these addresses hope to offer material for reflection.

Literary analysis is in a privileged position here. The four evangelists proceed side by side and invite a comparison which will bring out their personal characteristics, their relationships with one another, their common or differing traditions, their sources and what they made of them. The means of making this comparison are given at the beginning of each chapter, where the texts to be commented on are printed in parallel columns;[2] the comparison is then carried out and developed in the exposition which follows.

---

[1] A bibliography can easily be found in other works of a more scholarly kind, among others in J. BLINZLER, *Der Prozess Jesu*, 3rd ed., Regensburg, 1962, E.T. *The Trial of Jesus*, Westminster, Md., 1959.
[2] This reproduces, except in a few details, the arrangement used in *Synopse des quatre évangiles en français* Ed. du Cerf, 1965, vol. I.

For the most part, each of the gospels is first read for its own sake, in order to bring out better the peculiarities of style or thought characteristic of its author. In this way one gets to know the colourful, impulsive, faulty but vivid language of Mark, the more correct and intellectual but somewhat colourless expressions of Matthew, the fine, delicate style of Luke who can come close to that of the classical authors when he does not yield, as he so often does, to the desire to imitate the consecrated language of the Septuagint, and lastly the plain, correct, and very simple hand of John, whose lack of literary means does not prevent his thoughts from soaring high.

The comparison which follows, in addition to bringing out even more clearly their individual characteristics, also reveals their interdependence. Here, more than anywhere else, Matthew depends on Mark, whom he uses, retouches and completes by adding certain somewhat minor details. Luke too depends on Mark but also knows another tradition which yields him some new subject-matter and a better ordering of events. John follows his own special tradition which shows definite affinities with that of Luke; in several important cases, such as the appearances before the Jewish authorities or the discovery of the empty tomb, the agreement of Luke and John allows us to re-establish an order of events which has been disturbed in Mark and Matthew. Apart from deliberate borrowings at a particular stage of its composition (e.g. Jn 19:38; 20:11–14a) the fourth gospel does not depend directly on the synoptics, and its agreement with them, due to a parallel tradition, represents a very valuable reinforcement of the evidence.

Literary analysis however does not stop there. Behind the narratives of the four gospels, and from their resemblence or divergence, it is possible to get some idea of the more primitive forms of the tradition, when it was still oral or in the process of being written down, and of the brief and simpler stories which must have existed and circulated individually before being grouped together: various versions of the agony at Gethsemane, for example, which drew different lessons from it and of which two are already amalgamated in Mark's account; or again, primitive narratives which perhaps contained no more than one or two denials by Peter.

This involves problems of historical criticism. Was there only one session of the Sanhedrin, and is the brief account of it that we are offered anything other than a summary with a theological slant? If the appearance of Jesus before Herod Antipas seems to withstand critical attack, can one say as much for the dream of Pilate's wife, or the guard over the tomb? There are many details of facts or words which the divergence between the gospels makes it impossible to restore with absolute certainty. All these very real difficulties will be faced, but without ever losing sight either of the rational principles of sound criticism, or of the theological principles which must be employed when one is concerned with scriptural texts.

On the one hand, indeed, divergence in detail does not throw doubt on the soundness of the whole narrative if this itself has the appearance of being true, is supported by witnesses who are honest and in agreement on essentials, and is confirmed by contemporary documents. It is for this reason, for example, that the trial of Jesus by the Jewish authorities and its obligatory transfer to the executive power of the Roman authority appear to us to conform to historical truth.

On the other hand, Christians believe that the men who fashioned the gospel tradition were directed in their work by the Spirit of God, and that even the transformations which this tradition received on their lips or at their hands are safeguarded by divine authority. They were willed and inspired by God, whether it be to reduce the importance of many details and relegate them to their proper place as accessories, or to express the complex riches of the mystery in various ways by adapting it to the differing needs of the people of Christ and, through this very diversity, conveying better what is of itself inexpressible.

The theological teaching too stands out all the more strongly on this account. Reduced to essentials when such details are put in their proper perspective, the teaching makes itself heard even more forcefully in the fundamental agreement of the four discordant voices. This teaching, which will be harvested as we go along, revolves round the two principal actors in the drama, God and man – God first, whose love and power direct the drama from end to end: the love which expresses itself in the total giving of a perfect victim and in the inescapable demands of a plan of salvation which is to pardon and re-establish man in justice ('it is necessary', the scriptures must 'be fulfilled'); the power which draws good out of this evil, triumphs over the satanic forces and causes life to spring from death. And facing God, man – with all his cowardice and stupidity, his perversity even, but also his immeasurable wretchedness which calls down pardon and love – whether it be the Roman, closed and indifferent, who becomes an accomplice through his cowardice, or the Jew in the crowd who allows himself to be involved in cursing him whom only the day before he had been acclaiming; whether it be the leader of the Jews whose jealousy and ill-will are accompanied by an ignorance which diminishes his guilt; or lastly, the sinner in each of us who was already associated in advance with the murder of the Just One.

Thanks be to God, there were also friends: there was his mother, Mary; there were the holy women, there were Peter and John, Joseph of Arimathaea and Nicodemus, the good thief and the centurion, all those who could surround the death of the firstborn with some love and thus deserved to become his first brothers. I pray that there may be, among those who read these pages, many whose hearts are full of faith and love and who will draw from them, through the necessary discipline of criticism, a fresh understanding of the drama by which they were saved and a strengthened will to follow Christ through death to life.

Pierre Benoit

Jerusalem, Easter 1966

1. The Agony at Gethsemane

Mt 26:36–46	Mk 14:32–42
[36] Then Jesus came with them to a small estate called Gethsemane	[32] They came to a small estate called Gethsemane
and he said to his disciples, 'Stay here, while I go over there to pray'.	and Jesus said to his disciples, 'Stay here, while I pray'.
[37] He took Peter and the two sons of Zebedee with him And sadness came over him, and great distress. [38] Then he said to them, '*My soul is sorrowful*, even to the point of death. Wait here and keep awake with me.' [39] And going on a little further he fell on his face and prayed.	[33] Then he took Peter and James and John with him. And a sudden fear came over him, and great distress. [34] And he said to them, '*My soul is sorrowful* to the point of death. Wait here, and keep awake.' [35] And going on A little further he threw himself on the ground and prayed that, if it were possible, this hour might pass him by.
'My Father,' he said 'if it is possible, let this cup pass me by. Nevertheless,	[36] 'Abba (Father)!' he said 'Everything is possible for you. Take this cup away from me. But
let it be as you, not I, would have it.'	let it be as you, not I, would have it.'

Lk 22:40–46

John 18:1^b

⁴⁰ When they reached
the place,

¹ᵇ . . . There was a garden there,

and he went into it
with his disciples

he said to them,

'Pray
not to be put to the test'.

12 ²⁷ 'Now
my soul is troubled!

⁴¹ Then he withdrew from them,
about a stone's throw away,
and knelt
and prayed.

What shall I say? Father,

save me from this hour?' . . .

⁴² 'Father,'
he said
'if you are willing,
take this cup
away from me.
Nevertheless,

14 ³¹ 'But
the world must be brought to know
that I love the Father and that
I am doing
exactly what the Father told me.'

let your will be done,
not mine.'

12 ²⁷ '. . . But it was for this
very reason
that I have come to this hour.
²⁸ Father, glorify your name!'

⁴³ Then there appeared,
coming from heaven,

A voice came from heaven,
'I have glorified it,
and I will glorify it again.'

Mt

40 He came back
to the disciples
and found them sleeping,

and he said to Peter,

'So you had not the strength
to keep awake one hour
with me?
41 You should be awake and
praying
not to be put to the test.
The spirit is willing,
but the flesh is weak.'
42 Again,
a second time,
he went away
and prayed:
'My Father,'
he said
'if this cup

cannot pass by
without my drinking it,
your will be done!'
43 And he came again back
and found them sleeping,
their eyes
were so heavy.

44 Leaving them there,
he went away again
and prayed
for the third time,
repeating the same words.
45 Then he came back

Mk

37 He came back

and found them sleeping,

and he said to Peter,
'Simon, are you asleep?
Had you not the strength
to keep awake one hour?

You should be awake, and
praying
not to be put to the test.
The spirit is willing,
but the flesh is weak.'
39 Again

he went away
and prayed,

saying the same words.

40 And once more he came back
and found them sleeping,
their eyes
were so heavy;
and they could find no answer for
him.

41 He came back
a third time

Lk   Jn

an angel
to give him strength.*

44 In his anguish he prayed even
more fervently, and his sweat
fell to the ground like great
drops of blood.

45 When he rose from prayer
he went
to the disciples
and found them sleeping
for sheer grief.

46 He said to them,
'Why are you asleep?'*

Get up and pray

not to be put to the test.'

29 ... others said,
'It was an angel
speaking to him.'

18 **11** 'The cup
that the Father has given me,

am I not to drink it?'*

Mt	Mk
to the disciples and said to them, 'You can sleep on now and take your rest.	and said to them, 'You can sleep on now and take your rest. It is all over. The hour has come.
Now the hour has come when the Son of Man is to be betrayed into the hands of sinners. ⁴⁶ Get up! Let us go! My betrayer is already close at hand.'	Now the Son of Man is to be betrayed into the hands of sinners. ⁴² Get up! Let us go! My betrayer is close at hand already.'

Lk   Jn

12 [23] 'Now the hour has come
for the Son of Man
to be glorified.'

14 [31] 'Come now,
let us go.
[30] . . . the prince of this world

is on his way . . .'

The narrative of Mark

Mark here gives the essential plan of the scene:

They came to a small estate called Gethsemane (Mk 14:32). They came, that is to say all of them, Jesus and his followers. Jesus is not distinguished from his apostles. As has been pointed out, it is very possible that we have here an echo of Peter's preaching. You can almost hear him saying, 'We arrived at such and such a place, and Jesus did this'. This is the way in which a narrator associated with the events would express himself. It is tempting to believe that Mark reproduces the teaching and animated style of Peter; if so, there would be an indication of it here.

The small estate to which they came is called Gethsemane. Various etymologies have been suggested for this name. The most likely is the Aramaic *gat chemani*, which means 'a press' (gat) for oil (chemani) – in Arabic the related word *samn, samne*, means 'butter'. We are concerned, then, with a property which must have contained oil-presses by reason of its numerous olive trees. The place is well known to us through an ancient tradition, fixed by the building of a Byzantine church, on the site of which the existing church stands.

And Jesus said to his disciples, 'Stay here while I pray'. Jesus, then, is going apart to pray. During his life he has often gone apart to pray, but this vigil takes on exceptional significance since it is now a question of life and death.

Then he took Peter and James and John with him (Mk 14:33). These are the three favourite apostles, already selected to witness the resurrection of Jairus' daughter and the transfiguration. As a general rule the gospel says that Jesus prays all alone, apart, on the mountain. Here, because of the special significance of this prayer, he takes three witnesses. The apostles, at least the three most privileged, must be present at their master's final combat and take part in it as far as possible, accepting with him, as his companions, the cross which looms ahead.

And a sudden fear came over him, and great distress. The two Greek words are very strong. The first, which Mark is fond of using, means 'to be stupefied', 'struck with amazement'; here it is the fear which comes of stupefaction, as though Jesus felt himself suddenly face to face with death; he had, of course, been expecting it for a long time, but, as with all of us, it had not yet become an immediate event. Now death is imminent; the fear which he experiences is a kind of stupefaction of human nature. Distress, also, is a very expressive word in the Greek; it is used of a man who is rendered helpless, disorientated, who is agitated and anguished by the threat of some approaching event. We see Jesus in his human nature, suffering what all men suffer, the anguish of death, but with exceptional sensitivity in face of an exceptional death. Jesus wishes to pass through this state and so undergo the last trial.

And he said to them, 'My soul is sorrowful to the point of death. Wait here, and keep awake' (Mk 14:34). These words echo Ps 42:5, 'Why so downcast, my soul, why do you sigh within me?' where the same Greek word is used. 'To the point of death' reminds us of Jn 4:9, 'I am very sorrowful, even to the point of death'.* (See also Si 51:6.) These scriptural expressions serve to show that the sorrow Jesus suffers is part of God's plan and accepted by him as such. 'Wait here, and keep awake.' After leaving the main group of the apostles some distance behind, Jesus now leaves even the three who are closest to him and goes still further away to be alone to pray. He asks them to keep awake, an important theme which we shall examine later.

Jesus' prayer

And going on a little further, he threw himself on the ground and prayed (Mk 14:35). A more literal translation would be 'and was praying'. This would reproduce the Greek of Mark, which is often rough and abrupt. His imperfect tense expresses eloquently the sense of an action being prolonged, 'he was praying and praying'. Jesus' flinging himself on the ground is equally rare and remarkable. Nowhere else do we hear of his doing so and this attitude must indicate the prostration, the utter dejection of his human nature.

And prayed that, if it were possible, this hour might pass him by. This hour, which we know of particularly from St John, is the moment chosen by God for the beginning of the passion. Jesus asks that this hour pass him by, that is, that it may not come upon him, that it may pass over his head, that he may not have to live it out. In his human nature, Jesus can and does ask God to spare him this

suffering. We have to face the facts, as they are, since this is the truth
– Jesus will triumph at once over this appeal of his human nature,
but that nature is in him. We must not make him a 'pretender',
someone who in everything, from his birth to his death, merely
pretends to escape, pretends to question, and so on. Jesus lived as
we do, with everything that is implied in human nature; even though
he is God, he is truly man and as man he wants to escape death and
asks his Father to allow this if it is possible.

Verse 36 repeats the same plea in a direct form: '*Abba [Father]*'
he said. '*Everything is possible for you. Take this cup away from me.*'
This time Jesus uses the expression 'cup' instead of 'hour'. 'Cup' is a
scriptural image for an ordeal or a harsh destiny (see Isaiah, Jeremiah, the Psalms, Revelation). The cup, or chalice, is a bitter drink
of suffering that has to be swallowed.

The word 'Abba' (Father) is also to be noted since it is very striking.
It seems certain that it was a familiar mode of address, and one that
Jews did not use towards God. According to the research of a
contemporary scholar[1], 'Abba' does not mean simply Father, but
Papa, suggesting the familiar tones of a Jewish child speaking to his
father. While the Jews out of respect did not dare to use it towards
God, Jesus did so, thus permitting us to glimpse his intimacy with
his Father. And this fact so struck Christians that they kept the
word just as it was; in the Greek texts they transcribed the Aramaic
word 'Abba', taken from the lips of Jesus himself, and added
'Father' so that Greek or Roman readers might understand it.[2]

In an outburst which is nevertheless tender and humble, Jesus
says frankly to his Father, 'Everything is possible for you. Take this
suffering away from me', but goes on at once to add, '*but let it be
as you, not I, would have it*'. Human nature is put in its place, the will
of God is to be supreme; and that will is that Jesus is to agree to
drink the cup, to enter upon the hour.

Only an abbreviation of Jesus' prayer is given here; it could have
lasted half an hour or an hour.

---

[1] Cf. JOACHIM JEREMIAS, *The Prayers of Jesus*, S.C.M. Press, 1967, pp. 57–65,
108–12. 'Kennzeichen der ipsissima vox Jesu', in *Synoptische Studien*, Alfred
Wikenhauser . . . dargebracht, Munich 1953, pp. 86–9; *idem. Theologische
Literaturzeitung*, LXXIX, 1954, pp. 213f. See also W. MARCHEL, *Dieu Père
dans le Nouveau Testament*, Paris, 1966.
[2] In the epistles to the Galatians and the Romans (Ga 4:6 and Rm 8:15) St. Paul
says that we are children of God and that the Holy Spirit helps us to find the
words we need when we pray; the inspired prayer is 'Abba, Father', the very
words used by Jesus. Like little children, we can say Papa to God.

After this prayer, *He came back and found them sleeping, and he said to Peter, 'Simon, are you asleep? Had you not the strength to keep awake one hour?'* (Mk 14:37). Even the three closest disciples, tired perhaps, but also not very brave and hardly understanding what is going to happen, have let themselves drift off to sleep. Jesus realises he is alone. Then he adds a remark of general significance, capable of many particular applications:–

'You should be awake, and praying not to be put to the test. The spirit is willing, but the flesh is weak' (Mk 14:38). The willing spirit, ready and eager – as it were the 'Be prepared' of the Scout motto – is opposed by the weakness of the flesh, like a Sancho Panza who does not want to follow Don Quixote and tries to hold him back. Everyone knows this conflict. In such a situation you must 'watch and pray that you may not enter into temptation' as the older translations have it. But the word 'temptation' must not be taken in a banal sense, the temptation presented to a child by a pot of jam. The temptation which Jesus is speaking of is a technical term of the gospel – it is the eschatological test, the great ordeal, the pangs of childbirth of which the Bible often speaks, a necessary crisis in which one has to pass through a crucible of suffering in order to experience the era of salvation. Jesus is to be the first to endure this ordeal and all Christians will have to endure it after him.[1] Not to enter into temptation, it is necessary to stay awake and pray.

Again he went away and prayed, using the same words (Mk 14:39) This new prayer Mark indicates only by an allusion.

And once more he came back and found them sleeping, their eyes were so heavy; and they could find no answer for him (Mk 14:40). A second time Jesus finds his apostles in the same state of incapacity, their eyes simply overcome with sleep!

He returns *a third time*. Mark does not even describe the third prayer, merely indicating it with the words 'a third time'.

He came back a third time and said to them, 'You can sleep on now and take your rest. It is all over. The hour has come. Now the Son of Man is to be betrayed into the hands of sinners' (Mk 14:41). This is a difficult verse. First, the phrase, 'You can sleep on now and take your rest.' Here the translation has made a choice. The Greek text could be understood either as a question – 'Are you still asleep?' –

---

[1] In the Lord's Prayer, we ask God not to lead us into temptation, i.e. to spare us, if possible, this ordeal in which, since we do not know how to choose as Jesus did, we risk taking the wrong road.

or an order – 'Now sleep on.' Another interpretation, which was defended by Père Lagrange and which seems preferable to me, suggests a certain irony – 'Good, you can sleep, but I shall stay awake.' After two visits, on both of which he finds his apostles incapable of staying awake with him, Jesus allows himself this friendly irony. But he adds immediately:

'*It is all over.*' These words translate a Greek verb which is not easy to understand. Three main solutions may be considered. The word normally means 'to receive', for example to receive a sum of money, as on those ancient receipts which have survived among the Egyptian papyri. It could therefore be understood to mean, 'Judas is receiving, is laying his hands on his money at this moment.' The same word can also have another meaning, 'to be far off', and so would signify here, 'Judas is far off, you still have time to sleep.' The third possibility, which, with many other exegetes, is the one I have adopted, is this: the word can be used impersonally, meaning, 'That is enough', or, as it is translated here, 'It is all over'.

'*The hour has come. Now the Son of Man is to be betrayed into the hands of sinners.*' Jesus refers to himself as the Son of Man, a title which he is fond of using at important moment in his life to indicate the nature of his mission and his destiny. He is to be betrayed. '*Get up! Let us go! My betrayer is close at hand already*' (Mk 14:42). The moment has passed for sleeping or staying awake or praying, it is time for action. Judas is on the point of arrival, and the arrest of Jesus, which will be commented on in the next chapter, follows. Thus Mark's account ends.

The narrative of Matthew

It is striking to see how closely Matthew's text resembles that of Mark; there are only some slight modifications, but they are worth noticing for what they can teach us of the style and practice of the Greek gospel of Matthew. He starts straight off with one of his familiar expressions, 'Then . . .'

Then Jesus came with them (Mt 26:36). Whereas Mark said, 'They came', Matthew says, 'Jesus came with them.' There is a shade of difference: in Mark, Jesus is lost in the crowd, and only later separates off from them. For religious and theological reasons, at a slightly later date, Matthew is careful to give Jesus the leading role; Jesus comes, that is the important thing, the others are only his companions. Matthew works in the same way throughout the gospel; whenever we encounter this plural in Mark, he takes care to make Jesus stand out. Here is an example of the kind of literary habits which we must learn to recognise in each of the evangelists.

Then Jesus came with them to a small estate called Gethsemane; and he said to his disciples, 'Stay here, while I go over there to pray' (Mt 26:35). Matthew dots the i's; what was already intelligible in Mark becomes even more so in Matthew, who contrasts 'here' with 'over there'.

He took Peter and the two sons of Zebedee with him. And sadness came over him, and great distress (Mt 26:37). Matthew prefers 'the two sons of Zebedee' to Mark's 'James and John' (cf. Mt 20:20 and 27:56). It comes to the same thing, although, according to Père Lagrange, Matthew's phrase has perhaps a more archaic flavour. *And sadness came over him, and great distress*; Matthew has kept Mark's word 'distress', but has changed 'fear', a term which may have appeared to him to be too strong. Matthew's style is correct but dull, in contrast to that of Mark which is spontaneous and full of colourful expressions. Here Matthew simply uses the word 'sadness'.

Verse 38 in Matthew is almost identical with verse 34 in Mark. In verse 39, *he fell on his face* smoothes out the somewhat violent expression of Mark; instead of the collapse of a man throwing himself on the ground, Matthew's more traditional phrase (cf. Gn 17:3; 1 Co 14:25, Rv 7:11) suggests prostration in adoration and prayer, as the lepers prostrated themselves before Jesus (Lk 5:12; 17:16), a prostration which includes a sense of religious awe (Mt 17:6).

He fell on his face and prayed. 'My Father,' he said, 'if it is possible, let this cup pass me by' (Mt 26:39). Notice here Matthew's literary procedure. Mark gives the prayer twice, first in indirect (Mk 14:35) and then in direct speech (Mk 14:36). Matthew takes 'pass me by' from verse 35 and adds it to 'the cup' of verse 36, fusing the two formulas of Mark into one as though there were something abnormal about the repetition. As we shall soon see, this detail has some bearing on the actual origin of the various traditions.

'Nevertheless, let it be as you, not I, would have it' (Mt 26:39). The end of verse 39 differs from Mark only in one unimportant detail.

In verse 40, the reproach addressed to Peter is in the plural. In Mark, it is in the singular and addressed to Peter alone. Behind

Mark's words we can hear St Peter remembering that he once denied his Lord and blaming himself in all humility. Here he recalls how Jesus spoke to him alone. But Matthew, wishing to deal gently with the chief of the apostles, uses the plural: Peter no longer appears as the only guilty party.

'*You should be awake, and praying not to be put to the test. The spirit is willing but the flesh is weak*' (Mt 26:41). This verse is practically identical with the parallel in Mark. Such complete similarity can only be explained if one author knows the work of the other. The examination of cases in the gospels leads to the conclusion that it is Matthew who depends on Mark, rather than the other way round. Nevertheless it is also possible that both depend on a common source, perhaps a Greek translation of the original Aramaic.

Again, a second time, he went away and prayed (Mt 26:42). Matthew again dots the i's in regard to the second and third prayers. Whereas in Mark they are barely sketched in, Matthew emphasises them. Then, where Mark had said, 'the same words', Matthew formulates the prayer and gives the actual words: 'My Father, if this cup cannot pass by without my drinking it, your will be done.' The end of this prayer is exactly the same as the phrase in the Lord's Prayer (Mt 6:10).

And he came back and found them sleeping, their eyes were so heavy (Mt 26:43). The text is identical with that of Mark, except that 'heavy' is represented by a different word in the Greek. And Matthew does not reproduce the somewhat painful remark, 'and they could find no answer for him'.

Leaving them there, he went away again and prayed for the third time, repeating the same words (Mt 26:44). Mark indicates this third prayer only indirectly by saying that Jesus came back 'a third time'. Here again, Matthew is more definite, making use of Mark's verse 39.

Verse 45 in Matthew is identical with verse 41 in Mark, except that Matthew avoids the difficult and ambiguous expression, 'It is all over', preferring to leave it out.

Everything which follows, up to the end of the agony, is similar to the text of Mark.

The narrative of Luke

When we pass on to the text of Luke, we notice at once the existence of a very different tradition. On the one hand, Luke resumes the facts, as told by Mark, in a much briefer form, on the other hand he adds a whole section which is proper to himself – the angel of the agony and the sweat of blood. Let us take first of all that part of the text which corresponds to Mark's; we shall see how freely Luke treats it.

When they reached the place (Lk 22:40). In the context in Luke (Lk 22:39), Jesus has only just left the Upper Room: 'he then left to make his way as usual to the Mount of Olives'. So Luke here merely says 'the place'. *He said to them, 'Pray not to be put to the test'.* Luke does not mention the way in which the three closest disciples are taken apart from the main group. He does not report the words 'Stay here while I pray', nor the fear, nor the distress. If he leaves all this out, it is because he is going to describe the Lord's distress in another way, following another tradition he knows – the drops of bloody sweat, of which he will shortly speak. Here he is content to give, in an abridged form, the command to pray which Mark places further on (Mk 14:38) and which he himself will resume to conclude the scene (Lk 22:46).

Then he withdrew from them, about a stone's throw away (Lk 22:41). 'He withdrew from them' is a word proper to Luke, stylistically elegant. Luke is a more distinguished writer than Mark and even than Matthew. Mark's style is popular, vigorous and crisp, but far from elegant and sometimes even incorrect. Matthew's is more careful, but a bit dull. Luke's style is that of a distinguished and cultivated man, a physician as he is said to have been. The verb which he uses here means literally 'to tear oneself away from', but in an alternative sense is the equivalent of 'to withdraw'. The expression 'a stone's throw away' is a classical one and is found for example in Thucydides.

And knelt, and prayed (Lk 22:41). Luke alone, in the New Testament, notes this attitude of prayer which was not usual among the Jews. It was normal to pray standing up, as among Eastern peoples today.[1] Here Luke does not show us Jesus falling to the earth or prostrating himself, as in Mark and Matthew; he offers us a different picture of Jesus' prayer. It is useless to try to discover what Jesus actually did; we should rather try to appreciate how Mark, Matthew and Luke, each in his own way, make us feel the urgency of Jesus'

---

[1] Luke notes this attitude of prayer four times in the Acts of the Apostles: Stephen (Ac 7:60), Peter (Ac 9:20) and Paul (Ac 20:36 and 21:5) pray on their knees.

prayer. This is the essential thing; we are dealing with different ways of contemplating the mystery of the Lord's human nature in his dejection and grief, here kneeling, there prostrate. Basically they reveal the same thing, the differing literary expressions are mutually enriching.

'*Father*,' *he said* '*if you are willing, take this cup away from me. Nevertheless, let your will be done, not mine*' (Lk 22:42). This verse resumes that of Mark in a shorter form. Luke leaves out the hour, which Jesus wishes would pass him by, he keeps in only the taking away of the cup, and the essential thing, the doing of the Father's will.

Verses 43 and 44 may be left aside for the moment, to be studied later.

When he rose from prayer he went to the disciples and found them sleeping for sheer grief. He said to them, 'Why are you asleep?' (Lk 22:45). The text is very close to that of Mark and Matthew, except that it adds a rather delightful note, characteristic of the tender-hearted and indulgent Luke – they were sleeping 'for sheer grief'. It was not out of negligence or laziness, but because they were so sad, that they fell asleep, poor men! It is well in character for Luke to find an excuse for the apostles.

'*Get up, and pray not to be put to the test.*' With these words Luke ends his account, rather abruptly. Why has he abbreviated it so? Because he wanted to include a piece of evidence known only to himself.

The bloody sweat

Then there appeared, coming from heaven, an angel to give him strength. In his anguish he prayed even more fervently, and his sweat fell to the ground like great drops of blood (Lk 22:43–44). Scholars have raised and discussed the question whether these two verses are authentic, since they are omitted by certain manuscripts. Some have decided that they were inserted later and are not from the hand of Luke. I myself, in company with numerous other critics, am convinced that they are really his. There is evidence for the existence of the passage from the second century. It is true that we no longer have actual manuscripts dating from that period, since the papyri which have been found are very incomplete and go back only to the third century and the manuscripts begin only in the fourth. But the second-century authors Justin, Tatian and Irenaeus all know this text.[1] We need not, therefore, be afraid to follow the oldest tradition and accept this precious passage.

There is another indication of its authenticity – stylistically it is wholly Lucan, typical of his writing and of his usual manner. Luke is fond of mentioning the prayers of Jesus as well as the appearance of angels (see the narratives of the infancy and the resurrection, and those in Acts where angels appear to Peter and Paul). Lastly, Luke is not afraid to emphasise the humiliation and distress of the Lord for whom, in his tenderness, he feels such compassion. So, like the majority of exegetes, I believe these verses to be authentic. From the theological point of view they are interesting in that on the one hand they insist on the weakness of Jesus in so far as he is man while on the other they demonstrate the power of the aid which comes from God to strengthen him.

The language used by Luke is so precise that it may very well be that of a doctor. It is indeed thought that Luke is the 'beloved physician' mentioned by Paul (Col 4:14) and it is agreed that his style contains medical terms such as might be used by an educated man; here, the drops of blood, sweat, etc. The terms express a very great physical distress which doctors explain as the sign of extreme inward conflict.[2]

At the same moment, however, Luke shows us how the power of heaven upholds Jesus, by means of an angel who strengthens him. Like a true disciple of Paul, Luke reminds us that it is the power of God which sustains our weakness. Paul said, 'It is when I am weak that I am strong' (2 Co 12:10) and, 'There is nothing I cannot master with the help of the One who gives me strength' (Ph 4:13). This is pre-eminently true of Jesus Christ in so far as he is man; he is weak in the very anguish of his flesh that is to suffer and die, but strong in the heavenly strength his Father sends him. It was to find room for this valuable lesson that Luke abridged the rest of the narrative.

[1] The manuscripts which omit it are later than the year A.D. 300 and there is no proof that these verses were omitted earlier than that. In addition, the witnesses for its omission are very much localised and under Egyptian influence. Their doubts are easily understood: they were scandalised by so realistic a scene. To show Jesus in such a state of prostration and sweating blood was to over-humanise the Lord.
[2] A priest, who assisted one of his brethren shot by the Germans in 1914, told me that he could understand this sweating of blood by a man in good health at the moment of execution.

The evidence of John

We must now turn to St John, whose evidence is strange and very interesting. He does not mention the agony. He says only ' . . . there was a garden there, and he went into it with his disciples' (Jn 18:1), and immediately begins his account of the arrest.

It is not that John is ignorant of the agony; the ideas and even the expressions connected with the scene at Gethsemane reappear curiously in chapter 12 of his gospel.

Some Greeks want to see Jesus, they mention it to Philip, Philip goes to tell Andrew and both go to tell Jesus. John's narrative continues: *Jesus replied to them, 'Now the hour has come for the Son of Man to be glorified'* (Jn 12:23). This recalls in a striking way Mark 14:41b. In John 'being glorified' is used of the death and resurrection, glorification comes about through the cross. And John continues: *'I tell you, most solemnly, unless a wheat grain falls on the ground and dies, it remains only a single grain; but if it dies, it yields a rich harvest. Anyone who loves his life loses it; anyone who hates his life in this world will keep it for the eternal life'* (Jn 12:24–25). There are other passages in the synoptics (Mt 16:25; Mk 8:35; Lk 9:24) which are equivalent to these verses. Their meaning here parallels what Mark says of the willing spirit and weak flesh (Mk 14:38), that is the conflict within man between the spirit which should triumph and the flesh which resists. The same dialectic can be seen; one must die in order to live, lose one's life in order to keep it. More important, however, is what follows immediately, in the same passage of John:

'Now my soul is troubled. What shall I say: Father, save me from this hour?' (Jn 12:27). In Mark and Matthew, Jesus said, 'My soul is sorrowful, even to the point of death' (Mk 14:34 and Mt 26:38); in Mark he prayed 'that, if it were possible, this hour might pass him by' (Mk 14:35). The texts are very similar indeed. And the following verse *'Father, glorify your name'* (Jn 12:28) is surely the Johannine equivalent of Matthew's 'Your will be done!' (Mt 26:42).

To the prayer 'Father, save me from this hour' Jesus himself replied, *'But it was for this very reason that I have come to this hour, Father, glorify your name.'* (Jn 12:27). The thought behind it is the same acceptance of the divine will as in Mark and Matthew, only it is expressed in the idiom of John. John then continues his narrative: *A voice came from heaven, 'I have glorified it, and I will glorify it again'. People standing by, who heard this, said it was a clap of thunder; others said, 'It was an angel speaking to him'. Jesus answered, 'It was not for my sake that this voice came, but for yours.'* (Jn 12:29–30). This angel who speaks from heaven and brings strength from God with the words 'I have glorified it and I will glorify it again' offers a striking parallel to the angel in Luke, as all exegetes recognise. Jesus is troubled, Jesus asks that the hour may pass him by, Jesus wills that the Father's name be glorified and says, 'the hour has come for the Son of Man to be glorified', a voice comes from heaven like an angel to strengthen him – all these features are paralleled in the scene of the agony.

If John does not recount the agony in Gethsemane, it is because he has already used the substance of it in a preceding episode. This is not the only instance in his gospel. John gives us no narrative of the Last Supper but he has reported the discourse on the Bread of Life in chapter 6. He does not describe the trial before Caiaphas, but he has already used more than once the dialogue between Jesus and the Jews, 'Are you the Son of God? Are you the Messiah?' John works with a freedom permitted and willed by the Holy Spirit; he does not feel himself bound down to details of wording or even of episodes provided that, while respecting the substantial truth, he can bring out better his own theological design.

The parallelism noted here appears to be quite certain. And the fact that John has used the scene of the agony in his own special way is confirmed by a curious detail. In the middle of the discourse after the Supper the following words occur, 'The prince of this world is on his way . . . Come now, let us go' (Jn 14:30–1). Surely this is the same utterance that Mark has put at the end of the agony, whether in identical terms, 'Get up! Let us go!'[1], or in an analogous form, 'My betrayer is close at hand' (Mk 14:42). The same idea which in Mark occurs at the end of the agony, in John has found a place in the middle of the discourse after the Supper. Literary evidence like this forces us to take account of a certain evolution of the gospel tradition.

Before the written gospels

It is a fact that in these varying versions one can discern different but parallel traditions of one and the same episode. In Luke and John we have discovered the episode of the angelic help which is not found

---

[1] The words are identical in the original Greek and in the French edition of the Jerusalem Bible (Trans. note.)

in Mark and Matthew. Even in the two latter, if we follow a Protestant exegete[1] who has produced serious arguments for it, we can recognise two traditions which have been combined. One of these emphasises the soteriological theme: Christ prays that the hour may pass him by and accepts it with the declaration that the hour has come – a theme where everything centres on the Son of Man and his acceptance of this hour. The theological interest of this presentation principally concerns the person of Jesus, the Son of Man, who accepts death for us. The other theme, a hortatory one, is addressed to us: stay awake and pray not to be put to the test; the spirit is willing but the flesh is weak. This is directed towards the Christian, who is to imitate Christ in his vigil of prayer.

A literary analysis, which cannot be given in detail here[2], allows us to see how two parallel narratives, one focused on the theme of the hour of Christ, the other on the counsel to watch and pray, two ways, that is, of telling the agony of Christ, circulated separately in primitive tradition before being brought together in a single narrative by Mark. One of the indications of this is the doublet already pointed out in verses 35 and 36 in Mark, where Jesus' prayer is first given in indirect speech, then in direct: 'He prayed that, if it were possible, this hour might pass him by. "Abba, Father," he said "everything is possible for you. Take this cup away from me".' Why this repetition? Matthew felt it to be an anomaly and suppressed it by fusing Mark's two phrases into one. But these two almost identical phrases are surely the relics of two earlier parallel texts which Mark has combined. This is as far as we may go here. But it is open to us to believe that, before the gospels were written down, the Lord's agony was told from different points of view among the first Christians. Three great traditions can thus be distinguished.

In the earliest of these traditions (I believe that a certain chronological order can be discovered in them) the emphasis was on the person of Jesus himself, on his ordeal, his prayer that the hour might pass him by, and his final acceptance – what could be summed up as the Christological theme.

Another theme, perhaps a little later, perhaps contemporaneous with the first but originating in a different milieu, emphasised, in a context of preaching, the application to the faithful themselves –

[1] K. G. KUHN, 'Jesus in Gethsemane', in *Evangelische Theologie*, 12 (1952–3), pp. 260–85.
[2] See P. BENOIT, 'Outrages à Jésus Prophète', in *Neotestamentica et Patristica* (a symposium presented to Oscar Cullman), Leiden, 1962, pp. 103–4.

just as Jesus had stayed awake and prayed on the day of this great
ordeal, the faithful must stay awake and pray with him, since, as he
said, the spirit is willing but the flesh is weak. A moral lesson was
drawn from this gospel of Gethsemane. Christians could not be told
that their hour had come since they were not the Son of Man, but
it was the duty of each of them to stay awake and pray with the Lord
that they might escape from being put to the test.

Lastly, a third way of presenting it, which we found in Luke and
John, emphasised the distress of the Lord and the help he received
from heaven in order to teach the faithful how Jesus had been
strengthened by his Father in his supreme ordeal.

These three presentations, far from contradicting one another,
are mutually enriching. First, there is a mystery which cannot be
conceived or described – the Son of Man, the Son of God made man,
suffers in the sight of his Father and accepts that he has to die. This
is beyond all our imagination. Peter, James and John were present
at and witnessed this conflict, and later recounted it. The first
Christian community, the Church, meditated on and assimilated
this experience; in her preaching she drew various lessons from it,
emphasising sometimes Jesus' heroic acceptance, sometimes the
divine aid which did not fail him. These traditions were collected
and, to a greater or lesser extent, combined by the evangelists who
emphasised this or that aspect of the mystery according to their own
cast of mind. As for us, we must take it all without trying to fit all
the details into a consecutive narrative. The different accounts echo
the different preachers. Thanks to this very diversity, it is possible
for us, after a little exegetical discipline, to appreciate the wonderful
riches contained in these pages, even if we have to undergo first the
discipline of exegesis.

Lastly, we must be sure we understand to what degree the scene
is historical. Although we cannot be certain about every word and
may think that it has been manipulated and presented for the sake
of instruction, and although we may detect instances where texts
have been conflated or edited for didactic purposes, it remains that
the basis of the narrative is most certainly an experience which has
been lived through. Some scholars have doubted this and suggested
that it is a legend which has been invented. But how could anyone
have dared to invent a scene that was so disturbing to faith – the
fear of Jesus in the face of death? This story was handed down because
it was true. And if we need confirmation, we can find it in a passage

from the epistle to the Hebrews where the author, in asserting that Christ is a priest for ever, seems without any doubt to be alluding to the agony: 'During his life on earth, he offered up prayer and entreaty, aloud and in silent tears, to the one who had the power to save him from death, and he submitted so humbly that his prayer was heard.[1] Although he was the Son, he learnt to obey through suffering; but having been made perfect, he became for all who obey him the course of eternal salvation' (Heb 5:7-9). These are words which we would not have dared of ourselves to utter: 'he was made perfect'. Jesus was of course perfect in himself from the moment of his birth, but as our brother, he walked in the ways we have to walk and chose to be tested, not by inward sin like us, but by outward temptation, by the perfectly legitimate desire to escape death. He did not deserve to die. He willed himself to make this choice on our behalf. In this way he was able 'to learn obedience' and so reply to his Father, 'Let your will be done, not mine'. This is the measure of the humiliation of our Lord.

[1] Jesus was heard, not in the sense that he did not have to suffer, but in this, that he entered wholly into his hour.

2. The Arrest of Jesus

47
He was still speaking
when

43 Even while
he was still speaking,

Judas,
one of the Twelve,
appeared,
and with him
a large number of men
armed with swords and clubs,
sent by the chief priests

and elders of the people.

Judas,
one of the Twelve,
came up
with
a number of men
armed with swords and clubs,
sent by the chief priests
and the scribes
and the elders.

48 Now the traitor
had arranged
a sign with them.
'The one I kiss,'
he had said
'he is the man.
Take him in charge.'

44 Now the traitor
had arranged
a signal with them.
'The one I kiss,'
he had said
'he is the man.
Take him in charge,
and see he is well guarded
when you lead him away.'

49 So
he went straight up to Jesus
and said, 'Greetings, Rabbi',
and kissed him.
50 Jesus said to him,
'My friend,

45 So when the traitor came,
he went straight up to Jesus
and said, 'Rabbi!'
and kissed him.

do what you are here for'.
Then they came forward,
seized Jesus
and took him in charge.

46 The others seized him
and took him in charge.

Lk 22:47–53   Jn 18:2–11

² Judas the traitor knew the
place well, since Jesus had
⁴⁷   often met his disciples there,
He was still speaking
when
a number of men appeared,
and at the head of them
the man called Judas,   and he
one of the Twelve,

brought
the cohort to this place
together with a detachment of guards
sent by the chief priests
and the Pharisees,

all with lanterns and torches
and weapons

who
went up to Jesus

to kiss him.
⁴⁸ Jesus said,
'Judas,
are you betraying
the Son of Man with a kiss?'

⁴⁹ His followers,
seeing   ⁴ Knowing everything
what was happening,   that was going to happen to him,
                                          Jesus then came forward
                                          and said, 'Who are you
                                          looking for?'
                                          ⁵ They answered, 'Jesus the

| | |
| Mt | Mk |

51 At that,	47 Then
one of the followers of Jesus	one of the bystanders
grasped his sword	
and drew it;	drew his sword
he struck out	and struck out
at the high priest's servant,	at the high priest's servant,
and cut off his ear.	and cut off his ear.

52 Jesus then said,

'Put your sword back,
for all who draw the sword
will die by the sword.
53 Or do you think that I
cannot appeal to my Father
who would promptly send
more than twelve legions of
angels to my defence?
54 But then, how would the
scriptures be fulfilled that
say this is the way it must be?'
  26 42 'If this cup cannot pass by

without my drinking it,
your will be done!'

Nazarene'. He said, 'I
am he'. Now Judas the
traitor was standing among
them.

⁶ When Jesus said, 'I am he',
they moved back and fell to
the ground

⁷ He asked them a second time,
'Who are you looking for?'
They said, 'Jesus the Nazarene.'

⁸ 'I have told you that I am he'
replied Jesus. 'If I am the one
you are looking for, let these
others go.'

⁹ This was to fulfil the words he
had spoken, 'Not one of those
you gave me have I lost'.

said, 'Lord, shall we use
our swords?'

⁵⁰ And
one of them   ¹⁰ Simon Peter,
                                who carried a sword,
                                drew it
struck out   and wounded
at the high priest's servant   the high priest's servant,
and cut off his right ear.   cutting off his right ear.
                                The servant's name was Malchus.

⁵¹ But at this Jesus spoke,   ¹¹ Jesus said to Peter,
'Leave off!' he said 'That will do!'

'Put your sword back in its scabbard;

Am I not to drink
the cup
that the Father has given me?'

And touching the man's ear
he healed him.

Mt	Mk
55 It was at this time that Jesus said to the crowds,	**48** Then Jesus spoke,
'Am I a brigand, that you had to set out to capture me with swords and clubs?	'Am I a brigand' he said 'that you had to set out to capture me with swords and clubs?
I sat teaching	**49** I was among you teaching
in the Temple	in the Temple
day after day and you never laid hands on me.'	day after day and you never laid hands on me. But
56 Now all this happened to fulfil the prophecies in scripture. Then all the disciples deserted him and ran away.	this is to fulfil the scriptures.' **50** And they all deserted him and ran away. **51** A young man who followed him had nothing on but a linen cloth. They caught hold of him, **52** but he left the cloth in their hands and ran away naked.

Lk   Jn

⁵² Then Jesus spoke to the chief
priests and captains of the
Temple guard and elders
who had come for him.
'Am I a brigand' he said
'that you had to set out

with swords and clubs?

                          18 ²⁰ I have spoken openly
                          for all the world to hear.
                          I have always

⁵³ When I was among you

                          taught
                          in the synagogue
in the Temple   and in the Temple
                          where all the Jews meet together;
                          I have said nothing in secret.'

day after day
you never moved
to lay hands
on me.
But
this is your hour;   16 ⁴ᵃ . . . 'When their hour
                          comes . . .*'

this is the reign of darkness.'

The narrative of Mark

After the agony, there follows the scene of Jesus' arrest, still at Gethsemane. Here too it is convenient to begin with Mark's narrative.

Even while he was speaking, Judas, one of the Twelve, came up. Mark opens with an apparently meaningless word*, but one which is entirely characteristic of him.

Inspired though they are, the evangelists each have their own mannerisms, one might almost call them 'fads'. We ourselves have certain expressions which help us to make transitions in conversation, such as 'Well', 'So', 'Then', 'After that', 'Do you see?' In the same way, the evangelists have their own tricks of speech. Mark is fond of saying, 'And immediately', being a spontaneous man who sees things in flashes. Matthew likes 'Then', a very common word. Luke, who deliberately borrows the style of the Bible, uses a biblical expression, 'And it happened that'. John prefers, 'After that'. Nowadays the Sunday gospel begins 'In those days'.

Even *while he was still speaking*, speaking, that is, the words with which the preceding scene concludes, 'Get up! Let us go! My betrayer is close at hand already', *Judas comes up*. Once again Mark uses the historic present, a turn of speech which is more vivid than the imperfect and characteristic of his lively, accurate and realistic style. *Judas, one of the twelve*: we can guess the grief which it cost Mark to have to put this down. Matthew and Luke both take up his phrase. It reminds us of the tragedy of the scene: he who betrays the Master is one of the Twelve themselves. Not a man in the street, or a hostile Jew, but someone close to him, someone he had chosen to be among his companions. This is a mystery of God's providence. Why did Jesus, who foresaw the outcome, select him as one of the Twelve? How did Judas, who must certainly have been chosen for his good qualities, come to this? The mystery of Judas' psychology is disturbing. We find ourselves disconcerted by the tragedy of a

* The Greek *euthus*, 'immediately', is not represented in the English translation (Trans.)

soul which, though specially chosen, took this course in this way. And yet God allowed this to happen in order to bring about what he had planned from eternity, the arrest and execution of his Son.

One of the Twelve, with a number of men armed with swords and clubs. These words hardly suggest a body of regular troops. They are not soldiers armed with the latest weapons, they have brought very simple ones – the sword, the *Chibrieh*, which every Bedouin today still carries in his belt, and sticks that could have been picked up anywhere. But even if they are not regular troops, they are men commissioned by the Sanhedrin, doubtless porters or attendants who were at its disposal. The Sanhedrin was a kind of tribunal, a great assembly of Israel's leaders, which, especially before the Hasmonaean and Roman periods, wielded political, legislative and judiciary powers. Its sentences were carried out by porters or attendants, like a household police. The Sanhedrin is not mentioned here, but we are told that these men were *sent by the chief priests and the scribes and the elders.* These in fact form the three classes of which the assembly was composed.

This Jewish institution plays an important role in the gospel. The term 'Sanhedrin', which comes from the Greek *sunedrion*, refers to an assembly which appears in history after the return from the Babylonian exile, in the third to second century before Christ. This aristocratic senate was set up in the theocratic state which was established after the exile to replace the vanished kingship. On the orders of the Prince of the people (that is, God) a collective agent, the Sanhedrin, governed, did justice and directed the Jewish people. Under the domination of the Hasmonaean kings, and of Herod, and then of the Romans, this senate lost some of its importance, particularly in the political field. Nevertheless, it still maintained a religious role of legislation and control, including even the power to punish offenders. It was composed of three principal classes.

(i) The chief priests. This class included in the first place the high priest in office, who was changed from time to time, dismissed by the king or the Roman governor; then, former high priests (these kept the title 'high priest' in the same way as, for example, former presidents are still addressed as 'president'); lastly, the members of the great priestly families, from among whom it was the custom to select the high priest (in the same way as, during the Renaissance, the Pope was chosen from certain aristocratic Roman families, such as the Orsini or the Farnese). By the term 'chief priests', therefore, was meant the priestly nobility, the heads of the Temple who directed the religious aspect of the cult and of Judaism.

(ii) The scribes are very different; they are the teachers. Their name means only men who could write, but we must not think of them as mere village letter-writers. In that age, when not everyone could write, this talent was the key to knowledge. Those who studied books were in fact teachers. But they were essentially laymen, and were of modest social rank. Much in favour with the people, this democratic element had risen into prominence after the exile and its influence more or less rivalled that of the chief priests. The latter represented tradition. But the people held it against these hereditary leaders that they were not religious enough and that, in the time of the Maccabees, they had even collaborated with foreign powers. The people instead favoured the scribes, the teachers, who were for the most part Pharisees and who insisted on the study of the Torah and trying to keep in check the high priesthood in order to impose a stricter view of religion. Thus the scribes had achieved membership of the Sanhedrin; although expelled for a time, they had made their way back. By the beginning of the first century they had acquired great importance. In the course of his ministry Jesus was frequently involved in discussions with these scribes, most of whom were Pharisees.[1] They were, in short, lay theologians, in contrast to the high priesthood.

(iii) The elders. These are the rich landowners, the heads of the great families, i.e. the landed aristocracy. They are neither specialists in worship and temple service, nor theologians, but the heads of clans and an element of great importance for the balance of this senate. The chief priests, the scribes and the elders are the three classes which make up the Sanhedrin. And it is this, the supreme tribunal of Judaism, which sends armed men, led by Judas, to arrest Jesus.

Now the traitor had arranged a signal with them. 'The one I kiss,' he had said, 'he is the man. Take him in charge, and see he is well guarded when you lead him away' (Mk 14:44). The men from the Temple, servants of the Sanhedrin, do not all know Jesus, and, even if they know him by sight, they might fail to recognise him at night among the trees in Gethsemane. Judas is sure to, and so tells them to watch him, while he goes forward to meet Jesus: then they can take him. For a signal he suggests a kiss. This gesture appears to us a terrible

[1] The word Pharisee denotes a religious sect, not a social class.

one – as indeed it is – but for all that it is not an unusual one; it was the usual way for a disciple to greet his rabbi. Just as today we shake hands when we meet, in those days one went up to one's master and kissed him. It was an everyday greeting which Judas and others must often have given Jesus. So much so that the apostles saw nothing extraordinary in it; Judas arrives late, goes to meet Jesus and embraces him. But he has made this apparently innocent gesture the vehicle of betrayal. That is what is tragic, and all the more tragic because the gesture is so ordinary. It recalls an analogous incident, another very simple action which is the sign of a tragic reality – the morsel which Jesus gives Judas at the beginning of the Supper. Jesus has just announced that someone is going to betray him; his disciples are bewildered and do not know who it is; Peter and John, as John himself tells us, are near the Master and ask him. For their hearing alone Jesus says, 'He to whom I give the piece of bread', then he takes a morsel from the dish and gives it to Judas. This too is a perfectly ordinary gesture which anyone who knows the East will understand. At the feasts which take place in the tent, round the roast sheep and the dish of rice, it is quite natural for the Sheikh or the master of the household to make a small ball of the best meat and offer it, as a mark of honour, to one of his guests. Jesus makes the same gesture of friendship and respect to Judas. Jesus knows of the betrayal and shows it in this way to Judas, as well as to Peter and John. But he chooses a mark of honour which will in no way humiliate Judas, as a last appeal to his heart. Judas accepts it. And so this everyday action hides a tragic reality, like the kiss in Gethsemane but in reverse. On the Lord's part it is an act of condessension each time; on the part of Judas, with evil in his heart, a fall[1].

At Gethsemane, Judas takes strict precautions – when you recognise him, *take him in charge, and see he is well guarded when you lead him away*. The Greek word translated by 'see he is well guarded' means actually 'so that he does not slip'; it is the same word as 'asphalt', the kind of surface on which cars should not skid. Jesus must not be allowed to slip away between the hands of those who are going to arrest him. Judas remembers that Jesus has slipped between their fingers several times already, at Nazareth and elsewhere; he had been arrested but, as the gospel tells us, he escaped

---

[1] Note that Judas did not receive communion at the Last Supper, as is sometimes imagined. The morsel was not the Eucharist. It was only after Judas left that Jesus pronounced the words, 'This is my Body, this is my Blood'. See P. BENOIT, *Exégèse et Théologie*, Paris, 1961, I, p. 215.

as he pleased. Judas is afraid that the Lord may slip away once again and so warns them to be on their guard and keep good hold of him. *So when the traitor came, he went straight up to Jesus and said, 'Rabbi!', and kissed him* (Mk 14:45). He accosts him and kisses him, just as he does every day. Here the translation is more elegant than the Greek original, which is literally 'and coming, immediately coming up to him, he said'. We notice again Mark's rough, visual style: Judas comes, and immediately (the 'immediately' Mark is so fond of) he sees Jesus and comes up to him. The phrase is unpolished and Matthew will smoothe out its awkwardness so that it runs better. Notice also that, in Mark, Jesus makes no reply to the kiss.

The others seized him and took him in charge (Mk 14:46). The text is simple: a hand on the shoulder, no resistance, nothing even said.

Then one of the bystanders drew his sword and struck out at the high priest's servant, and cut off his ear (Mk 14:47). The Greek text says: 'a certain person among those who were there', giving the impression that it was someone who was well enough known. John tells us that it was St Peter, but Mark is not so precise. Was it that Peter wanted to keep this piece of bravado dark, that seemed in the end somewhat ridiculous? Who was this servant of the high priest? Was he a high-ranking official of the Temple, as some think? More probably, he was a particular servant whom the high priest had delegated to watch what happened and keep him informed. The high priest himself does not come out but he is to hear all about it. It seems as if Peter knows this servant, and, in order to take vengeance and get at the high priest through the servant, cuts off the outer edge of the latter's ear.[1]

Then Jesus spoke. 'Am I a brigand,' he said 'that you had to set out to capture me with swords and clubs?' (Mk 14:48). With sovereign irony, Jesus forces them to take note that they did not need to make so much preparation to seize him. It is as though he had said: 'I am a "gentleman", take me and let that be an end of it. It is neither polite nor distinguished to attack me with such weapons, as though I were going to defend myself like a man in the street.' This interpretation takes the word 'brigand' in its usual sense of a highway robber.

---

[1] This is what is meant by the Greek word, which is the diminutive form of the word for 'ear'. There are some picturesque parallels in ancient literature which refer to the unfortunate boxers of the time who fought bare-fisted. Some of them have left a record of their exploits in their epitaphs, such as this: 'He had a nose, a chin, eyelashes, ears and eyelids: he became a boxer, and lost them all.' *Palatine Anthology*, xi, 75.

Certain exegetes would like to give it a technical sense, which is possible. In Greek, the word can mean professional bandits, revolutionaries, the terrorists of that age. Struggling against the government, they were armed with daggers (hence their Latin name, *sicarii*) and organised like the *maquis*. According to this interpretation, Jesus is alluding to them and defending himself from the charge of being a political enemy. It fits in with the theory that Pilate saw Jesus as a political agitator. But it is not very probable. The general meaning, brigand, is quite sufficient. It is met with in the gospel in the story of the good Samaritan, where the traveller is stripped by brigands, or again in the parable of the good Shepherd who protects his flock against sheep-stealers. The same word is used of the thieves crucified with Jesus. Jesus then is saying: I am not the kind of man you need such weapons to arrest.

Jesus immediately adds; '*I was among you in the Temple day after day and you never laid hands on me. . . .*' (Mk 14:49). I give myself up to you, I am not defending myself, arrest me if you wish. This attitude, which Matthew and Luke will underline still further, indicates the deeper meaning of the scene: Jesus dominates the situation, accepting everything. It is the moment willed by his Father, he must therefore let himself be taken. Besides, he adds, even in Mark, '*But this is to fulfil the scriptures.*' He knows that the divine intention and the prophecy of the passion of the Servant must be accomplished in his person. Perhaps he is thinking of a text, which is even more precise, quoted by Luke (22:37), in which Isaiah says that the Servant 'let himself be taken for a criminal'.

And they all deserted him and ran away (Mk 14:50). Brief words, but how heavy! After sleeping while Jesus stayed awake, the disciples surrender at the first hint of danger: a single sword-stroke, and then, when Jesus allows himself to be taken, they all flee, even Peter. Later, Peter is to recover himself and follow at a distance, right to the high priest's palace. But for the moment the flight is general. The apostles may seem cowardly to us, but we should ask ourselves what we would have done in their place.

A young man who followed him had nothing on but a linen cloth. They caught hold of him, but he left the cloth in their hands and ran away naked (Mk 14:51-2). What is this rather odd episode doing here? Some exegetes see it as a pretext for introducing an extra witness. Others draw attention to the build-up – all the bystanders flee, even a boy who is wearing only a cloth. Others again think that

this detail was intended to show the fulfilment of a scriptural text –
you need a very good Concordance to find it! The prophet Amos
(2:16) describes the disarray at the moment of God's wrath in these
words, 'The bravest warriors will run away naked that day', i.e.
leaving behind their weapons and baggage. So according to them
an anecdote has been invented for this text to apply to! The explanation may display erudition, but it seems very artificial. It is best to
accept the episode as factual. Why then has it been recounted here?
The solution suggested by many exegetes, and a very attractive one,
is that the young man in question is Mark himself, here giving us a
personal reminiscence and, as it were, affixing his signature. In the
same way, perhaps, Matthew has put his signature to his gospel
when he speaks of the 'scribe who becomes a disciple of the kingdom
of heaven . . . who brings out from his storeroom things both new
and old' (Mt 13:52). How did Mark come to be in the garden of
Gethsemane? We cannot answer this without becoming somewhat
fanciful.[1] Whatever the reason is, Mark alone among the evangelists
has retained this inexplicable detail, like a personal reminiscence
engraved in his memory.

The narrative of Matthew

By contrast with the episode of the agony, Matthew here furnishes
us with some details differing from those of Mark; he also employs
phrases which are more semitic, and which are noteworthy since they
suggest that he does not depend uniquely on Mark but also has
access to another source which is closer to the semitic idiom and
perhaps more primitive.

He was still speaking when Judas, one of the Twelve, appeared.
Two brief notes on the grammar: Matthew uses the word 'behold',
(omitted in the translation) between 'when' and 'Judas', it is a formula
frequently used by Matthew and Luke, drawn from the Bible. He
also uses the aorist 'appeared' which he normally prefers to the
historic present of Mark.

[1] According to one author (Dom L. NOLLE, in *Scripture*, II, 1947, pp. 113f.)
Mark's family owned both the house in which the Last Supper took place and
Gethsemane. After the supper, the house was so full that some went off to lie
down in the garden of Gethsemane. The men, Jesus and his disciples, were
going to spend the night there; the young Mark, twelve to fourteen years old,
went with them. He was sleeping in a corner, covered only by a linen cloth.
At the noise of the troop he woke up, looked and ran to see what was happening.
They wanted to lay hold of him too, but he chose to leave his cloth in the
soldiers' hands and ran away naked.

*And with him a large number of men armed with swords and clubs,
sent by the chief priests and elders of the people* (Mt 26:47). Why
has Matthew left out the scribes? The reason is perhaps that,
belonging as he did to this class, he wants to avoid showing them
to have been mixed up in the affair. This is not the only occasion in
his gospel that he has suppressed mention of the scribes. If he is in
fact, as one is very ready to believe, a tax-gatherer, a scribe who has
become a disciple of Jesus, one can understand his not liking to
focus attention on them in painful episodes. A last detail; as often,
Matthew emphasises the *'elders of the people'* to show that those
great landlords represented the people.

Now the traitor . . . The text which follows is identical with that of
Mark. Matthew omits 'see he is well guarded when you lead him
away' because he felt it to be superfluous, or perhaps too disrespectful.

So he went straight up to Jesus (here the style is more correct than
Mark's) *and said, 'Greetings, Rabbi' and kissed him* (Mt 26:49).
Jesus makes a reply to the kiss which Mark has not reported: *Jesus
said to him, 'My friend, do what you are here for'* (Mt 26:50). The
translation here has made a choice between alternatives and is open
to question. The Greek word translated 'friend' means companion,
comrade, an expression which is both polite and familiar – my
friend. *'Do what you are here for'.* The Greek expression is difficult
to translate here. Literally it means, 'for what you are here', and has
given rise to much discussion. Some read it as a question, 'For what
are you here?' It is taken in this way by the Vulgate text, which is
sung on Palm Sunday. But this translation is not correct. It is not an
interrogative pronoun but a relative, and must be translated 'that
for which you have come'. The phrase, then, is elliptical and has to
be completed. Some understand it to mean, 'I know why you have
come'; others, for example Père Lagrange, to mean, 'A kiss! for
what you have come to do!' The solution which I prefer sees it as a
stereotyped, proverbial expression, used to remind someone of
what they have to do, 'Do what you are here for'.[1] 'Do your job.'
It is a reproach which is at one and the same time gentle and dignified.
Jesus says: that is enough for now, it is time for action, carry out

---

[1] Here are two texts which support this interpretation. In the acts of the martyrs
Carpus and his companions, a woman called Agathonica is pressed by the
crowd to deny her faith out of pity for her son. She replies: it is God who will
have pity on my son, I, 'what I am here for'. Which means: I am carrying out
my task; what I have to do here is to confess Christ and die; God will take
care of my little boy. (See A. HARNACK, 'Die Akten des Karpus, des Papylus

your task. Up till now the Lord has been patient, shut his eyes and tried to bring Judas back; but this is the climax, Jesus stops him, now is not the time for embraces, 'My friend, no more pretending, do your job'. John tells us of a parallel at the Last Supper (Jn 13:27): Jesus, who has shown Judas that he knows of the betrayal by giving him a morsel from his dish, tells him, 'What you are going to do, do quickly'. The disciples, says John, do not understand and think that Judas has to distribute some alms or buy what is needed for the Passover. But Jesus is thinking of the betrayal, 'Let's get it over, do your job'.

Then they came forward, seized Jesus and took him in charge (Mt 26:50). The text is similar to Mark's. *At that, one of the followers of Jesus grasped his sword and drew it* (Mt 26:51). There is a point of philological interest here. There is no need to say that someone grasps (literally, 'stretched out his hand') his sword *and* draws it, but it is a biblical turn of speech. When Samson snatches up the jawbone of a donkey to attack his enemies, the Bible, first in the Hebrew, then in the Greek, says, 'he reached out and snatched it up [the jawbone]' (Jg 15:15). Again, when David fights Goliath, he stretches out his hand and takes a stone from his bag to kill him (1 Sam 17:49). Matthew takes up this biblical expression, a small point but one which must be carefully noted since it shows that Matthew does not depend solely on Mark and that his style may betray another source.

He struck out at the high priest's servant, and cut off his ear (Mt 26:51). As with the kiss, Matthew includes a reply by Jesus which is not given in Mark, '*Put your sword back, for all who draw the sword will die by the sword*' (Mt 26:52). This sounds like a proverb, comparable to the quotation in Revelation (13:10). A sword is answered by a sword, the law of human vengeance. Jesus sets himself on a higher plane. He is soon to tell Pilate: I have no soldiers, my kingship is not of this world (Jn 18:36). Here he adds, '*Or do you think that I cannot appeal to my Father who would promptly send more than twelve legions of angels to my defence?*' (Mt 26:53). Jesus points out that his army, his kingdom and his cause are of a wholly

---

und der Agathonike', in *Texte und Untersuchungen*, III, 3–4, Leipzig, 1888, p. 452).

Another parallel: the following inscription (see *Supplementum Epigraphicum Graecum*, vol. VII, Leiden, 1934, no. 811) has been found engraved on a number of ancient glass cups: 'Be glad, what you are here for', i.e. 'Be glad and get on with your business, you're here to drink.'

different order. If he wished for it, the omnipotence of God would be at his disposal and the angels at his service; if he allows himself to be arrested, it is because he wills it and does not conduct his case on the political level.

Why twelve legions of angels? It is a curious expression. It suggests Roman legions, regiments. Are we then to suppose that angels are regimented and grouped in legions? The texts found at Qumrân, near the Dead Sea, now throw some light on this. They are documents of a Jewish sect contemporary with, and even a little earlier than, the New Testament, and they reveal a doctrine in which angels play a large part, especially the bad angels and the good. There the sons of darkness are distinguished from the sons of light, like two great opposing camps in which evil and good, Satan and God, face each other. The prince of darkness and the prince of light have under their command angels as well as men. The *War Scroll*, a manual which deals with the last great conflict, describes all the manoeuvres with which the armies on earth, and above them the angelic armies, confront one another. This is the climate of thought to which Jesus' saying belongs; the angels are like heavenly reinforcements, his true army. If he wished he could call on them, but – '*Then how would the Scriptures be fulfilled that say this is the way it must be?*' (Mt 26:54). Jesus says, 'If I defend myself with the help of God's angels, I shall not die. The scriptures will my death, so I must submit to arrest without resisting.' His attitude is voluntarily passive.

Everything which follows is identical with Mark's narrative, up to the end. There is no need to say anything about it, except that Matthew omits the episode of the naked youth which has no interest for him: one can understand why.

The narrative of Luke

In Luke the account of the arrest is somewhat shorter.

He was still speaking when a number of men appeared, and at the head of them the man called Judas, one of the Twelve (Lk 22:47). Luke mentions neither the swords and clubs, nor the priests and scribes; nor does he speak of the agreed signal, although he is not ignorant of these facts. We shall see further on that Jesus' reply to Judas presupposes that he recognises the kiss to be a signal, and the chief priests are mentioned in verse 52. Luke reserves these details for later and goes straight to the kiss.

He reports a saying of Jesus which is different from that in Matthew: *Jesus said, 'Judas, are you betraying the Son of Man with a kiss?'* (Lk 22:48). The phrase is a fine one, with strong theological overtones; it emphasises the contrast between the kiss, the sign of friendship, and the betrayal it achieves. The expression 'Son of Man' is a major messianic title which Jesus uses to proclaim the sorrow and glory to which he is destined. The tragic character of the scene is condensed into the phrase: a friend fulfils the destiny of the Son of Man – with a gesture of friendship. Since the sayings of Jesus, as reported by Matthew and Luke, differ, it may be asked what Jesus actually said. We do not know, and the question is somewhat pointless. The evangelists have not handed the sayings on to us with the literal exactness of a tape-recording. Each of them has rendered the scene in the terms of his own psychology and his own theology. Matthew records a reply thoroughly worthy of Jesus, Luke gives a majestic summing up of the situation. Both are right, expressing profoundly as they do the spirit of Jesus and his encounter with Judas. Were these sayings spoken in succession? Must they both have been actually uttered? If we had to choose, we might take Matthew's as the more likely, without, for all that, saying that Luke's was incorrect.

His followers, seeing what was happening, said, 'Lord, shall we use our swords?' (Lk 22:49). Here we no longer have Simon Peter taking the initiative and attacking. Respectfully, the disciples ask their master's permission to defend him. From the psychological point of view, this is less truthful. It is difficult to imagine Peter saying, 'Lord, may I strike out?' since Jesus would at once have refused.

And one of them struck out at the high priest's servant, and cut off his right ear (Lk 22:50). Why his right ear, a detail confirmed by John? Face to face with an enemy it is more natural to cut off the left one. It might be suggested that Peter struck from behind, but this would be cowardly[1]. It is probably nearer the truth to say that Peter deliberately chose the right rather than the left ear in order to inflict greater shame. In ancient times, and still today, the limbs on the right are more competent, and are therefore considered more honourable, than those on the left. The Mishnah (*Baba Qamma*, VIII, 6) imposes a fine on a man who administers a slap with the palm of his hand, i.e. a slap on the left cheek; this fine is doubled

---

[1] It might also be suggested that Peter was left-handed, but this would surely be mere evasion.

if the slap is administered with the back of the hand, i.e. is on the right cheek. An Egyptian papyrus (P. Tebt. 793) records another example: a Roman soldier is attacked by the watchman and riff-raff of a village. He defends himself and, in order to get rid of his opponents, cuts off the watchman's right ear. Rather than kill his enemy, the soldier is content to shame him in this way. Peter's action at Gethsemane is analogous.

Jesus' reaction is not the same as in Matthew; according to Luke, Jesus says, *'Leave off! That will do!'* (Lk 22:51); he does not ask for actions of this kind. Already, during the Supper (Lk 22:36–8), Jesus has foretold, in figurative language, the coming of a time when the Son of Man will be persecuted and when he who has a cloak will have to sell it and buy a sword. The apostles, taking these words literally, replied, 'Lord, there are two swords here now'. And Jesus said, 'That is enough', i.e., you don't understand, that's not what I mean. It is the same here: Peter makes a gesture of bravado, which perhaps he is proud of, but Jesus interrupts, 'Leave off! That will do!'

And touching the man's ear he healed him (Lk 22:51). Luke is the only evangelist to record this moving gesture, being both tender-hearted and a doctor. Neither Matthew, Mark nor John mentions such a thing; as far as they are concerned we might think the servant went away wounded. But, according to Luke, the Lord would not allow that to happen. This does not necessarily mean that he invented it, it could be that he has kept in a detail which the other evangelists neglected, since he is compassionate and likes to record stories of healing.

Then Jesus spoke to the chief priests and captains of the Temple guard and elders who had come for him (Lk 22:52). The term 'captains of the guard' refers to the officers of the Temple police. We know that there existed a religious police charged with guarding the holy places, like the Swiss Guard at the Vatican; the captains of the guard were its officers. From the way Luke puts it, it sounds as though Jesus was speaking to the chief priests, the captains of the Temple guard and the elders face to face, as though these high personages had gone themselves, during the night, to Gethsemane, in order to take part in the arrest. No word of this is to be found in Matthew, Mark or John. Did Luke have the benefit of special information? Or did he, as seems more likely, simplify the situation? It is much more probable that only the servants and guards came to Gethsemane and that their chiefs waited for Jesus to be brought to them. Whoever the audience was composed of, however, Luke reports the same saying of Jesus: *'Am I a brigand that you had to set out with swords and clubs?'* (Lk 22:52).

'But this is your hour; this is the reign of darkness' (Lk 22:53). The struggle of Satan against Christ, the clash of the two great empires, is a theme as dear to Luke as it is to John. As early as the temptation in the desert, Luke tells us – he is the only evangelist to do so – that Satan left Jesus, to return at the appointed time, as though he only left Jesus alone in order to lay hands on him later. Now 'the time' has come; when Judas goes to find the chief priests and deliver Jesus to them, Luke asserts that it is Satan who has entered into him and is moving him to act in this way (Lk 22:3). Similarly, according to John (13:27), Satan enters into Judas when he accepts the morsel of bread. Thus Luke and John both indicate that the unhappy man is the instrument of an evil power. Satan has several times been vanquished by the Lord in the healing of the possessed (Lk 10:17–18), but he has not given up the struggle and now he exerts his power again. Satan is to put Jesus to death, believing that he has thus gained the victory while in fact it is his defeat. This is the meaning of the saying which Luke records here: this is your hour, the reign of darkness. God grants Satan permission to act; as Revelation says, he allows the forces of evil to be unloosed. The righteous succumb, but God's purpose is accomplished.

The narrative of John

John adds two new elements which are of some importance. The first is the presence of the cohort.

Judas brought the cohort to this place together with a detachment of guards sent by the chief priests and the Pharisees, all with lanterns and torches and weapons (Jn 18:3). We already know of the detachment of guards sent by the chief priests from Mark and Matthew; they are the hired assassins of the Sanhedrin. The mention of the Pharisees mixes up sects, such as Pharisees and Sadducees, with social classes, such as chief priests and scribes. But the mention of the cohort is still more surprising. This term suggests the Roman army, in which it meant a body of troops six hundred strong. This fresh detail seems to be confirmed by the episode which follows, in which Jesus is led bound by the 'Chiliarch', translated by the Vulgate as 'tribune' (Jn 18:12). This raises a serious difficulty: who is responsible for the trial and death of Jesus, the Jews or the Romans? One answer, espoused particularly by the Jews, even today, is that it was the Romans who arrested Jesus and put him to death by crucifixion, a Roman penalty. John here, therefore, is admitting that the Romans themselves carried out the arrest, with the collaboration of certain Jews. In a recent work[1], a German-Jewish scholar, resident in London, claims that the whole responsibility rests with Pilate. According to him, Pilate has for a long time been saying to Caiaphas, 'Get rid of this man, he is embarrassing me; if you don't act, I shall have to intervene myself'. Caiaphas calls a meeting of his council (Jn 11:47f.) and says, 'If we let him go on in this way everybody will believe in him and the Romans will come and destroy the Holy Place and our nation. . . . It is better for one man to die for the people, . . .' Caiaphas acts only under Roman pressure. Pilate sends his soldiers to Gethsemane to make sure that his orders are carried out. The Jews, then, are not responsible for Jesus' death. This problem, a very serious one, will be discussed later. As regards the arrest at Gethsemane, however, it is not the only possible solution. It is quite possible to believe, on the contrary, that the Jews themselves took the initiative and arrested Jesus, but, knowing that they would have to hand him over to the Romans later, since they did not have the power to execute the death penalty themselves, they asked the Roman army for a small body of troops to guarantee that the arrest would succeed. This explanation is quite convincing, but there could be yet another – is it a fact that the Greek terms translated 'cohort' and 'tribune' or 'captain' necessarily refer to the Romans? This is not obviously so, for the Greek words (literally 'officer over a thousand' and 'squad of troops') can also be used of another body of police, perhaps a Jewish one. We may end by asking ourselves whether John was well informed, or whether he was being somewhat inaccurate, compared with the synoptics who make no mention of the Romans.

Verses 4–9 convey another original element, the majestic attitude of Jesus at the arrest.

Knowing everything that was going to happen to him, Jesus then came forward and said, 'Who are you looking for?' They answered, 'Jesus the Nazarene'. He said, 'I am he'. Now Judas the traitor was standing among them. When Jesus said, 'I am he', they moved back

[1] PAUL WINTER, *On the Trial of Jesus*, 1961; see my review in *Revue Biblique*, 1961, pp. 593–9.

and fell to the ground. He asked them a second time, 'Who are you looking for?' They said, 'Jesus the Nazarene'. 'I have told you that I am he' replied Jesus. 'If I am the one you are looking for, let these others go.' This was to fulfil the words he had spoken. 'Not one of those you gave me have I lost' (Jn 18:4–9). This presentation differs from that of the synoptics and has its own value and interest. John obviously wishes to put the accent on the majesty of the Lord, the master of his own destiny. It is an aspect of the 'Johannine Christ', which, without falsifying the facts, hints from the very beginning of Jesus' earthly life at the 'glory' which he has from his Father and which is to shine out through his resurrection. Just as painters encircle the head of saints with a halo, John deliberately surrounds Jesus with this divine majesty which is less apparent in the synoptics. John is expressing differently something which they have already said – Jesus fulfils the scriptures, refuses to defend himself, controls his own destiny. He shows himself and says, 'I am'. This expression occurs often in the gospel of John; it suggests powerfully the divine presence of Jesus – at Sinai Yahweh says, 'I am who I am' (Ex 3:14), and 'I am' is the divine being. In fact, the soldiers shrink back and fall to the ground at this word. This is quite likely. There is no need to exaggerate the element of the marvellous and imagine them crashing like pillars in an earthquake. It is enough if, awed by the majesty of Jesus, they recoil a little, trip over the roots of the olive trees and some of them fall over backwards. Mark and Matthew have not retained this stray detail, but John develops it because he sees in it a symbolic expression of a deeper truth: these men fell to the ground before the Lord, Jesus deliberately allowed himself to be arrested, preventing any of his own from being taken for trial too.

Apart from these important elements, John gives us two other details. One is the identification of Simon Peter, which is not made by any of the synoptics. This is very likely and absolutely in character: Peter draws his sword in a gesture which is generous and spontaneous but more or less useless.

The other detail is the name of the servant Malchus. This feature, which is unlikely to have been invented, indicates an ancient tradition in John. John knew the household of the high priest and, if not the high priest himself, at least the servants, including this Malchus. The name is known and probably Nabataean, showing that this is a particular servant, a slave of the high priest. John was an eye-witness; like Luke he notes that it was the right ear.

Other than this, John tells us nothing new. The ending is very brief: '*Am I not to drink the cup that the Father has given me?*' (Jn 18:11). It proves that John knew of the agony at Gethsemane although he did not recount it. Here he uses the cup of Gethsemane, which Jesus accepted, to signify that Jesus fulfils the scriptures.

Such is the scene of the arrest. It is based on four strands of evidence, statements which have many features in common and include others peculiar to one or other of the evangelists. This only confirms the historicity of the event. The arrival of Judas, the exchange of words, the sword-stroke, have been recorded in different ways to convey different aspects of the mystery. The chief thing we learn from it is Jesus' own desire to do his Father's will. In the trial which is to follow we shall find the same dignified attitude in Jesus when he gives his adversaries to understand that he obeys them only in obedience to his Father in order to fulfil his role of saviour.

3. Peter's Denials

Mt 26:57-58, 69-75	Mk 14:53-54, 66-72
[57] The men	[53] They
who had arrested Jesus	
led him off	led Jesus off
to Caiaphas the high priest,	to the high priest;
where the scribes and the elders were assembled. [58] Peter	and all the chief priests and the elders and the scribes assembled there. [54] Peter
followed him at a distance	had followed him at a distance,
and when he reached the high priest's palace, he went in	right into the high priest's palace,

Lk 22:54–62	Jn 18:12–18, 25–27
54 They	**12** The cohort and its captain and the Jewish guards
seized him then	seized Jesus and bound him.
and led him away, and they took him	**13** They took him first
	To Annas,
to the high priest's house.	because Annas was the father-in-law of Caiaphas, who was high priest that year.
	14 It was Caiaphas who had suggested to the Jews, 'It is better for one man to die for the people'.
Peter	**15** Simon Peter, with another disciple,
followed at a distance.	followed Jesus. This disciple, who was known to the high priest, went with Jesus into the high priest's palace,
	16 but Peter stayed outside the door. So the other disciple, the one known to the high priest, went out, spoke to the woman who was keeping the door and brought Peter in.
	17 The maid on duty at the door said to Peter, 'Aren't you another of that man's disciples?' He answered, 'I am not'.
55	**18** Now it was cold, and the servants and guard had lit a charcoal fire
They had lit a fire in the middle of the courtyard	
	and were standing there

Mt	Mk
and sat down with the attendants to see what the end would be	and was sitting with the attendants warming himself at the fire
[69] Meanwhile Peter was sitting outside in the courtyard, and a servant-girl came up to him and said, 'You too were with Jesus the Galilean'. [70] But he denied it in front of them all.	[66] While Peter was down below in the courtyard, one of the high priest's servant-girls came up. [67] She saw Peter warming himself there, stared at him and said, 'You too were with Jesus, the man from Nazareth'. [68] But he denied it.
'I do not know what you are talking about' he said.	'I do not know, I do not understand, what you are talking about' he said.
[71] When he went out to the gateway another servant-girl saw him and said to the people there, 'This man was with Jesus the Nazarene'. [72] And again, with an oath, he denied it, 'I do not know the man'.	And he went out into the forecourt (and a cock crew) [69] The servant-girl saw him and again started telling the bystanders, 'This fellow is one of them'. [70] But again he denied it.
[73] A little later the bystanders	A little later the bystanders themselves

Lk   Jn

	warming themselves;
and Peter sat down	so Peter
among them,	stood there too,
	warming himself with the others.

[56] and as he
was sitting there
by the blaze

a servant-girl   [17] The maid on duty at the door

saw him,

peered at him,
and said,   said to Peter,
'This person was   'Aren't you another
with him too'.   of that man's disciples?'
[57] But he denied it.

'Woman,' he said   He answered,
'I do not know him,'   'I am not'.

                                     [25] As Simon Peter stood there
                                     warming himself,

[58] Shortly afterwards
someone else
saw him
and said,   someone said to him,

'You are another   'Aren't you another
of them'.   of his disciples?'
But

Peter replied,   He denied it, saying,
'I am not,   'I am not'.
my friend'.
[59] About an hour later
another man   [26] One of the high priest's servants,
                                     a relation of the man whose

Mt	Mk

came up
and said to Peter,   said to Peter,
'You are   'You are
one of them   one of them
for sure!   for sure!
Why,   Why,
your accent gives you away.'   you are a Galilean.
⁷⁴ Then he started calling down   ⁷¹ But he started calling down
   curses   curses
on himself   on himself
and swearing,   and swearing,
'I do not know   'I do not know
the man'.   the man
                                       you speak of'.
At that moment   ⁷² At that moment

the cock crew,   the cock crew
                                       for the second time,

⁷⁵ And Peter remembered   and Peter recalled
what Jesus had said,   how Jesus had said
                                       to him,
'Before the cock crows   'Before the cock crows
                                       twice,
you will have disowned me three   you will have disowned me three
   times   times'.
And he went outside
and wept   And he burst into tears.
bitterly.

Lk   Jn

ear Peter had cut off,

insisted, saying,   said,
'This fellow   'Didn't I see you
was certainly
with him.   in the garden with him?'
Why,
he is a Galilean.'
⁶⁰ 'My friend,'
said Peter   ²⁷ Again Peter
                                denied it;

'I do not know

what are you talking about.'
At that instant,   and at once
while he was still speaking,
the cock crew,   a cock crew.

⁶¹ and the Lord turned
and looked straight at Peter,
and Peter remembered
what the Lord had said
to him,
'Before the cock crows
today,
you will have disowned me three
times'.
⁶² And he went outside
and wept
bitterly.

After reflecting on the agony of Gethsemane and the arrest of Jesus, we should, at least if we follow Mark and Matthew, turn next to the appearance before the Sanhedrin. However, I prefer to follow the order of Luke, who places the session of the Sanhedrin in the early hours of the morning instead of during the night. A problem is involved here which we shall deal with later. I believe, with Luke, that all that took place during the night was the denials of Peter and, according to John, a swift interrogation before Annas.

In this chapter we shall see Jesus led to the high priest's palace and disowned by his chosen disciple. The narratives of the evangelists diverge so much from one another that one cannot hope to get an absolutely coherent picture of what took place. The best way to understand the gospels is to read each carefully for its own content and then, by comparing them with each other, form a general idea of the deeper significance of the scene.

The narrative of Mark

They led Jesus off to the high priest; and all the chief priests and the elders and the scribes assembled there (Mk 14:53). Jesus has just been taken prisoner at Gethsemane; now he is led to the high priest's house. Notice that Mark does not give the name of the high priest; this is important because his name cannot be taken for granted. It may, of course, have been Caiaphas, the high priest in office, but it could also have been Annas, a former high priest who still had considerable influence. In fact, it was to the latter's house that Jesus was led, as we shall learn from John. For the moment, it must suffice that Jesus was taken to the palace of the high priests. These had, as a family, a residence in Jerusalem. Mark adds that the whole Sanhedrin assembled there; in the chief priests, elders and scribes can be recognised the three classes of which the Sanhedrin was made up. Mark says they *all* gathered there; so, according to him, it was a full session of the Sanhedrin which was now going to be held. It was night, and the text must not be smoothed over with the suggestion that only a small group was involved; according to Mark, it was the whole assembly of the Jews. We shall see later what we are to make of this information.

Peter had followed him at a distance, right into the high priest's palace (Mk 14:54). After fleeing like everyone else, Peter has regained control of himself and wants to follow his master. He is generous, impulsive, at times fearful, but he has nevertheless the courage to come as close as possible to the events which are in train. He follows at a distance to avoid being reprimanded by the guards.

Mark's style is not elegant: 'he followed him right inside, into the court of the high priest'. The translation has smoothed this out. Matthew too improves the phrase. The Greek word *aule*, the equivalent of the Latin *aula*, can in fact mean either the palace or the court[1]. It can refer to the building as a whole as well as the people to be found there or the central courtyard of the palace.

Peter then goes into the high priest's palace *and was sitting with the attendants warming himself at the fire*. The translation has again been kind to Mark, who says literally 'warming himself at the light', an example of the clumsiness to which he is addicted, but nevertheless a picturesque and pertinent detail, since it is this light which will help the servant girl to recognise Peter.

Mark then records the session of the Sanhedrin (14:55-65) which will be studied in chapter 5. Here we take up the story again at verse 66.

While Peter was down below in the courtyard, one of the high priest's servant-girls came up (Mk 14:66). 'Below, in the courtyard', this time the word *aule* means courtyard. Clearly, Mark is distinguishing between the upper floor of the palace and the lower where the courtyard was. He imagines – we must assume, since he does not tell us in so many words – that the Sanhedrin is sitting in a room upstairs, while the servants are waiting round the fire, below in the courtyard.

One of the high priest's servant-girls came up. She saw Peter warming himself there, stared at him and said . . . (Mk 14:67) She stares at him and, as Mark suggests, it is because he is close to the fire that the light from it allows her to recognise him. The Greek verb suggests an attentive scrutiny; Mark uses the same word when he describes Jesus looking at the rich young man, 'Jesus looked steadily

---

[1] In the same way, the 'court' of the Queen is not a courtyard with a fountain and so on, but the palace and its inhabitants.

at him and loved him' (Mk 10:21) . . . *And said, 'You too were with Jesus, the man from Nazareth'* (Mk 14:67). So the servant-girl guesses that Peter was with Jesus, though Mark does not tell us how she did.

But he denied it. 'I do not know, I do not understand what you are talking about' he said (Mk 14:68). We must take note of the two verbs which give us the impression that Peter is stammering. Peter does not know what to do, he stutters, 'I . . . I . . . don't know, I . . . I . . . don't understand what you're talking about'. This is not a formal denial yet; Peter pretends to be taken aback, withdraws, looks for a way of evading the question without a formal repudiation – at least this is what the Greek text suggests. Some exegetes, however, think that this is a poor Greek translation of an Aramaic original which could mean, 'I do not know *him* of whom you are speaking'. In Aramaic the same particle can be both masculine and neuter, 'who' and 'what'. If we accept that there was an Aramaic original, and that the masculine was intended, then Peter would indeed be making a formal repudiation, 'I do not know Jesus.' But I prefer to abide by the Greek as we have it, and here it is neuter: 'I do not know what you are talking about', along with the two verbs which suggest stammering.

And he went out . . . Peter feels that the situation is becoming dangerous, he wants to leave, he goes out, but . . . *into the forecourt.* This is odd; he could get away but he stops there and is going to be questioned twice more. This is slightly incoherent but should be retained; it can perhaps be explained by his going out but stopping in the forecourt.

And a cock crew should be added here. Although many manuscripts do not contain these words, I believe they should be included since Mark will tell us, and even repeat it, that before the cock crew *twice*, Peter denied Christ three times. The cock will crow for the last time after the third denial, so it must crow once before that. If these words have been suppressed in certain manuscripts, it must be because neither Matthew nor Luke tells us that the cock crew at this point. So the cock crows here for the first time. It is strange that Peter does not notice it; it ought to have attracted his attention and reminded him of the words of Jesus. But apparently he takes no notice.

The servant-girl saw him and again started telling the bystanders, 'This fellow is one of them' (Mk 14:69). Here it is the same servant-girl who had stared at him. Are we to imagine that she has followed him into the forecourt? No, since it seems that she is speaking to the people round the fire. The actions of the characters are obscure; there is a slight incoherence which we shall need to try and explain. The same girl, then, tells the bystanders, 'This fellow is one of them'.

But again he denied it. In Mark, the second denial is not expressed in words, the fact is merely stated.

A little later the bystanders themselves said to Peter, 'You are one of them for sure! Why, you are a Galilean' (Mk 14:70). 'A little later', how long? We do not know, the expression is very vague. 'The bystanders': this time it is not the servant-girl but the whole group who say, 'You are one of them.' Mark does not say why they took Peter for a Galilean; and it is not obvious. Perhaps they recognised it from his dress. Matthew explains that it was by his accent, but it is not impossible that it was a question of dress. Today a man from Hebron can be recognised by a particular kind of head-dress, Arab women from each village wear different embroidery. It was possible, then, to recognise Peter by his manner or his dress.

The third denial, following on this new attack, becomes much stronger: *But he started calling down curses on himself and swearing, 'I do not know the man you speak of'* (Mk 14:71). Here the Greek uses *anathematizein*, to pronounce an anathema. This is a scriptural expression characteristic of the Septuagint which means either to curse someone or, more often, to call down curses on oneself. It is not rare to find the following expression in the Bible, 'May this happen to me and that happen to me, if I am not speaking the truth'. Even today, in the East, you can hear people take God to witness by calling down curses on themselves and their family if they are wrong. So Peter reaches the point of saying, 'My God curse me if I ever knew this man!' It is a violent expression, a paroxysm of repudiation. The first time he had said, 'I don't understand what you are talking about'; the second it seems he contented himself with a mere denial; this time he is deeply involved, 'I do not know the man you speak of.' You could hardly have a more formal denial.

At that moment the cock crew for the second time. We have seen that the cock crew once before. *And Peter recalled how Jesus had said to him, 'Before the cock crows twice, you will have disowned me three times'* (Mk 14:72). While they were walking from the supper room to Gethsemane, Jesus had told them that the time was coming when the shepherd would be struck and the sheep scattered.

Peter had said, 'Even if all lose faith, I will not.' To which Jesus had replied, 'I tell you solemnly this day, this very night, before the cock crows twice, you will have disowned me three times' (Mk 14:27–30). Peter had forgotten this; even the first crowing of the cock, it seems, had failed to recall it to him. But this time, suddenly, after three denials, he realises his sin.

And he burst into tears. The Greek expression is difficult to understand and there is much uncertainty about its exact meaning. The verb means literally, 'to throw oneself on', but it can take on many different shades of meaning according to its context. According to Theophylact, a writer of the Byzantine period, it means 'having covered [his head]', that is, Peter has thrown a cloak or a veil over his head, perhaps to weep. But there is no mention of a cloak here as there is in the passage of Mark where the disciples throw their cloaks over the ass's back (Mk 11:7). Others suggest that the word 'mind' should be understood – 'casting his mind', that is, 'reflecting'. According to this interpretation, Peter reflects in order to weep – which is highly academic! Others translate it as 'beginning to speak', since in certain cases it can have this meaning. In my opinion a better solution is to take the verb to mean 'to rush'[1]. Here it could be said that Peter rushes ('outside' understood) or, to put it more colloquially, 'makes off'. This would come closer to the text of Matthew and Luke. But the best solution, again one proposed by Theophylact and upheld by the old translations, is that which takes the word in the sense 'to hasten to do something'. The word can in fact have this meaning[2]. Here we should have to interpret it to mean that Peter hastened to weep, i.e. he burst into tears.

The narrative of Matthew

The men who had arrested Jesus led him off to Caiaphas the high priest, where the scribes and the elders were assembled (Mt 26:57). As Matthew does not record the episode of the young man who had been arrested and fled naked, he recalls the action taken against Jesus: 'The men who had arrested Jesus'. Matthew here names

[1] Thus in Mk 4:37 the waves rush upon the boat. In the First Book of Maccabees, 4:2, Gorgias, a Greek general, rushes on the Jewish camp, irrupting on it in an unexpected movement.
[2] For example, an Egyptian papyrus (P. Tebt. 50:12) exists in which a villager wants to stop up the canal which feeds his neighbour's garden to get some water for himself; at length he finds a good opportunity and 'hastens' to block the canal.

Caiaphas where Mark was not so precise. It is not certain that this information is correct since we shall find it contradicted by John. We shall have to choose between them.

Where the scribes and the elders were assembled: like Mark, Matthew is certainly thinking of the Sanhedrin, though he does not say 'all'. If he does not mention the chief priests, this is probably because he imagines that they must already be present in the high priest's residence. Whatever the explanation, Matthew, like Mark, assumes that the Great Sanhedrin assembles during the night.

Peter followed him at a distance, and when he reached the high priest's palace, he went in and sat down with the attendants to see what the end would be. (Mt 26:58). Peter 'followed him'; in the Greek the imperfect is used, not the aorist, a slight stylistic change which is very expressive; the imperfect suggests better the length of time it took to reach the high priest's palace. *He went in*; this phrase is clearer than Mark's, we can see better both the approach to the palace and the moment of going inside. *He sat down with the attendants.* Matthew does not have the same feeling for the picturesque as Mark and alludes neither to the flame nor to the fire: these details seem unimportant to him and he drops them; we have already seen him do this several times in his gospel. This action of Peter's, however, in which he warms his hands to cover his embarrassment and so lets himself be illuminated by the fire and recognised, is a piece of true observation on Mark's part. Matthew, less imaginative than Mark, does not linger over this scene and says only that Peter stays with the attendants *to see the outcome.* This is what interests Matthew; Peter is there to see what turn events will take.

Here, Matthew, like Mark, places the sitting of the Sanhedrin during the night.

Meanwhile Peter was sitting outside in the courtyard, and a servant-girl came up to him and said, 'You too were with Jesus the Galilean' (Mt 26:69). Matthew does not say 'below', like Mark; he does not set the stage with an upper storey and a courtyard below. He imagines simply that the Sanhedrin is assembled in a room inside. As he has not mentioned the fire, he eliminates the nice detail about the girl recognising Peter by its light. *'You too were with Jesus the Galilean'.* Matthew's phrase resembles Mark's, but he says Galilean, perhaps because he wants to suggest how they recognise Peter; a man is identified by the district he comes from rather than the town. For the inhabitants of Judaea, Galilee was another province; each

could tell where the other came from, rather as in France nor-
therners can recognise southerners and vice versa.

*But he denied it in front of them all. 'I do not know what you are
talking about' he said* (Mt 26:70). Matthew adds that it was in front
of everyone that Peter denied Christ, thus aggravating this offence
since they all hear his reply, 'I do not know what you are talking
about'. The text is the same as Mark's but it contains only one verb
so that the stammering effect, which was so spontaneous and
striking, is lost. But here, as in Mark, Peter evades the question and
does not make a formal denial.

*When he went out to the gateway another servant-girl saw him and
said to the people there, 'This man was with Jesus the Nazarene'*
(Mt 26:71). In Matthew it is not the forecourt but the gateway, and
the cock does not crow. In Mark it was the same servant-girl and
not 'another'; the difference should be noted.

And again, with an oath, he denied it. 'I do not know the man'
(Mt 26:72). There are two things to be noticed here. First, Matthew
makes Peter's reply explicit, where Mark had merely said that he
denied without being more precise. We are reminded of what Matthew
has already done in the account of Gethsemane for the second prayer;
whereas Mark said that Jesus went off to pray saying the same words,
Matthew indicated what they were, 'Father, your will be done . . .'
He composes words for it to make it more clear. So too here he takes
the words from the third reply in verse 74, 'I do not know the man',
in order to be able to give an actual reply instead of Mark's vague
'he denied it'. Secondly, it must be noticed that in Matthew the
second denial is accompanied by an oath; he manages the crescendo
more skilfully than Mark. The first time Peter says, 'I do not know
what you are talking about'; this time the denial is more formal,
Peter swears an oath, 'I do not know the man'. The third time it will
be still more energetic.

*A little later the bystanders came up and said to Peter, 'You are
one of them for sure! Why, your accent gives you away'* (Mt 26:73).
'A little later' is as vague as Mark; 'the bystanders' indicates an
anonymous group. According to Matthew, just as in Mark, Peter
makes for the exit; perhaps the people from the central courtyard
come up to him. 'Why, your accent gives you away', Matthew
explains how they recognised him, which Mark left obscure; it is
his accent which betrays a man! A man from northern France
immediately recognises someone from Marseilles by his sing-song

intonation, and this is reciprocal. The Galileans did not speak like the inhabitants of Judaea.

Then he started calling down curses on himself and swearing, 'I do not know the man'. At that moment the cock crew (Mt 26:74). This is the climax to which Matthew has been building up and he has calculated the effect better than Mark: this time Peter accompanies his oath with a curse. *The cock crew,* not for the second time since Matthew has only one crowing of the cock.

And Peter remembered what Jesus had said . . . This verse resembles the parallel in Mark. *And he went outside and wept bitterly* (Mt 26:75). 'He went outside', Mark did not say so, unless this is what was meant by the difficult verb. In Matthew, all is clear; Peter at last goes out; he has been waiting at the gateway before doing so (why exactly we do not know), but at last he does go, and weeps bitterly.

The narrative of Luke

They seized him then and led him away, and they took him to the high priest's house. Peter followed at a distance (Lk 22:54). Luke did not say, in the scene at Gethsemane, that Jesus was arrested. According to Mark and Matthew it was at the moment that they laid hands on Jesus that Peter drew his sword and intervened. According to Luke, on the other hand, 'His followers, seeing what was happening, said "Lord, shall we use our swords?"' It is to prevent the arrest that Peter or some other un-named man draws his sword. Since Luke has not yet mentioned the arrest he does so now. He uses a Greek term different from that used by Mark and Matthew, a more elegant and more classical one, 'they seized him'; the word used by Mark and Matthew is more colloquial and would perhaps be better translated 'grabbed'. Luke does not name the high priest, it could be either Caiaphas or Annas. Again, it is the 'house', not the palace, and it sounds more as if a private residence were meant. We shall see too that according to Luke the session of the Sanhedrin is not held in the high priest's palace, but in a special courtroom near the Temple. Luke distinguishes clearly between the private residence of the high priest, where they spend the night, and the Sanhedrin to which they move in the early morning (Lk 22:66). Even now we begin to sense divergences of tradition between Luke on the one hand and Mark and Matthew on the other, between which we shall have to choose as best we can. *Peter followed at a distance*: Luke, like Matthew, uses the imperfect (literally, 'was following') that is so much more expressive than Mark's aorist. *They had lit a fire in the middle of the courtyard and Peter sat down among them* (Lk 22:55). As a writer, Luke knows how to tell a story, he makes things clearer; they are sitting round the fire, when Peter goes over and joins the group. Fire and light are better distinguished than in Mark; the fire at which Peter warms himself, the light of the flame which allows him to be recognised. *And as he was sitting there by the blaze a servant-girl saw him, peered at him, and said, 'This person was with him too'* (Lk 22:56). 'By the blaze', Luke uses the same word as Mark does in verse 54. 'Peered at him', this word is characteristic of Luke who uses it often elsewhere, it means 'to fix the eyes on someone, to stare them in the face'. The servant-girl's intervention is not addressed to him directly as it is in Mark and Matthew: Luke writes 'This person' where they had said 'You too'. It is impersonal, she speaks to everybody and says 'with him', not mentioning Jesus by name.

But he denied it. 'Woman,' he said 'I do not know him' (Lk 22:57). In the three denials Luke has completely ignored the sense of crescendo; there is even a slackening of tension. Here at the outset there is a formal denial: 'I do not know him', whereas in Mark and Matthew, we have 'I do not know what you are talking about, I don't understand'. Seemingly Luke did not intend the same effect.

Shortly afterwards someone else saw him and said, 'You are another of them'. Mark tells us that it was the same servant-girl, Matthew that it was another girl, Luke that it was a man. The details are different. For the second questioning, Luke adopts the style of a direct challenge, 'You are another of them'. *Peter replied, 'I am not, my friend'* (Lk 22:58). In Luke, Peter is not talkative and his second reply is less strong than the first.

About an hour later another man insisted, saying, 'This fellow was certainly with him. Why, he is a Galilean' (Lk 22:59). The precise time 'about an hour later' may be a piece of information which is true, but it could also be an instance of the storyteller's art, enlivening the narrative with extra details[1]. In Luke, the third encounter is with a man, 'another man', whereas in Mark and Matthew it is with the bystanders. These slight discordances should be noted. 'This fellow

---

[1] At Gethsemane, where Matthew and Mark said that Jesus went on a little further, Luke is more precise, 'about a stone's throw away'.

was certainly with him', Luke reverts to the indirect approach, *'My friend,'* said Peter, *'I do not know what you are talking about'* (Lk 22:60). Luke's third denial is the weakest, resembling Mark's first. Notice the slackening tension: first it was, 'I do not know Jesus', then 'I don't belong with them', lastly 'What do you mean? I don't understand'. The psychological point of view is different, less successful perhaps than in Mark and especially in Matthew. But Luke is going to redeem this failure by recording a truly precious detail.

At that instant, while he was still speaking, the cock crew, and the Lord turned and looked straight at Peter (Lk 22:60-1). Luke alone records for us this action of the Lord, an action which is very important not only from the historical but also from the theological and spiritual points of view. This is the actual, historical situation: the Lord is there, in the courtyard, where these events take place. Neither Mark nor Matthew had told us so. Nor in fact does Luke, but he notes that the Lord turned round; he has only to turn round, he is therefore somewhere there, in the corner of the courtyard. When Peter has made his three denials, he turns and looks at him. If you try to combine the three accounts, you have to say that Jesus descends from the upper storey at that very moment and as he passes looks at Peter. But this is not in the text; to get this you have to merge the accounts of Matthew and Luke. If we do not merge the two, but read Luke by himself, there is no question yet of the Sanhedrin. This does not assemble for its session until the morning. My conclusion, and I am certain that this is historically true, is that Jesus spent that night in the courtyard, or rather, taking John also into account, that Jesus was briefly interrogated in private by Annas and a few of the leaders, that after this quick examination he was left in a corner of the courtyard, where the mocking took place, after which they waited for daybreak, and that it was during this interval that the unhappy Peter repudiated him. Jesus heard it all, and when his disciple had denied him for the third time, he looked at him, a deeply moving look, which caused Peter's breakdown, full as it was of a tender reproach – 'I told you so, my poor Peter'. Luke is a writer of deep understanding and this detail recorded by him is one we should carry into our lives. When we have some denial, small or great, to reproach ourselves with, we may imagine this look of the Lord fixed on us – 'You promised to be faithful, and look what you have done!' – and, like Peter, repent.

And Peter remembered what the Lord had said to him . . . And he went outside and wept bitterly (Lk 22:61–2). Peter is in tears, it is contrition that wins pardon.

Before leaving Luke, we should notice one detail; he uses here the same expression as Matthew, 'and he went outside and wept bitterly'. This raises a problem of literary analysis connected with the synoptic problem. We are continually forced to conclude that both Luke and Matthew knew the work of Mark and often enough the resemblances between them can be explained by their having had this common source. But the cases where Luke and Matthew resemble one another and are *not* following Mark raise a difficulty: how do they come to use the same phrases? Judging by their divergences on texts of major importance, such as the Our Father or the infancy narratives, it does not seem possible that they knew one another's work. If they did, they would have made their accounts agree more closely. We have then to explain how it is, in a case like this, that the same saying occurs in identical form in Luke and Matthew. Various solutions are possible; one, which I think is the correct one here, is to ask whether the manuscript tradition is reliable or whether some ancient copyist has not modified Luke's text to make it agree with Matthew's. The words in which we are interested here are not found in all the manuscripts of Luke, or at any rate are not always found in the same form. It is quite possible that one of the monks of antiquity who copied the manuscripts, knowing the gospel by heart, introduced into Luke the phrase found in the parallel passage in Matthew. This phenomenon, common enough in the manuscripts, produces 'harmonisations' which are not the work of the original authors at all but of the copyists.

The narrative of John

The cohort and its captain and the Jewish guards seized Jesus and bound him (Jn 18:12). Here again are the terms of which I spoke in the preceding chapter. The Greek word can mean 'cohort', and its captain is called a 'tribune', but it is not certain that this is the meaning, and we cannot assert definitely that the 'cohort' consisted of Roman soldiers. *They seized Jesus and bound him.* These bonds have not been mentioned by any other evangelist, we shall meet them again later in John.

They took him first to Annas, because Annas was the father-in-law of Caiaphas, who was high priest that year (Jn 18:13). John is quite definite; Jesus is taken to Annas, not to Caiaphas as Matthew said. This Annas or Ananos is well-known to historians: after occupying the position of high priest himself for a long time, he was succeeded by not less than five of his sons, Caiaphas, according to John, was his son-in-law. We may justly question the accuracy of Matthew's information, according to which it was Caiaphas to whom Jesus was taken. For reasons which I shall give later, I believe that John's is more probable and more historical.

The following verse reminds us who Caiaphas is: *It was Caiaphas who had suggested to the Jews, 'It is better for one man to die for the people'* (Jn 18:14). John is alluding to an earlier incident in his narrative (Jn 11:47–53): fearing that Jesus' fame would disturb the Romans, the members of the Sanhedrin assembled; Caiaphas suggested doing away with Jesus because it was better 'for one man to die for the people'. John adds that with these words Caiaphas, the high priest, was prophesying without knowing it: 'Jesus was to die for the nation – and not for the nation only, but to gather together in unity the scattered children of God.' Notice that Caiaphas himself has not yet appeared; he is only mentioned as being Annas' son-in-law, and it is to Annas they go first, during the night.

Simon Peter, with another disciple, followed Jesus. This disciple, who was known to the high priest, went with Jesus into the high priest's palace, but Peter stayed outside the door (Jn 18:15–16). John always says 'Simon Peter'; he keeps both names, whereas the others say 'Peter', or, at the beginning, 'Simon'. Who is this 'other disciple' whom we also meet in other passages of John (20:2, 3, 4, 8)? He is often identified with John himself; this is possible: John would be cloaking himself with a sort of discreet anonymity. But John is identified also with 'the disciple Jesus loved' (13:23; 19:26; 20:2; 21:7, 20); are they the same person? This problem will occur again later (pp. 251f). 'He went with Jesus into the high priest's palace' – literally 'court', but it is better to translate it 'palace'. This disciple, who knows the high priest, can come and go freely in the palace; he is allowed in with everyone else. But Peter has to stay outside since he is not known to the members of the household.

So the other disciple, the one known to the high priest, spoke to the woman who was keeping the door and brought Peter in (Jn 18:16). According to an ancient Syriac translation, it should read 'the porter'; this is plausible: it would be more normal for the entrance to the high priest's palace to be guarded by a doorkeeper. The porter lets Peter in, and it is his servant-girl who later addresses Peter.

Now it was cold, and the servants and guards had lit a charcoal fire and were standing there warming themselves; so Peter stood there too warming himself with the others (Jn 18:18). The picture is even more concrete and precise than in Luke. We may well believe we are seeing the scene as reported by an eye-witness.

The maid on duty at the door said to Peter, 'Aren't you another of that man's disciples?' He answered, 'I am not'. Here it is a servant-girl, as in Mark and Matthew, but she is on duty at the door. According to Mark, Peter is in the centre of the courtyard, near the fire, when the girl addresses him; here, it happens the moment he comes in. The denial remains very vague, 'I am not, I am not a member of that group'.

John places the examination by Annas here; it will be dealt with in the chapter which follows. Annas interrogates Jesus, who scarcely replies; Jesus receives a slap, and it is then, I think, that the maltreatment takes place. John then separates the first denial from the second and third by the examination before Annas.

As Simon Peter stood there warming himself, someone said to him, 'Aren't you another of his disciples?' He denied it, saying, 'I am not' (Jn 18:25). Peter says neither more nor less than he did the first time, he merely asserts that he does not belong to the group.

One of the high priest's servants, a relation of the man whose ear Peter had cut off, said, 'Didn't I see you in the garden with him?' Again Peter denied it; and at once a cock crew (Jn 18:26–7). The servant is indicated with a certain exactness. John knows Malchus by name, he knows the high priest's household, and he knows that it is a relation of Malchus who questions Peter, 'Didn't I see you in the garden with him?' According to Mark, Matthew and Luke, Peter was recognised because he was Galilean; here it is quite different: he is recognised because he was seen at Gethsemane. John does not give the actual wording of Peter's denial. 'And at once a cock crew.'

Before the written gospels

Here we have, then, four accounts of the same scene which do not agree too well together. We can, however, firmly claim its historicity, first because there were witnesses – Peter and the other disciple – who were present and could relate what happened. Moreover, it is

incomprehensible that the Christians should have imagined a scene
so painful and humiliating for St Peter. Certain critics, for example
Goguel, think that the whole thing was invented to demonstrate the
fulfilment of Jesus' prophecy, 'You will deny me three times'. But
this is turning things upside down; the scene actually took place, and
Jesus foretold it because it was going to happen. Most critics admit
its historicity. And it is again confirmed by the triple question put to
Peter on the lake's edge by the risen Jesus in order to rehabilitate
him, 'Do you love me?' (Jn 21:15–18). This will compensate for
Peter's denial. Similarly in Luke (22:32) Jesus had foretold Peter's
denial and subsequent recovery.

But though there is no need to doubt the historicity of the scene
itself, it must be admitted that the details are not clear and sometimes
evade us altogether. Peter's interlocutors are different in each gospel.
In Mark: a servant-girl, the same servant-girl, the bystanders;
in Matthew: a servant-girl, another servant-girl, the bystanders;
in Luke: a servant-girl, a man, another man; and in John: the man
on duty at the door, 'someone', and then one of the high priest's
servants related to Malchus. As the accusers vary, so do their questions and Peter's replies. How are we to deal with these discrepancies?
Some exegetes, with a narrow conception of inspiration and inerrancy, accept every detail as literally true, add them together and
arrive at a total of seven or eight denials – Peter denies Jesus before a
servant-girl, another servant-girl, a group of people, and so on. This
multiplication is improbable and slightly ridiculous. Others try to
harmonise the details by imagining stage-directions, entrances and
exits; the result is a passage from a novel. It is far better to admit that
the sacred writers, like any other writers, used a certain freedom in
their narrative. The same event is always told differently by different
witnesses, even eye-witnesses. It is easy to make this experiment in
one's daily life, by getting several people to describe a scene which
they have all witnessed. The basis will be the same, but each will
have noticed different details, or even, having forgotten the details,
will imagine them in their own way. So it is with the evangelists: the
Holy Spirit has not suppressed these limitations of human nature,
which have no theological importance. We are not then to expect
perfect agreement between them, but must be content with approxi-
mations.

Perhaps it is possible to go still further. I think it will be of interest
here to give the outline of a new and ingenious theory, which has

been put forward by a Protestant exegete, a minister and professor at Lausanne.[1] It need not necessarily be accepted, but it is an example of stimulating and perceptive criticism. He draws attention, as I have done, to a discrepancy in Mark's narrative: after the first denial Peter 'goes outside' . . . and yet he does not go. In the Greek the expression 'he went out', on the evidence of other passages in Mark, means a real exit (as for example when Jesus heals a blind man outside Bethsaida, Mk 8:23).[2] But here, after Peter has 'gone out', he turns out to be still inside. This is not coherent. Mark says 'into the forecourt', but these words could have been added to smoothe over the incoherence. Again, as I have pointed out, the cock crows after the first denial as though the episode has come to an end, but without Peter noticing it. The second denial repeats the first in an almost identical form – the same servant-girl says practically the same words to the same people.

The solution which Professor Masson proposes is that we have here in Mark the combination of two accounts. In one, Peter, questioned by a servant-girl, replies, 'I don't know, I don't understand what you are talking about'. Then he went out, and the cock crew. The account stopped there, with a single denial. Another parallel narrative told the denial of Peter in two episodes, perhaps because two witnesses were needed to confirm an event. This second narrative was added to the first and is represented in our present text by the second and third denials; each narrative ends with a crowing of the cock. The two narratives were welded together in Mark, with this addition of 'into the forecourt' (Mk 14:68) and 'again' (Mk 14:69). This has resulted in there being three denials instead of one or two. This solution explains the oddities to which I have drawn attention; a first crowing of the cock which Peter does not notice, and the fresh onset of accusations just as Peter means to go out.

In confirmation of this theory, it is possible to show how Matthew and Luke, especially the former, have tried to smooth out the roughness in Mark: they suppress the first crowing of the cock, and, instead of saying that Peter goes out, they indicate only that he goes towards the door. John himself also provides interesting support for the theory: in his account, the first denial is separated from the

[1] C. MASSON, 'Le reniement de Pierre', in *Revue d'Histoire et de Philosophie Religieuses*, XXXVII, 1957, pp. 24–35.
[2] See also Mk 11:19 and 12:8.

other two by the examination before Annas. It seems, therefore, very
probable that there were originally two narratives, one with one,
the other with two denials, and that these were later combined.

I have outlined this theory because I believe that it is plausible
and even illuminating. It can be shown on other occasions that Mark
knew different traditions which he combined in his gospel[1].

Literary and historical analysis has, then, to envisage, in the period
which preceded the writing of the gospels, a stage in which these
primitive versions of each narrative existed separately before they
coalesced. One by one the episodes were told and re-told in short
narratives which diverged in varying degrees from one another, and
the writers reduced them gradually to a single coherent narrative.
There is no difficulty in recognising this process, it is a normal law
of literary development. Neither does such an evolution detract from
the substantial truth of the narrative. And, besides, we have a
guarantee in the Church, which carried these narratives within
herself, aided by the Holy Spirit, whose inspiration controlled and
directed the formation of the text we possess. We need not be troubled, then; the text which has resulted from these literary origins,
and which the Church has accepted as canonical, is trustworthy:
it does not give the exact historical details – I have pointed out
certain small divergences – but it does give us the atmosphere, the
totality of the scene presented in four different ways and the same
fundamental lesson.

It is a salutary lesson, even if it is also a terrible one. If the first
Christians felt obliged to perpetuate the story of the fall of the chief
apostle, this was certainly in order to put us on our guard against
too great a confidence in ourselves. 'The man who thinks he is safe
must be careful that he does not fall' (1 Co 10:12; cf. Rm 11:20f;
Ga 6:1). But at the same time they mentioned the tears which prepared the way for the Lord's forgiveness, and so taught us that any
sin, however great, can be redressed if it is mourned with love.

[1] Here it is sufficient to recall, in the agony at Gethsemane, the one account
focused on 'the hour of the Son of Man' and the other on 'Stay awake and
pray not to be put to the test'. These were two different ways of recounting the
same episode which Mark fused together (Mk 14:32–41). Perhaps it is possible
to explain the fact that there are two sessions of the Sanhedrin in Mark; it
would mean that he had two distinct traditions at his disposal and decided to
combine them.

4. The Examination by Annas, Mockery and Maltreatment

THE EXAMINATION BEFORE ANNAS

Mt	Mk

26 [55b] 'Day after day	14 [49b] 'Day after day
	I was among you
I sat teaching	teaching
in the Temple . . .'*	in the Temple . . .'*

14 [65b] And the attendants
rained blows on him.

MOCKING OF JESUS AS PROPHET

Mt 26:67–8	Mk 14:65
[67] Then	[65] Some of them

	started
they spat in his face	spitting at him
	and, blindfolding him,
and hit him with their fists;	began hitting him with their fists
others said	and shouting,
as they struck him,	

Lk

Jn 18:13, 19–24

13 They took him first to Annas ...
19 The high priest questioned
Jesus
about his disciples and his teaching.
20 Jesus answered, 'I have spoken
openly for all the world to hear;

22 53 'Day after day
when I was among you

I have always

taught
in the synagogue
and in the Temple
where all the Jews meet together:
I have said nothing in secret.
21 But why ask me? Ask my
hearers
what I taught: they know what
I said.'
22 At these words, one of the
guards
standing by gave Jesus a slap in
the face, saying, 'Is that the way
to answer the high priest?'
23 Jesus replied, 'If there is
something wrong in what I said,
point it out; but if there is no
offence in it, why do you strike
me?'
24 Then Annas sent him, still
bound, to Caiaphas the high priest.

in the Temple ...'*

Lk 22:63–65

63 Meanwhile the men who
guarded Jesus
were mocking and beating him.

64 They blindfolded him

and questioned him.

Mt	Mk
[68] 'Play the prophet, Christ! Who hit you then?'	'Play the prophet!' And the attendants rained blows on him.

Lk   Jn

'Play the prophet' they said.

'Who hit you then?'

18 ²² At these words,
one of the guards
standing by
gave Jesus a slap in the face,
saying, 'Is that the way
to answer the high priest?'

⁶⁵ And they continued heaping
insults on him.

We turn now to study what happened during the same night that Peter denied his master: an appearance before the Jewish authorities, then the mockery inflicted on Jesus. Two problems will arise regarding each of these episodes, since the narratives of the evangelists do not agree.

(i) The Appearance before Annas during the Night

The narratives of Mark and Matthew

This appearance of Jesus before 'the high priest' raises a difficulty.[1] Even in the synoptic gospels, there is already a divergence between Mark and Matthew on the one hand and Luke on the other. In Mark and Matthew, a session of the Sanhedrin takes place during the night immediately after Jesus arrives from Gethsemane, then comes the mocking which follows the session, and only after that Peter's denials. These events all take place during the night. In Luke, on the contrary, the session of the Sanhedrin is held in the morning; all that happens during the night, after the arrival from Gethsemane, is the denials and the mocking.

Again, Mark and Matthew follow Peter's denials with a fresh session of the Sanhedrin in the early morning, at which the assembly decides to send Jesus to Pilate. So there are two meetings of the Sanhedrin in Mark and Matthew, one at night, the other in the morning, while Luke records only one, and that in the morning. At first sight we might be tempted to think that Luke had omitted one of the sessions. But it is perfectly clear from his text that his morning session is identical with the one Mark and Matthew place during the night. Moreover, even within the narratives of Mark and Matthew, the situation is not clear; it is not obvious how these sessions of the Sanhedrin are to be arranged. The night session is odd; it seems contrary to the procedure of the law since the Sanhedrin normally met only by day, like courts of law all over the world. During the

[1] See P. BENOIT, 'Jésus devant le Sanhédrin' in *Exégèse et Théologie*, Paris, 1961, I, pp. 290–311.

night, the courtroom annexed to the Temple was closed, like the Temple itself. Lastly, this night session goes against psychological probability; it is difficult to imagine the members of the Sanhedrin leaving their homes in the middle of the night on this business. It seems more likely that they would attend in the early morning, after passing a peaceful night at home. So this night meeting of the Sanhedrin seems unnatural, even taken by itself. Moreover, in Mark and Matthew, the morning session is indicated only in an enigmatic way; they record briefly that the whole Sanhedrin meets and sends Jesus on to Pilate. Nothing is said of any formal deliberations, and we may well ask what need there was for them to meet again. From all this we get the impression that the session during the night described by Mark and Matthew is identical with the morning one in Luke, and even with the one they themselves place in the morning. If this is true, then there must be a reduplication of the session of the Sanhedrin in Mark and Matthew, one recorded as happening during the night, the other in the morning.

For a long time critics have explained this reduplication as the combining of two traditions, two strata of literary formation; a first short notice had furnished Mark and Matthew with what they tell us of the morning session; another, which is more detailed and which came to them through some other channel, has become their night session. But these critics add, wrongly, that this second account is late and of no historical value, that only the brief notice of the morning session is well founded. While I do not accept this value-judgement, I do believe that the double session in Mark and Matthew is to be explained by the joining together of different traditions, as we have already seen happening at several points in the episodes of Gethsemane and of Peter's denials.

One difficulty remains: if Mark knew two different traditions of the same session, why did he not put the two narratives side by side? He could very well have placed the more detailed account immediately after the brief one. Why then distinguish them as a night session and a morning session? This is a real difficulty for which, it seems to me, the critics do not provide a solution.

The narratives of John and Luke

In John and Luke, however, we shall find the clues which will help to solve the difficulty.

John mentions two appearances of Jesus before the authorities: a first appearance before Annas – '*They took him first to Annas*', (Jn 18:13), as well as an examination carried out by the high priest, who seems to be the Annas already mentioned (Jn 18:19–23). After this examination we read, '*Then Annas sent him, still bound, to Caiaphas the high priest*' (Jn 18:24). John thus records two appearances of Jesus, not before the same authorities, as in Mark and Matthew, but once, during the night, before Annas, and once, it seems, in the early morning before Caiaphas. This information is extremely interesting; as so often happens in John, especially in the narrative of the Passion, historical reminiscences of great value have been preserved side by side with later theological developments. It is not for allegorical reasons that John makes a distinction between Annas and Caiaphas, but because he has actual historical reminiscences at his disposal; this is the way things must have happened.

When we turn to Luke, in the light of John's account, it is noticeable that the text fits in very easily with that of John. Actually, Luke records only one session, the morning one, but what he does tell us about the night is easily adjusted to John's account. According to Luke, Jesus is apparently in a corner of the courtyard, where he can look at Peter after his denials; then Jesus is mocked and beaten by the men guarding him. Everything is explicable if during the night there is a preliminary examination by Annas which ends with one of his guards slapping Jesus. It is easy to accept that the semi-official examination was followed by a night without sleep during which Jesus was kept in the courtyard and could watch Peter.

How are we to conceive of this examination by night, the existence of which seems to be guaranteed by the twofold occurrences in John on the one hand, Mark and Matthew on the other? I think it has to be understood in the light of John's account, in which we see the high priest questioning Jesus about his disciples and his teaching. If it is objected that 'high priest' would normally have meant Caiaphas, we must remember that Annas, his father-in-law, was a man of such stature that he had kept the title of high priest[1]. We can go farther, and say that he was the high priest in all but the official

---

[1] Annas himself had been high priest from A.D. 6 (or perhaps even 4) to A.D. 15. After his own spell of office, Annas had seen his son Eleazar fill it from A.D. 16 to 17 his son-in-law Caiaphas from 18 to 36, another son Jonathan from 36 to 37, his son Theophilus during and after 37, then his son Matthias, and lastly his son Ananos in 62; in short, a son-in-law and five sons high priests. Annas was a man who, although he had quitted office himself, managed to fill it with his own creatures so that he could continue to direct affairs.

duties of the office. Luke gives us the proof of this in one of those historical notes that he collected from tradition. At the moment when Jesus begins his ministry, Luke lists the authorities at that time (Lk 3:1–2): Tiberius was the emperor, Pontius Pilate the governor, Herod Antipas tetrarch, etc., and *the* high priest Annas and Caiaphas. Luke lists Annas and Caiaphas as though there were two high priests; to be more precise, he says *the* high priest in the singular, making it appear as though Annas were the high priest and Caiaphas his deputy[1]. Such information, though it concerns our problem only indirectly, fully justifies the way in which John speaks (Jn 18:19): the high priest is Annas. The examination therefore takes place before Annas.

However, before commenting on John's narrative (Jn 18:19–23), I would like to deal with a suggestion which I do not accept but which has often been put forward by exegetes; it is that verse 24, where Jesus is sent from Annas to Caiaphas, should be placed elsewhere. This modification is to be found in an ancient manuscript, an old Syriac translation, contained in a precious codex preserved at the monastery of Mt Sinai: in it, verse 24 is displaced and is found after verse 13. This is how it then reads: 'They took him first to Annas, because Annas was the father-in-law of Caiaphas, who was high priest that year. (24) Annas sent him, still bound, to Caiaphas the high priest. (14) It was Caiaphas who had suggested to the Jews . . .' With this one change, the whole examination takes place before Caiaphas, since Annas does not keep Jesus with him but sends him on at once.

Certain exegetes, of whom Père Lagrange was one, have approved of this change and thought it a good solution. Personally, I am doubtful, and I am not the only one. I suspect that this Sinai manuscript and the handful of authorities which support it, including Cyril of Alexandria, made the correction in order to get rid of the difficulty. They recognised the problem of reconciling the synoptics and the fourth gospel where this session of the Sanhedrin was concerned: in the synoptics it was before Caiaphas, in John it was before Annas. By displacing one verse they obtained an appearance before Caiaphas in both John and the synoptics. This was their correction, and here is the proof: the Sinai manuscript is so anxious to restore

---

[1] In the same way, when Peter and John appear before the Sanhedrin (Ac 4:6), Luke names the high priest Annas first and only mentions Caiaphas with the rest of the high-priestly family.

order that it displaces other verses too. It puts the examination by the high priest (Jn 18:19–23) before Peter's first denial (Jn 18:16–18) It is true that, in John, the second and third denials are separated from the first in an odd way by the examination. In order to get rid of this embarrassing fact, the Sinai manuscript puts the first denial after the examination, and so gets the three denials together, one after the other. These are alterations made by a copyist who is intelligent but takes liberties, and I refuse to follow him. To me it seems preferable to keep the text as it is, even if we have to find another way of explaining it. Besides, the solution offered by this manuscript is not a happy one. Perhaps it looks satisfactory at a first glance, since it obtains an appearance before Caiaphas in John as well as in the synoptics, but the content of the examination is quite different: there is no similarity between the high priest's questions and the replies of Jesus as they are found on the one hand in John and in the synoptics on the other. So much so that nothing has been gained except to situate before Caiaphas two totally different episodes. It is much better to admit that there was an examination before Annas, recorded by John and not mentioned by the synoptics, and an examination before the Sanhedrin, recorded by the synoptics but passed over in silence by John.

The examination before Annas. Gethsemane

This is how John describes the examination before Annas:

The high priest questioned Jesus about his disciples and his teaching. Jesus answered, 'I have spoken openly for all the world to hear; I have always taught in the synagogue and in the Temple where all the Jews meet together: I have said nothing in secret. But why ask me? Ask my hearers what I taught: they know what I said.' At these words, one of the guards standing by gave Jesus a slap in the face, saying, 'Is that the way to answer the high priest?' Jesus replied, 'If there is something wrong in what I said, point it out; but if there is no offence in it, why do you strike me?' (Jn 18:19–23)

This narrative presents an interesting detail which could explain the divergence of the tradition of the synoptics from that of John. Jesus' reply to the high priest (Jn 18:20) is curiously similar to the one the synoptics put into his mouth at Gethsemane: 'I was among you in the Temple day after day and you never laid hands on me' (Mk 14:49; Mt 26:55; Lk 22:53). This bears a striking resemblance to

'I have always taught in the synagogue and in the Temple where all the Jews meet together' (Jn 18:20). Moreover, in Luke's narrative it was surprising to find this saying, at Gethsemane, addressed by Jesus to the chief priests, the captains of the Temple guard and the elders as though all these Sanhedrin authorities had come to take part in the arrest. It seems as if this saying was uttered only once, in the place which John gives it, that is before Annas, during the night and at his palace. In the synoptic tradition it has moved from the palace of Annas to the olive trees of Gethsemane.

There are two possible explanations: either Jesus' reply to Annas has found a place in the scene at Gethsemane in Mark and the other synoptics because they have replaced the examination by Annas with the night session of the Sanhedrin; or – and this, I think, is more probable – having already recorded at Gethsemane an essential saying of Jesus that belongs properly to the scene of the examination by Annas, Mark and Matthew have made a void in the narrative of the night at the palace and, since it was remembered in the tradition that there had been an examination during the night, they brought forward the session of the Sanhedrin to fill this void and satisfy the tradition. This is a possible explanation.

In any case, I believe the historical truth rests with John. During the night there took place an examination before Annas. But comparison with the synoptics and especially with Luke indicates perhaps that Annas was assisted by some high officials at the Temple. It is very probable that certain more fanatical people were waiting with Annas to hear the result of the arrest, and unofficially interrogated Jesus as soon as he had arrived from Gethsemane, to try and get some admission out of him.

This, then, is how I believe the events of that night are to be reconstructed. Jesus is arrested and taken to the house of Annas. He spends the night there, since the Sanhedrin cannot meet before daybreak. During this vigil, Annas and certain officials of the Temple question Jesus on the subject of his teaching and his disciples; this examination is unofficial, but Annas' authority lends weight to what is really a private enquiry. With great dignity Jesus refuses to reply, saying that he has always taught openly and asking why he should be questioned now. 'I have said what I thought before all the world.' A servant then slaps him and this unleashes general mockery. At the same time, in the courtyard, Peter is struggling to ward off those who are questioning him. In the end he repudiates his master; Jesus looks at him, Peter remembers and hurries away weeping.

It is quite possible that the examination by Annas was held in a room and did not take long. When the high priest realises that Jesus does not intend to answer, he sends him down again into the court-yard, where Jesus can look at Peter after the denial and where he is to stay until morning. At first light, Jesus is taken to Caiaphas, that is, before the Sanhedrin, where a legitimate examination takes place.

(ii) Mockery and Maltreatment[1]

The examination before Annas ends with maltreatment perpe-trated by a servant who slaps Jesus (Jn 18:22). This episode seems to be connected with the one recorded by the synoptics where Jesus is mocked as a prophet (Mt 26:67–8; Mk 14:65; Lk 22:63–5).

We shall look carefully at each of the gospels and bring out the differences between the three narratives. There is no question of following the usual practice and harmonising their texts; each evangelist has the right to be heard separately, each has benefited from the inspiration of the Holy Spirit in the way in which he presents what happened and should be listened to respectfully.

Who inflicted the maltreatment?

In Mark and Matthew, the episode of insults takes place after the night sessions of the Sanhedrin, so that those who perpetrated it are the members of the Sanhedrin itself – chief priests, scribe-theologians and noblemen; all these high personages demean them-selves and carry on like a platoon of soldiers. After they have said, 'He deserves to die' (Mk 14:64), the text goes on, *Some of them started spitting at him*, suggesting that the same people are meant (Mk 14:65). Mark then alludes to the servants who rained blows on him. He therefore seems to distinguish two categories, the members of the Sanhedrin and the servants.

In Matthew this distinction is no longer to be found. The members of the Sanhedrin answered the high priest, 'He deserves to die' (Mt 26:66). *Then they spat on his face*, continues Matthew (Mt 26:67.)

---

[1] Cf. P. BENOIT, 'Les outrages à Jésus Prophète (Mk 14:64 par.)' in *Neo-testamentica et Patristica* (a collection in honour of Oscar Cullman), Leiden, 1962, pp. 92–110.

Here, as in Mark, it is the leaders of the Jews who maltreat Jesus. But this is still surprising, for it is difficult to imagine these respectable judges, whatever their sentiments may have been, stooping to such behaviour.

Luke says no such thing, only *the men who guarded Jesus were mocking and beating him* (Lk 22:63). It is no longer a matter of the highest officials, only of those poor devils who had arrested Jesus and guarded him through the night. They are cold and are passing the time mocking their prisoner, as, unhappily, is so often done in every country. This is still horrible, but it is less monstrous and more probable.

What was the maltreatment?

Other differences are to be noticed between the narratives, concerning the actual character of the treatment: in John simply a slap, in Mark and Matthew not only a slap but blows and spitting. The words 'blow' and 'slap', which are almost synonymous, translate two Greek words which are also almost synonymous. In theory, the word translated 'slap' refers to a blow given with the palm of the hand, and that translated simply as 'blow' to one given with the fist or the back of the hand. The two words render the sense of the two Greek words very well.

Luke's text is not so precise and mentions neither blows nor spitting: *The men were mocking and beating him*. He is mocked and beaten. But Luke records another detail, *They blindfolded him and questioned him. 'Play the prophet' they said, 'Who hit you then?'* (Lk 22:64). We often take this to mean that a bandage covered Jesus' eyes, but the Greek word suggests instead a large piece of cloth which would cover the upper part of the body.

This cloth seems to occur again in Mark, but is wanting in Matthew. It raises a difficulty: if Matthew knew Mark and used him, as so many indications elsewhere seem to show, why does he not mention the cloth too? Moreover, this absence of the cloth in Matthew is awkward: *They spat in his face and hit him with their fists; others said as they struck him, 'Play the prophet, Christ! Who hit you then?'* If Jesus is not covered with a cloth, it is not difficult for him to point to whoever has struck him, while in Luke he has to guess. By leaving out the cloth, Matthew has deprived himself of a necessary element of the situation.

A further problem of literary analysis occupies the attention of exegetes. Matthew and Luke quote the same words, 'Who hit you then?' But these are not found in Mark. Since Matthew and Luke are not known to one another, what is the common source from which they took this detail? Here, it cannot be Mark.

In such cases it is often useful to have recourse to textual criticism, that is, to the examination of the text as it is found in ancient manuscripts. There are thousands of manuscripts, of both the Old and the New Testament, between which scholars have to choose in order to find the variant reading which seems most authentic. In the case with which we are concerned, some excellent manuscripts, known as 'Western', omit the cloth in Mark; the old pre-Vulgate Latin translation, codex Bezae, and other valuable manuscripts indirectly support this omission. I believe that they are correct, and would be prepared to change the text of the ordinary editions to adopt this better reading, 'They began spitting in his face and hitting him with their fists . . .' leaving out any mention of the cloth. If this reading is accepted, the difficulty disappears; it is not that Matthew has omitted the cloth which Mark mentions, it is simply that it was not there in the text. The cloth which now figures in Mark's text comes from later copyists who borrowed it from Luke.

It is tempting to propose a similar solution for the other difficulty, 'Who hit you then?' Some manuscripts of Mark include this phrase. If they were right, we would have in Mark a sufficient explanation of the agreement between Matthew and Luke[1]. Nevertheless I would not defend this solution since the authority of the manuscripts on which it rests is weak. I want now to turn away from these technical problems and come back to the scene itself.

The narrative of Luke

The narratives of the synoptics are not in agreement, and we have therefore to try to understand the aim and meaning of each.

Luke's account is the easiest to grasp. At Jesus' expense, the guards play a guessing game which has existed always and everywhere; they cover him with a cloth and make him guess who has hit him. In ancient Greek texts this game is described under the name of *myinda*: one of the players puts his hand over his eyes and has to guess what object has been presented to him or who has

[1] Cf. above, p. 67.

touched him. If he guesses right, he wins, and the other player has to cover his eyes in his turn. If wrong, he has to begin guessing again. This, according to Luke, is the game the guards play with Jesus; they cover his head, and Jesus has to guess without looking who hits him. As the offences alleged against Jesus are of a religious character, they try to provoke him to speak as a 'prophet', since a prophet ought to know everything.

The narrative of Mark

Mark's text is less easy to interpret. Jesus is covered with a cloth, hit and told, 'Play the prophet!', without any further details being given. Since there is nothing for him to guess, what is the cloth for, if indeed it is to be kept in the text? Some exegetes reply that the cloth was part of a prophet's dress; they cite an Arab custom in which the tribal soothsayer or 'Kahun' – the name corresponds to the Hebrew 'Kohen' – puts on a cloth before uttering his oracles in order to emphasise that his supernatural vision in a mysterious way surpasses natural sight. The guards would then have presented Jesus with the cloth of a prophet for him to play the part. At the session of the Sanhedrin which in Mark precedes the maltreatment, the Jewish accusers have recalled a saying of Jesus, 'I am going to destroy this Temple . . . and in three days build another' (Mk 14:58). Jesus, then, has spoken as a prophet. Their mockery consists in inviting him to continue prophesying. This explanation is possible. But if the cloth was not in the original text of Mark, there is no point in trying to explain it.

Another aspect of Mark's text needs to be considered: its quite striking resemblance to a text of Isaiah (50:6). In interpreting a passage from the New Testament, it is always necessary to ask oneself whether it can be explained by some Old Testament text which the writer had at the back of his mind. This very proper question often leads to a positive answer. The first Christians read, re-read and meditated on the Old Testament to draw from it all the prophecies concerning Jesus Christ, his life and his Passion. Every time they noticed a saying or a fact which had been fulfilled in him, they noted it down carefully, or at least used the Old Testament wording to draw the Christian reader's attention to the accomplishment of God's plan.

Various texts have been suggested regarding our passage of Mark. Some exegetes point to a text in Numbers (24:3-4): from the plateau of Moab in Transjordania, Balaam pronounces oracles upon the Israelites, who are in the plain; of him it is said, 'the oracle of the man with far-seeing eyes, the oracle of one who hears the word of God . . . He sees what God makes him see, he receives the divine answer and his eyes are opened.' These lines certainly mean that the prophet Balaam's eyes are opened to a vision of Israel's future which God gives him, but the analogy with Mark's text is slender. There is no question of a covering over Balaam's eyes, all that is said is that God opens his eyes and makes him far-seeing.

A text from the First Book of Kings has also been suggested (22:24). Here the kings of Israel and Judah are preparing a campaign against Ramoth-gilead and have summoned the prophets to Samaria to find out if the campaign will succeed. The kings then consult the prophets, many of whom, like courtiers, assure him of victory. One, however, dares to say that it will end badly. He, Micaiah, is then struck by one of those present, who demands, 'Which way did the spirit of Yahweh leave me, to talk to you?' Micaiah retorts, 'That is what you will find out the day you flee to an inner room to hide', and defends his prophecy of misfortune. In this narrative we see a prophet struck and provoked by mockery into enlarging on the blow he has just received. This is not without analogies to the scene in the gospel, but here too there is nothing which helps us to a full explanation.

There is, however, another and more important parallel in the Old Testament: this is the oracles of Isaiah (50:6) on the Servant of Yahweh, a mysterious figure sent by God to save the world, Israel and even the gentiles, through his humiliation and his sufferings. Of him Isaiah says that he does not turn his face from insults and spitting. They are the same words as we have here; it is very likely that the evangelists, at any rate Mark, had the figure of Isaiah's Servant in mind. This is not to say that the evangelists invented the insults and the spitting; the episode is true, and when they relate it they use the very expressions of Isaiah to bring out a theological truth; Jesus fulfilled what God had announced concerning his Servant.

Thus understood, the scene of the maltreatment as told by Mark takes on a different colouring from Luke's. Luke's account has an atmosphere of barrack-room camaraderie and horseplay with the soldiers making fun of their prisoner. Mark's has theological overtones; Jesus undergoes the humiliations of the suffering Servant. Christian readers, who knew the Bible by heart, coming on this passage of Mark would immediately recall the text from Isaiah;

like the Servant, Jesus suffered insults and was told, 'Play the prophet!' The Servant was a prophet who had to suffer for his mission, and whom God had destined for death because his very mission was to fail and yet by his failure to save. To play the prophet by undergoing insults and spitting was the Servant's part. Without any doubt Mark intends to show that Jesus has fulfilled Isaiah's prophecy.

The narrative of Matthew

Matthew's account resembles Mark's: spitting, blows, mockery aimed at a prophet. It includes also the question, 'Who hit you, then?', which is surprising since there has been no mention of the covering. But there is in Matthew a new word, which should be noticed although it may seem obvious, 'Christ'. The use of this word is not natural in the gospel. Jesus won this name through his resurrection, it is the name which believing Christians give him. But it is very seldom that he is called Christ when he is spoken of. Christ means Messiah. If Matthew records this highly unusual innovation, it is because he attaches importance to it. What does this insult mean?

A contemporary exegete[1] has drawn attention to the fact that we are too much concerned with the kingly Messiah. The Jews certainly were waiting for such a Messiah, a descendant of David, who was to reign and liberate Israel. Jesus was this king, though in a spiritual sense and of a transcendent kingdom; he became *Kyrios*, Lord. But the Jews had another hope, that of a priestly Messiah, a Messiah who would be high priest, not king; beside the king, there was to be the high priest. The Qumrân texts in particular – these texts found by the Dead Sea have renewed our problems – contain the expectation of two Messiahs, the Messiah of Aaron or Messiah High Priest, and the Messiah of Israel, who is the Messiah King. In these writings the first place is reserved for the priestly Messiah; the kingly Messiah comes after him. Surely then we ought to expect to find this notion of the Messiah High Priest more often in the New Testament. There may be texts which call Jesus 'Christ' in this sense[2]. When, at the session of the Sanhedrin, the high priest asks Jesus, 'Are you

[1] G. FRIEDRICH, 'Beobachtungen zur messianischen Hohepriestererwartung in den Synoptikern', in *Zeitschrift für Theologie und Kirche*, LIII, 1956, pp. 265–311, esp. pp. 291f.
[2] The whole of the epistle to the Hebrews is taken up with showing in what sense Jesus is the true High Priest.

the Christ, the Son of God?' perhaps he is not thinking so much of the kingly as of the priestly Messiah. For Jesus has been accused of wanting to destroy the Temple and rebuild it, he claims to be establishing a new form of worship. Who is interested in forms of worship, if not a priest? Thus the Jewish trial of Jesus would centre on his title of Messiah High Priest, rather than Messiah King; and there would be an echo of it here too. The high priest was by definition a prophet[1]. The maltreatment could be explained in the light of this: 'Play the prophet, Messiah'. If the two titles are taken together it brings out the full meaning of 'Christ'; 'If you are really the high priest, the high priest of the eschatological age, prove it, prophesy!' If this explanation of Matthew's narrative is correct, the word prophet stands out afresh; it is one of the marks of the messianic High Priest Jesus claims to be and whom the Jews will not accept.

This, then, is how each of the three narratives presents what happened. At the centre of the historical fact, like a flint in a bed of chalk, lies the word 'prophet', which all three narratives have in common. This is the most reliable datum; Jesus was mocked as a prophet. Each tradition presents the fact in its own way. For Luke, in a context of barrack-room horseplay, 'Play the prophet' has merely the trite meaning, 'Guess who hit you'. In Mark's account the figure of the Servant is to be discerned, the prophet who was despised, insulted and spat on; Jesus is that prophet. Lastly, in Matthew, there appears the Christ-prophet, the Messiah High Priest, whom Jesus claimed to be before the Sanhedrin and with whom the Jews would have nothing to do. These three ways of presenting the facts complete one another and reveal different aspects of this mystery of the shame Jesus endured.

This, however, is not the only scene of mocking which the passion includes. The evangelists record another before Herod Antipas, and yet another at Pilate's residence organised by the Romans. This latter is recorded in two different places. Are we then to distinguish five such scenes – one before the session of the Sanhedrin (Luke), one after the session (Mark and Matthew), one in front of Herod Antipas (Luke), one at Pilate's in the middle of the trial (John) and, lastly, one at Pilate's at the end of the trial (Mark and Matthew)?

---

[1] Prophecy was one of the gifts of the high priest. Josephus, for example, attributes it to John Hyrcanus, one of the Hasmonaean kings and high priest (*Ant.* xiii, 299: *Wars*, i, 68f). John records in his gospel (11:51) Caiaphas' words, 'It is better for one man to die for the people', and then adds, 'He did not speak in his own person, it was as high priest that he made this prophecy.

This would be to make too many distinctions. In fact we need retain only two great scenes of mockery; one, which we have just been studying, takes place at the end of the examination by Annas, and not after the meeting of the Sanhedrin; the other is that organised by the Romans, recorded by John in the middle, by Mark and Matthew at the end of the trial; it is, however, one and the same episode, and can also be linked with the scene before Herod Antipas described by Luke[1].

These two scenes of mockery are, as it were, at the two poles of the trial of Jesus. He was mocked by the Jews as prophet, by the Romans as king. This corresponds to the underlying pattern of his trial: the Jews rejected Jesus as a religious leader, high priest and messiah. Although they did not accept him as their king, they presented him to the Romans as such. The trial became political and Jesus was condemned by Pilate as King of the Jews. The maltreatment inflicted by the Romans, then, is directed against the Messiah King.

Thus we see our Lord mocked and rejected by men according to his different titles. It is as a prophet whose message they refuse that he is insulted by the Jews, and he accepts these insults as the servant of Isaiah. Among the Romans, he is rejected by men who will have nothing to do with a king, but who is nevertheless the true king.

This scene leaves a deep impression on us and teaches us a powerful lesson, both from the spiritual and the theological point of view: questioned by Annas and the Jewish leaders the Lord with dignity declines to answer: he asserts that there is nothing secret about his life; he undertakes willingly the part of the prophet such as it had been foretold, the part of the Servant who allows himself to be insulted and his face to be spat on, since this is indeed the part the prophet must play – 'A prophet is only despised in his own country and in his own house' (Mt 13:57), 'It would not be right for a prophet to die outside Jerusalem' (Lk 13:33), 'Jerusalem, you that kill the prophets' (Mt 23:37). Jesus assumes this destiny and allows himself to be insulted and killed by men. His disciples in their turn will have to accept it, in order to build the Kingdom of God. For, 'A servant is not greater than his master. If they persecuted me, they will persecute you too' (Jn 15:20).

[1] See below, p. 150f.

5. Jesus before the Sanhedrin

Mt 26:59–66   Mk 14:55–64

⁵⁹ The chief priests and the whole Sanhedrin were looking for evidence against Jesus, however false, on which they might pass the death-sentence.	⁵⁵ The chief priests and the whole Sanhedrin were looking for evidence against Jesus
⁶⁰ But they could not find any, though several lying witnesses came forward.	on which they might pass the death-sentence. But they could not find any. ⁵⁶ Several, indeed, brought false evidence
	against him but their evidence was conflicting.
Eventually two stepped forward ⁶¹ and made a statement,	⁵⁷ Some stood up and submitted this false evidence against him,
'This man said, "I have power to destroy the Temple of God,	⁵⁸ 'We heard him say, "I am going to destroy this Temple made by human hands,
and in three days build it up" '.	and in three days build another, not made by human hands" '. ⁵⁹ But even on this point their evidence was conflicting.
⁶² The high priest then stood up	⁶⁰ The high priest then stood up before the whole assembly and put this question to Jesus,
and said to him, 'Have you no answer to that? What is this evidence these men are bringing against you?' ⁶³ But Jesus was silent.	'Have you no answer to that? What is this evidence these men are bringing against you?' ⁶¹ But he was silent and made no answer at all.
And the high priest said to him, 'I put you on oath by the living God to tell us	The high priest put a second question to him,

Lk 22:66–71   Jn

[66] When day broke there was a meeting of the elders of the people, attended by the chief priests and scribes. He was brought before their council,

2 [19] 'Destroy this sanctuary,

and in three days I will raise it up'.

[23:9–10]

[67] and they said to him,

Mt	Mk

if you are the Christ,   'Are you the Christ,' he said
the Son of God'.   'the Son of the Blessed One?'

⁶⁴ 'The words are your own'   ⁶² 'I am,'
answered Jesus.   said Jesus
'Moreover, I tell you
that from this time onwards
you will see   'and you will see
the *Son of Man*   *the Son of Man*

seated   *seated*
at the right hand of the Power   *at the right hand of the Power*

and *coming on the clouds of heaven.*   and *coming with the clouds of*
                                            heaven.'

⁶⁵ At this, the high priest   ⁶³ The high priest
tore his clothes   tore his robes,
and said,
'He has blasphemed.
What need of witnesses   'What need of witnesses
have we now?   have we now?' he said.
There!
You have just heard   ⁶⁴ 'You heard

the blasphemy.   the blasphemy.
⁶⁶ What is your opinion?'   What is your finding?'
They answered,   And they all
                                            gave their verdict:
'He deserves to die'.   he deserved to die.

Lk   Jn

'If you are the Christ,   10²⁴ᵇ 'If you are the Christ,

tell us'.   tell us plainly.'
'If I tell you,' he replied   ²⁵ Jesus replied, 'I have told you,
'you will not believe me,   but you do not believe . . .'
⁶⁸ and if I question you,
you will not answer.

⁶⁹ But from now on,

the Son of Man
will be
seated
at the right hand of the Power
of God.'

⁷⁰ Then they all said,
'So you are the Son of God then?'
He answered,
'It is you who say
I am'. | 10 ³⁶ᵇ '. . . I am the Son of God'.

                                             ³⁶ᵇ '. . . You say,
                                            "You are blaspheming".'

⁷¹ 'What need of witnesses
have we now?' they said.

We have heard it for ourselves
from his own lips.'

It is now time to study the session of the Sanhedrin, which took place probably in the morning, as Luke says, rather than during the night, as Mark and Matthew say. It is an important scene, since it is at this moment that the chosen people, represented by their leaders, decide to put the Christ to death through the mediation of the Roman government.

The scene is recorded by the three synoptics, and John too alludes to it in other passages of his gospel. In Mark and Matthew it has two phases: the first is the depositions of witnesses concerning an utterance which Jesus is alleged to have made against the Temple; in the second, the high priest asks Jesus who he is and Jesus declares how he conceives his person and his mission. Finally, the Sanhedrin pronounces that he deserves to die.

The narratives of Mark and Matthew

Mark's witnesses say, 'We heard him say, "I am going to destroy this Temple made by human hands, and in three days build another, not made by human hands" ' (Mk 14:58).

In Matthew the saying of Jesus reported by the witnesses is briefer, 'This man said, "I have power to destroy the Temple of God, and in three days build it up" '.

Did Jesus actually utter these words? Some critics think it improbable that Jesus could have made such a violent pronouncement. Why destroy the Jerusalem Temple? Nevertheless, in slightly different forms, this saying is attested in the New Testament tradition not only by the texts of Mark and Matthew quoted here, but also by other passages in the gospels: at the foot of the cross, the passers-by taunt Jesus by wagging their heads and saying, 'Aha! So you would destroy the Temple and rebuild it in three days! Then save yourself: . . . come down from the cross!' (Mk 15:29 and Mt 27:40). At the beginning of John's account of the ministry, when Jesus drives the vendors out of the Temple, the Jews intervene and say, 'What sign can you show us to justify what you have done?' And Jesus answers, 'Destroy this sanctuary, and in three days I will raise it up' (Jn 2:19). A last text from the New Testament corroborates this tradition (Ac 6:14): the Jews accuse Stephen, 'This man is always making speeches against this Holy Place and the Law. We have heard him say that Jesus the Nazarene is going to destroy this Place and alter the traditions that Moses handed down to us.' These various statements all confirm one another and guarantee the historicity of this saying.

When properly understood, the saying is not unlikely; it is not merely negative, but positive; it is a question not only of destroying but of rebuilding. In his eschatological discourse (Mk 13; Mt 24; Lk 21), Jesus announces that Jerusalem is to be sacked and the Temple destroyed; already, on his entry into Jerusalem (Lk 19:41–4), he has wept over the city and foretold its destruction. But Jesus also speaks of rebuilding, by which he means that after the punishment willed by God there will be a renewal, a Temple 'not made by human hands', that is to say a new worship and a new age of religion. This outlook on the Temple finds an echo among Jesus' contemporaries. Certain more advanced and more spiritual Jewish circles were hoping for a better religious future and waiting for the day when the Temple, with its present materiality, would disappear to make way for a new Temple, a heavenly and spiritual one, in the eschatological era. The Jews of Qumrân in particular were waiting for this renewal and looked on their community as a Temple. The faithful of Qumrân were in revolt against the Jerusalem priesthood, and were scandalised by the deficiency of the religious spirit among the great families which directed the Temple worship and were not even pure-blooded descendants of Aaron. These fervent, puritanical, somewhat sectarian priests had abandoned the Temple, which they believed to be under a curse, and taken refuge in the desert. In their writings they regard their community as the true sanctuary, the 'Holy of Holies', a living spiritual temple[1]. This idea, then, of a new Temple coming to replace the existing one was nothing unusual in the climate of the time. Jesus could very well have put out a similar idea regarding his own ministry and mission. Among the first Christians some, such as Stephen, the Hellenists and Paul, were well aware that the old establishment had

---

[1] *Manual of Discipline*, VIII, 5–9. These Qumrân texts are interesting in the way they prepare for St Paul's idea of the Church as a spiritual temple (1 Co 3:16; 2 Co 6:16; Ep 2:21–2). Not so long ago this was thought to be a new and Christian idea; we see now that the way was prepared for it by the Jews of Qumrân.

been condemned and that the Temple was due to disappear. In his speech, Stephen inveighs powerfully against the Temple worship, against sacrifices and against an over-materialistic religion. This did not please the Jews and he was stoned for having spoken with such youthful fire and audacity. In short, the words imputed to Jesus by the Sanhedrin's witnesses are wholly probable, both as to their substance and in their context.

The meaning of Jesus' words

What does this utterance of Jesus mean? It has come down to us in different forms. According to Mark, he said, 'this Temple made by human hands' and 'not made by human hands'. These epithets, which are missing from the parallels in Matthew and John, could be editorial additions. They are qualifications, whose usage betrays a somewhat later date, and were no doubt added by Mark; besides, all they do is to make the meaning of the phrase more explicit.

It is more important to discover what is meant by 'in three days'. Jesus does not say merely that he will destroy the Temple and rebuild it, but that he will do this 'in three days'. The allusion to the resurrection is obvious. For this reason some critics assert that Jesus could not have made this prophecy himself, that it was put into his mouth by Christians later. There is, however, no reason at all to reject the fact that Jesus foretold his own resurrection. If these words had been added we should expect to find 'on the third day', which would be more correct since Jesus died on Friday and rose again on Sunday. There is little chance that it would have been formulated as it is, 'in three days', had it been written after the event: it must therefore depend on given facts and go back to the Lord himself.

It is important to notice that Jesus, in speaking subsequently of the new Temple, alludes to his own body. We are told this by John (Jn 2:19–22): after Jesus' words, 'Destroy this sanctuary, and in three days I will raise it up', John adds, 'The Jews replied, "It has taken forty-six years to build this sanctuary: you are going to raise it up in three days?" But he was speaking of the sanctuary that was his body, and when Jesus rose from the dead, his disciples remembered that he had said this, and they believed the scripture and the words he had said.' Thus, not only does Jesus announce the coming of a new religious era, but he gives them to understand that it is his own body that will be its centre, its Temple.

In order to grasp the depth of Jesus' thought here, we have to link it with other passages of scripture, in the first place with those in which Jesus himself speaks of the change and renewal that he is bringing. When the Samaritan woman tries to embarrass him by opposing the worship centred on Mt Gerizim to that of Jerusalem, Jesus replies, 'The hour is coming when you will worship the Father neither on this mountain nor in Jerusalem. . . . But the hour will come – in fact it is here already – when true worshippers will worship the Father in spirit and in truth' (Jn 4:21–3). Jesus announces a spiritual worship and a spiritual Temple, which will no longer be dependent on geographical circumstances. Elsewhere in the gospel we are told that one must not put new wine into old wineskins, nor sew a new piece of cloth on to an old garment (Mt 9:16–17 and parallels).

The idea 'Body of Jesus – New Temple' is also to be linked to certain themes of the Old Testament. According to Ezekiel, God himself became the sanctuary of his people in exile (Ezk 11:16). Echoing Ezekiel, Revelation tells us that God and the Lamb are to be the temple of the heavenly Jerusalem (Rv 21:22).

Ezekiel, Joel and Zechariah all announce that a spring of living water will issue from the eschatological temple – what riches for the semi-desert of Palestine! This will become a river; after a thousand cubits the water will come up to the ankle, after another thousand up to the waist. And from this miraculously overflowing water will spring life (Ezk 47:1–12; Jl 4:18; Zc 13:1 and 14:8). When Jesus proclaims that streams of living water will flow from his breast, it is of these prophecies as well as of the rock from which Moses struck water in the desert that he is thinking. This is yet another way in which he compares his person to the sanctuary and the new temple.

Jesus' words are indeed profound. He is telling us that he is inaugurating a new era of religion and that the spiritual temple from which the spring of grace will flow is to be his own body. This idea is the stock on which will be grafted all that the resurrection and the life of the Church have to add, all the sacraments. For the sacraments, beginning with baptism, are nothing else but the outpouring of the divine life which flows from the body of the Lord. The sacraments are more than mere symbols or ideas, they are mysterious physical contacts; they make use of the physical realities of this world to bring us the energy of the world in which Christ lives. In the sacraments we eat the food of the eschatological era, we are put in touch with the purity, life and grace which exist in the risen body of

Christ. Through the physical action which they imply, all the sacraments are contacts – contacts in faith, but real – with the risen body of the Lord which is in truth the new temple from which life flows.

All this leads to the conclusion that Jesus' saying about the Temple is perfectly plausible. Why, then, at the session of the Sanhedrin, is there mention of false witnesses? If this saying of Jesus is true, as we have decided it must be, the witnesses did not lie. One detail, however, appears to be false; the witnesses make Jesus say, 'I will destroy' or, according to Matthew, 'I can destroy'. Did Christ announce that he would carry out the destruction himself? No, according to John, who gives the saying in the form, 'Destroy this Temple'. It is with tears that Jesus foresees that men's sins will bring about its destruction (Lk 19:41–4). Himself he does not wish for this, but will intervene to rebuild. Thus to impute to Jesus violent intentions against the Temple is to bear false witness.

Mark adds that the witnesses were not in agreement with one another. Apparently it is because the witnesses differ that the high priest insists further. But at a deeper level we can understand very well – after analysing the meaning of Jesus' words – why the high priest intervenes and asks Jesus, 'Who are you, then?' The Jews are in no doubt as to the meaning of the saying about the Temple, they realise that the intention to build a new one is a messianic claim and even blasphemous. This first utterance of Jesus is already a blasphemy such as to bring about a death-sentence at the end of the session.

The gravity of the blasphemy becomes clear if we refer to earlier episodes in the Old Testament. When the prophet Jeremiah receives a divine mission to go and speak against the Temple in front of the Jews, God says to him – 'Say to them, "Yahweh says this: if you will not listen to me by following my law which I put before you, by paying attention to the words of my servants the prophets. . . . . I will treat this Temple as I treated Shiloh [which was already in ruins in Jeremiah's time] and make this city a curse for all the nations of the earth". The priests and prophets and all the people heard Jeremiah say these words in the Temple of Yahweh. When Jeremiah had finished saying everything that Yahweh had ordered him to say to all the people, the priests and prophets seized hold of him and said, "You shall die! Why have you made this prophecy in the name of Yahweh: This Temple will be like Shiloh, and this city will be desolate and uninhabited"?' (Jr 26:4–9). Jeremiah is saying what

Jesus has just said in the name of God, 'Because of your sins the
Temple will be destroyed and the city abandoned'. This is a scandal
and the people all crowd together to put Jeremiah to death. The
magistrates intervene and institute a hearing. Some of the people say,
'This man deserves to die, since he has prophesied against this city, as
you have heard with your own ears'. But Jeremiah replies, 'Yahweh
himself sent me to say all the things you have heard against this
Temple and this city'. Others are impressed by this and say, 'This
man does not deserve to die: he has spoken to us in the name of
Yahweh our God'. (Jr 26:11-12, 16).

On this occasion they recall the precedents. 'Micah of Moresheth –
another prophet – who prophesied in the days of Hezekiah king of
Judah, had this to say to all the people of Judah . . . "Zion will
become ploughland, Jerusalem a heap of rubble, and the mountain
of the Temple a wooded height!" ' (Jr 26:18). Like Jeremiah, Micah
had prophesied the destruction of the Holy Places as a punishment
by God, and the Jews go on to ask: Ought we to put a prophet to
death for this? Hezekiah and all the people of Judah accepted the
prophecy and repented.

In the same chapter of Jeremiah another precedent is recalled
(26:20-3). A certain Uriah from Kiriath-jearim uttered the same
threats against the city and the land as Jeremiah, but his lot was less
fortunate. King Jehoiakim sought to put him to death. Uriah fled to
Egypt, but was brought back before the king who had him put to the
sword and his body thrown into the common burial-ground.

Such is the fate of prophets who dare to speak against the Temple:
they expose themselves to death. Jeremiah only escaped because he
had powerful friends who managed to get him spared, but Uriah
before him had been put to death. We can get some idea, then, of the
indignation of the Jews when Jesus in his turn announces that their
city and their Temple are to be destroyed. In their eyes it is an inadmissible blasphemy. And this is why the high priest is led to ask the
definitive question – Who then are you?

The high priest's examination

The second phase of the trial opens. *The high priest then stood up
before the whole assembly and put this question to Jesus, 'Have you no
answer to that? What is this evidence these men are bringing against
you?* (Mk 14:60). The question is the same in Matthew (Mt 26:62).

The Greek can be translated slightly differently; if the interrogative pronoun is taken as a relative, it will read, 'Have you no answer to the evidence which these men are bringing against you?' But the first translation is to be preferred.

But he was silent and made no answer at all. The high priest put a second question to him. 'Are you the Christ,' he said 'the Son of the Blessed One?' (Mk 14:61). In Matthew the tone is much more solemn, *'I put you on oath by the living God to tell us if you are the Christ, the Son of God'* (Mt 26:63). In Matthew, the high priest calls God to witness by a solemn oath in order to force Jesus to speak. Jesus wishes to keep silence, but if he were to do so after this oath he would be treating God with contempt.

We must weigh the high priest's question carefully. It includes two terms, 'the Christ' and 'the Son of the Blessed One'. Christ is the Greek translation of Messiah. 'Son of the Blessed One' and 'Son of God' mean the same; 'the Blessed One' is a way of referring to God without naming him. In New Testament times, the Jews had scruples about pronouncing the name of God outright. Instead they substituted expressions like Adonai (the Lord), Heaven, the Most High or, as here, the Blessed One. Mark's expression then is more archaic than Matthew's but the meaning is the same.

What is the connection between these two titles, Christ and Son of God? We might be tempted to reply that the Christ is God's emissary, the son of David, while the Son of God is the second person of the Blessed Trinity. This is true, since the Christian faith, founded on the witness of the apostles, the early Church and the councils, has revealed the full range of this title, Son of God; but this would not be so for the high priest at the time of the Passion. What did 'Son of God' mean for a Jew? It was a metaphorical expression, indicating an intimate relationship with God, an immediacy of grace and love for a man or a group especially united to God by their devotion. In the Bible, many are called sons of God[1]: the angels because they belong to the court of heaven, the people of Israel because they are the chosen people, the object of God's love – 'Out of Egypt I have called my son'. Again, this title is given to the Messiah, the King, the Judges and even to the devout Jew who lives justly[2]. In consequence, 'Son of God' does not necessarily imply the

[1] Cf. P. BENOIT, *Exégèse et Théologie*, I, pp. 127f.
[2] This wide, metaphorical use of the idea of sonship is characteristic of the east; it is found in Hebrew, in Aramaic and even in Arabic.

equality of essence of the Father and the Word, but an intimate and affectionate relationship.

Here, the high priest merely adds to the notion of the Messiah a more precise idea of a special closeness to God. God had said of the Messiah King (Ps 2:7), 'You are my son, today I have become your father.' The high priest is perhaps thinking of those discussions in the Temple in which Jesus spoke of God as his Father, but he cannot see this man Jesus as the Son of God in the sense in which our faith understands it, thanks to the resurrection and to subsequent Christian reflection. This is not said to exculpate the Jews who committed the crime, but it should make one very careful how one uses the term 'deicide'. They did in fact kill the Son of God, but they cannot have known that he was the Son of God in the strongest sense of the word. Today the Church puts us on our guard against anti-semitic expressions, which may be true theologically, but not psychologically. The Jews did not really want to kill God.

Jesus' reply

Jesus then has to answer whether he is the Christ, the Son of God. In Mark, the answer is categorical, '*I am, and you will see the Son of Man . . .*' (Mk 14:62). In Matthew it is less clear, and Luke seems to confirm Matthew. I am willing to believe that Matthew is here the more exact, '*The words are your own*' (Mt 26:64). In Aramaic, as in Greek, this is an evasive reply which could be expanded as follows: 'I would not have said so myself, it's you who have said it. It's not wrong but I wouldn't have put it like that myself[1]'.

Jesus follows this immediately with a qualification and presents his own conception. In order to tell the high priest, 'I am the Christ, the Son of God, but not in the sense in which you understand it', he goes on: *Moreover, I tell you from this time onward you will see the Son of Man seated at the right hand of the Power and coming on the clouds of heaven* (Mt 26:64). The different meaning which Jesus gives to the high priest's idea is very important; he confronts him with two Old Testament texts.

The first of these is from Psalm 110, 'The Lord said to my Lord: Sit at my right hand.' The Messiah King is to sit at the right hand of

---

[1] Jesus had already replied in the same manner to Judas, who had asked who would betray him, 'Not I, Rabbi, surely?' – 'They are your own words'. (Mt 26:25). In other words, 'I didn't force you to say it, you said it yourself.'

God. 'The Power': this term refers to God in a veiled way, without actually naming him. Jesus knows that he is the Messiah, but not such as the high priest is expecting; he is not a warrior king who will march at the head of an army, nor is he simply a high priest who will transform the Temple. He is the Messiah of whom David's psalm speaks. Jesus had already quoted this text when he asked the Jews to explain how David could say this of the Messiah King and yet call him his Lord (Mt 22:44). The Jews did not know how to reply. Jesus meant to convey in this way that he was not the earthly, warrior-type Messiah they were expecting, but a Messiah of divine rank and transcendent dignity who would surpass their usual hopes. Similarly here, Jesus tells the high priest that he is the Messiah in the sense of Psalm 110, seated at the right hand of the Power.

Jesus quotes another text, '*and coming on the clouds of heaven*'. These words are borrowed from the prophet Daniel (Dn 7:13). When Daniel is describing his vision of the empires of the earth, their kings are symbolised by savage beasts such as the lion, the bear and the leopard. After that he sees the kingdom of the saints, the elect of God – the 'little remnant' called by God to the messianic salvation – and their sovereign who is 'like a son of man coming on the clouds'. Jesus took up this image to convey the idea that the messianic king is a mysterious, heavenly personage. He is called 'Son of Man' by contrast with the beasts, the kings of the earth. The kingdom of the saints will have as its sovereign a human being of heavenly origin, coming on the clouds of heaven. Jesus has said several times already that he is to be this Son of Man and that he is coming to bring into being that kingdom of the saints which Daniel foresaw. He says so again here: after asserting that he will be the Messiah announced by David, seated beside the Father, he adds also that he will be the Messiah who is the Son of Man, coming, crowned, on the clouds of heaven.

So Jesus does not reject the high priest's question out of hand: he does not deny that is is the Messiah, only that he is the kind of Messiah the high priest is thinking of. Similarly when Pilate, with earthly kings in mind, asks whether he is a king, Jesus replies, 'It is you who say it. Yes, I am a king, but my kingdom is not of this world.' In both these cases Jesus takes the notions of those who are accusing him on an earthly plane and transposes them to the truly spiritual plane that is his own.

Jesus also says, 'From this time onward you will see . . .' Does he mean that the high priest and the Sanhedrin are going to see the Parousia, the Son of Man coming to the Last Judgment? It is a serious question, since certain critics have used this occasion to say that Jesus was mistaken, that he proclaimed the Parousia to be close at hand, whereas in fact we are still waiting for it. But to take this text as referring to the Parousia is to misunderstand it: 'coming on the clouds of heaven' does not relate necessarily to the Last Judgment. In the New Testament certain texts (e.g., 1 Th 4:16–17) use the image of 'clouds' to describe how Jesus will come for the last time and how the dead will rise and go up to meet him. But the original implication of Daniel's text is not that the Son of Man comes down to men but that he himself ascends towards the throne of God. In Daniel's vision, the Son of Man ascends on the clouds to receive the everlasting sovereignty of the kingdom of the saints. The clouds are the steps, so to speak, which the Son of Man has to climb in order to present himself before the everlasting God and to be crowned by him. This is the image which Jesus takes up here. He is not saying, 'You will see the Son of Man coming towards you at the Parousia', but, 'You will see the triumph of the Son of Man, crowned by God and seated at his right hand'. Jesus is proclaiming his enthronement as Messiah in glory. The high priest and the Jews, if they are willing to open their eyes, will see Christ rise from the dead, the Church triumph and Judaism disappear. In A.D. 70, Jerusalem is to be destroyed and the Church will succeed to her position. So Jesus is not wrong in saying that they will see this change of regime in which the new worship will be inaugurated by Jesus himself risen from the dead.

The Jews refuse to accept this man who claims to be the Messiah, glorified at God's right hand, and who is to destroy their religious establishment. This claim is intolerable!

The high priest tore his robes, 'What need of witnesses have we now?' he said. 'You heard the blasphemy. What is your finding?' (Mk 14:63–4). Tearing one's robes was a ritual gesture that expressed indignation[1]. The high priest has detected blasphemy. The opinion of some critics is that it was not blasphemous to call oneself the Messiah. Many adventurers, Judas, Athronges, Theudas, Bar Cochba, gave themselves out to be the Messiah, gathered disciples and tried to

---

[1] Some commentators have gone so far as to claim that there was a ready-made slit in the tunic which could be drawn together again afterwards.

shake off the Roman yoke. Their enterprises may have come to a bad end but no one accused them of blasphemy. At most it was their good sense that was suspect. Here, then, where is the blasphemy? Jesus, as we have seen, claims for himself a rank and mission which are not human. For the Jews it is inadmissible that he should claim to be of divine rank.

And they all gave their verdict: he deserved to die (Mk 14:64). We must be careful not to interpret this as a real death-sentence, a verdict carrying with it the power of execution. The Jews no longer had the right to condemn anyone to death[1], they would be obliged to take this matter to the Roman governor to obtain a death-sentence. As a sentence, it is therefore a statement of intent, a vote, a private decision; they are all agreed that the death of the accused must be obtained, but it is not yet a verdict with juridical force. Before bringing out this point, we must ask what allowances have to be made for editing throughout this scene.

Certain critics have thrown doubt on the authenticity of the whole narrative of the session, on the grounds that it cannot be based on the evidence of eye-witnesses. This objection is worthless. It would be enough for a Nicodemus, a Joseph of Arimathaea, members of the Sanhedrin, to have given an account of what happened. Besides, it is naïve surely to imagine that the secrets of an assembly can be kept. Human nature is not like that; even if they are not supposed to, men talk. That some session of this kind took place in reality is overwhelmingly probable. Some consultation, some decision was necessary before the matter could be taken before the governor. There had to be some session like this in order to present him with plausible reasons for their action. In substance, then, the historicity of the scene seems absolutely assured.

Once this is admitted, though, can we expect to be given a precise and detailed account of the whole session? *A priori*, it would seem that an account as brief as this cannot possibly contain the complete minutes of the deliberations. The evangelists have apparently gathered the essential points from a fairly unsystematic summary. If we take a closer look at the narrative itself certain discrepancies come to light. For example, verses 57–9 in Mark 14 seem to have been inserted later, verse 60 follows on very well after verse 56. This suspicion is confirmed by the fact that Luke does not record the saying about the Temple. Perhaps he omitted it deliberately, or

[1] See below, pp. 113f.

110   JESUS BEFORE THE SANHEDRIN

perhaps, more probably, the tradition he was using did not include it.
Once again we sense behind our present texts an earlier, and perhaps
simpler, version with which other fragments have later been inter-
woven.

The narrative of Luke

Luke's narrative differs from those of Mark and Matthew at several
points. First, Luke distinguishes more clearly between the titles
'Christ' and 'Son of God' – 'If you are the Christ, tell us', then later,
'So you are the Son of God then?' Why are these two titles, which in
Mark and Matthew are associated closely as though they were
synonymous, here given a sense distinct from one another? Is it
perhaps because Luke is deliberately giving 'Son of God' a Christian
meaning and putting more into it than the high priest could? He is
thinking of his Christian readers who have a full knowledge of what
is meant by the expression 'Son of God', a title much superior to
that of 'Christ'. So Luke puts them in ascending order, first Christ,
then Son of God[1]. The version in Mark and Matthew is more suited
to the mentality of the Jews, for whom Christ and Son of God were
practically equivalent.

Another important difference: Luke suppresses the reference to
the text of Daniel. According to Luke, Jesus says, '*But from now on
the Son of Man will be seated at the right hand of the Power of God*'
(Lk 22:69). The expression 'Son of Man' is included in the text, but
not the phrase 'coming on the clouds of heaven'. Why has Luke
omitted it? Perhaps he wanted to guard against the difficulty to
which I have already drawn attention: in Christian circles, after
thirty years of the gospel, coming on the clouds of heaven meant the
Parousia. He did not want his readers to think that Jesus had
announced an almost immediate Parousia to the Sanhedrin, since
this would have already been proved wrong by the facts. Luke
preferred to suppress the ambiguous expression in order to avoid
misunderstanding. In any case, Luke's divergences from Mark and
Matthew are a clear warning that we should not expect the gospels
to give us a strictly accurate verbatim report of the session of the
Sanhedrin.

[1] The same thing happens in the two parts of the dialogue at the annunciation,
where Jesus is presented first as the Messiah, the Son of David (Lk 1:31-3),
and then as the Holy One, the Son of God (1:35).

The gospel of John

There is one last important thing to notice; here, once again, Luke resembles John. In fact, of course, John does not record the meeting of the Sanhedrin, but if we look further back in the fourth gospel we come across scenes very like it: Jesus is in the Temple, discussing his person and his mission with the Jews. They ask him, 'Who are you? Are you the Christ?' Jesus, speaking of his relationship to the Father, says, 'The Father and I are one' (Jn 10:30) or again, 'Before Abraham ever was, I Am' (Jn 8:58). Each time the Jews attempt to stone him.

A particularly striking case is that passage of John in which the same words are to be found as in Luke (Jn 10). In Luke, when the high priest asks him, 'If you are the Christ, tell us', Jesus replies, *'If I tell you, you will not believe me'* (Lk 22:67). In John (10:24–5), the Jews surround Jesus at the Portico of Solomon as they do in the Sanhedrin, and say, 'How much longer are you going to keep us in suspense? If you are the Christ, tell us plainly.' Jesus replied, 'I have told you, but you do not believe.' The two replies are indeed very alike. Jesus then goes on to speak about the works done in the name of his Father, and about his sheep, and he finishes, 'The Father and I are one.' The Jews fetch stones to stone him with, but he asks them, 'For which of these [my works] are you stoning me?' – 'For blasphemy', they answer (as in the Sanhedrin), 'you are only a man and you claim to be God.' And Jesus replies, 'You say, "You are blaspheming", because I said, "I am the Son of God" ' (Jn 10:36). The outline of this scene is very similar to that in the Sanhedrin: Jesus proclaims himself 'Christ' and 'Son of God' before the Jews, he tells them, 'You do not believe', he is accused of blasphemy, and they want to put him to death.

The synoptics report this discussion between Jesus and the Jews only once, at the end of the ministry, whereas John alludes several times to similar incidents in the Temple. Which is correct? Both traditions are true and complementary to one another; each has arranged the material in its own fashion. Following Mark's outline, the synoptics have chosen not to deal with Jesus' ministry in Jerusalem; Jesus only goes up there once, and that for the last Passover of the Passion. In John, on the contrary, Jesus goes up there several times; from a historical point of view this arrangement seems more correct. The differences in the presentation of the debate which concerns us here are a consequence of this difference in drafting the outlines of the gospels. In my opinion, discussions in the Temple between Jesus and the Jews were fairly frequent. The synoptics, since they made no mention of Jesus' ministry in Jerusalem, could not give an account of each of these discussions, and so chose to report them all together in one scene. They had the right to do this, since the final scene, the meeting of the Sanhedrin, did actually take place; but in doing so they put together in a schematic way the substance of several discussions and the arguments fundamental to the problem – Jesus speaks against the Temple, proposes a new worship, claims to be the Messiah, the Christ, the Son of Man, and the Jews refuse to accept him.

John took it on himself to report the whole of Jesus' ministry in Jerusalem; he gives several accounts of this same debate and from episode to episode the tone of the exchanges becomes sharper. For this reason John must have felt himself dispensed from reporting the last session of all.

The two traditions, disjointed though they are, are each correct in their own way. We have to take advantage of both; with John, we must believe that the debate between Jesus and the Jews regarding his mission began before the Passion, in repeated discussions in the Temple: with the synoptics, and despite John's silence, that these discussions reached their climax at the session of the Sanhedrin, the last encounter, where the final decision against Jesus was taken. Once again, the four gospels are complementary and reflect a tradition which is well founded and in substance true, although the details differ according to the point of view and underlying motive of each writer.

I will finish with two corollaries of a juridical character. Once it is understood that the gospel narratives do not give us a detailed verbatim report of the session, but instead a short theological summary, we must give up the idea of discovering whether or not there were any irregularities in its procedure. One type of Christian apologetics, which in my opinion is too short-sighted, draws up a list of the irregularities the Jews are supposed to have committed. Thus two priests named Lémann, who were converted Jews, exposed twenty-seven irregularities, from which they concluded that the sentence passed by the Sanhedrin had no judicial force.[1] In fact, of course, the way in which the gospels are written does not allow this

---

[1] *Valeur de l'assemblée qui prononça la peine de mort contre Jésus-Christ*, Paris, Lecoffre, 3rd ed., 1881.

kind of argument, since they do not pretend to give a complete recital of all that was said and done. And in addition this clumsy apologetic makes the mistake of arguing according to the Mishnaic law – the law of the Pharisaic Rabbis who drew up the Mishnah – whereas in Jesus' time the law in force was that of the Sadducees, about which little is known[1].

A last question remains to be asked: did the Jews still have the right to put a man to death? If they no longer had the right, as John says (Jn 18:31), the events of the Passion are easy to explain: the intervention of the Romans is necessary, they are the secular arm and they inflict crucifixion, a Roman penalty; nevertheless the initiative for the death sentence belongs to the Jews. This is the traditional Christian thesis.

However, the contrary thesis is defended today by Jews and others, who claim that at that time the Jews still had the right to put a man to death. If it had been they who put Jesus to death, as Christians allege, they would have stoned him. But in fact Jesus died on the cross and it was therefore the Romans who were responsible for his death. In an important book[2], J. Juster, who died in the First World War, tried to demonstrate that in Jesus' time the Jews had managed to keep this right. The book gave rise to considerable discussion, the details of which I cannot give here[3]. In my opinion the thesis of the gospels, in particular of John, remains true.

For in fact, throughout the empire, the Romans reserved to themselves the right to pass the death-sentence, which is a fundamental right of the crown; they withdrew it from the local authorities. Everywhere, whether in Cyrenaica, Egypt, Greece or elsewhere, power over life and death belonged to the Roman governor and not to the local courts. It must have been the same in Palestine. The historian Josephus, who records the appointment of the first procurator, Coponius, specifically says that Augustus gave him the right to put a man to death (*Wars*, II, 117); he does not tell us explicitly that this right was withdrawn from the Jews, but this can be taken for granted.

---

[1] See J. BLINZLER, *Le procès de Jésus*, Paris, 1962, Annexe 7, '*Le code pénal de la Mischna était-il en vigueur au temps de Jésus?*', pp. 219–38.
[2] *Les Juifs dans l'Empire romain*, Paris, 1914.
[3] There is a good account of the question with a bibliography by U. HOLZ-MEISTER, 'Zur Frage der Blutgerichtsbarkeit des Synedriums', in *Biblica*, XIX, 1938, pp. 43–59, 151–74. See also P. BENOIT, 'Le Procès de Jésus', in *Exégèse et Théologie*, I, pp. 278f.

Against this, it is possible to bring forward certain actual cases: the Jews killed both Stephen and James. But if these cases are examined carefully it becomes apparent that there were exceptional circumstances. In Stephen's case, for example, who was probably 'lynched', taken and stoned by the crowd without much of a trial, it is a question of execution by a mob. In addition, the Jews profited by the momentary absence of the Roman authority; it is probable that he was executed between the departure of Pilate and the arrival of Marcellus, who succeeded Pilate as procurator. In the case of James, we are told the following quite clearly by Josephus (*Ant.*, XX, 197f): Festus, the Roman procurator, had just died and his successor Albinus had not yet arrived; Ananos, the youngest son of the high priest Annas, seized the opportunity to summon a hasty court, pass sentence on James and execute him. The Jews themselves, disgusted by this violence, told the procurator the moment he arrived, saying that the high priest did not have the right to act in this manner and set up a court without the procurator's consent.

The principle remains true, then: the Jews no longer had the right to put a man to death. The gospel has good reason to show the Sanhedrin looking for a valid cause to present to the governor. Only the governor could give a verdict that would have executive force, and that would be the Roman penalty of crucifixion.

After examining the deeper meaning of this session of the Sanhedrin, we may grieve over the attitude of the Jews who rejected the emissary of God, but we shall avoid calling them 'deicides'; as Jesus and the apostles said, 'They did not know what they were doing'. What it is above all important to remember is that, at this crucial moment, the climax to the discussions in the Temple, Jesus solemnly admits before his own people, before history and before mankind, what he claims to be and what he is going to die for – a Messiah who is transcendent, spiritual and of divine rank. Jesus accepts a momentary abasement, but soon – raised by his Father and triumphant on the clouds of heaven – he will found in his risen body a new form of worship, by which the Church and all who believe in him will live for ever afterwards.

6. Jesus before Pilate

APPEARANCE BEFORE PILATE

| Mt 27:1–2, 11–14 | Mk 15:1–5 |

¹ When morning came,
all the chief priests
and the elders of the people

met in council
to bring about the death
of Jesus.

² They had him bound,
and led him away

to hand him over
to Pilate,
the governor.

---

¹ First thing in the morning,
the chief priests together
with the elders
and scribes,
in short the whole Sanhedrin,
prepared a council.*

They had Jesus bound
and took him away

and handed him over
to Pilate.

---

¹¹Jesus, then, was brought before
the governor,
and the governor put to him this

² Pilate questioned him,

Lk 23:1–5   Jn 18:28–38

22 **66** When day broke
there was a meeting
of the elders of the people,
attended by the chief priests
and scribes.
He was brought before their
    council, . . .

1 The whole assembly then rose,

and they brought him   **28** They then led Jesus
                                    from the house of Caiaphas

before Pilate.   to the Praetorium.

                                    It was now morning. They did
                                    not go into the Praetorium
                                    themselves or they would be
                                    defiled and unable to eat the
                                    Passover.
                                    29 So Pilate came outside to
                                    them and said,
2 They began their accusation   'What charge do you bring
                                    against this man?'
                                    They replied, 'If he were not a
                                    criminal, we should not be
                                    handing him over to you'.

by saying, 'We found this
man inciting our people to
revolt, opposing payment of the
tribute to Caesar, and claiming
to be Christ, a king'.
                                    31 Pilate said, 'Take him your-
                                    selves, and try him by your own
                                    Law.' The Jews answered, 'We are
                                    not allowed to put a man to death'.
                                    32 This was to fulfil the words
                                    Jesus had spoken indicating the
                                    way he was going to die.
                                    33 So Pilate went back into the
                                    Praetorium and called Jesus
                                    to him.

3 Pilate put to him this question,

| Mt | Mk |

question,
'Are you the King of the Jews?'   'Are you the King of the Jews?'

'It is you who say it'   'It is you who say it'
Jesus replied.*   he answered.

¹² But when he was accused
by the chief priests   ³ And the chief priests
                                          brought many accusations against
                                          him.

and the elders
he refused to answer at all.
¹³ Pilate then said to him,   ⁴ Pilate questioned him again,
                                          'Have you no reply at all?
'Do you not hear   See
how many charges they have   how many accusations they are
brought   bringing
against you?'   against you!'
¹⁴ But to the governor's   But, to Pilate's
complete amazement,   amazement,
he offered no reply   Jesus made no further reply
to any of the charges.

| Lk | Jn |

'Are you the king of the Jews?'

                     'Are you the king of the Jews?'
he asked.
Jesus replied, 'Do you ask this of
your own accord, or have others
spoken to you about me?'
   [35] Pilate answered, 'Am I a Jew?
It is your own people and the
chief priests who have handed you
over to me: what have you done?'
   [36] Jesus replied, 'Mine is not a
kingdom of this world; if my
kingdom were of this world, my
men would have fought to
prevent my being surrendered
to the Jews. But my kingdom
is not of this kind.'
   [37] 'So you are a king then?' said
Pilate.

'It is you who say it'
he replied.

'It is you who say it'
answered Jesus.
'Yes, I am a king. I was born
for this, I came into the world
for this: to bear witness to the
truth; and all who are on the
side of truth listen to my voice.'
   [38a] 'Truth!' said Pilate 'What
is that?'

23 [9] So he questioned him at some
length;

19 [9b] But Jesus made no answer.
   [10] Pilate then said to him,
'Are you refusing to speak to me?'

but without getting any reply.

[10] Meanwhile the chief priests and
the scribes were there, violently
pressing their accusations.

Mt   Mk

JESUS IS SENT TO HEROD AND SENT BACK TO PILATE

27 ¹² But when he was accused
by the chief priests

15 ³ And the chief priests

and the elders
he refused to answer at all.
¹³ Pilate then said to him,

'Do you not hear
how many charges they have
   brought
against you?'
¹⁴ But . . . he offered no reply
to any of the charges.

15 ³ And the chief priests
brought many accusations against
him.

⁴ Pilate questioned him again,

'Have you no reply at all?
See
how many accusations they are
bringing
against you.'
But . . . Jesus made no further
   reply.

Lk   Jn

18 38b and with that he went out
again to the Jews
4 Pilate then said   and said,
to the chief priests and the crowd,
'I find no case   'I find no case
against this man'.   against him'.
5 But they persisted, 'He is
inflaming the people with his
teaching all over Judaea; it
has come all the way from
Galilee where he started, down
to here'.

Lk 23:6–12

6 When Pilate heard this, he asked
if the man were a Galilean;
7 and finding that he came under
Herod's jurisdiction he passed him
over to Herod who was also in
Jerusalem at that time.
8 Herod was delighted to see Jesus;
he had heard about him and had
been wanting for a long time to
set eyes on him; moreover he
was hoping to see some miracle
worked by him.

19 9b But Jesus made no answer.
9 So he questioned him   10 Pilate then said to him,
at some length

'Are you refusing to speak to me?'

but without getting any reply.

10 Meanwhile the chief priests and

Mt	Mk
27 ²⁷ The . . . soldiers . . .	15 ¹⁶ The soldiers . . .
²⁸ made him wear a scarlet cloak . . .	dressed him up in purple . . . .
²⁹ to make fun of him.	

THE SENTENCE OF DEATH
Mt 27:15–26   Mk 15:6–15

Mt	Mk
¹⁵ At festival time it was the governor's practice to release a prisoner for the people, anyone they chose.	⁶ At festival time Pilate used to release a prisoner for them, anyone they asked for.

| Lk | Jn |

the scribes were there, violently
pressing their accusations.
¹¹ Then Herod,
together with his guards, | 19 ² The soldiers . . .
treated him with contempt
and made fun of him;
he put | dressed him
a rich cloak on him | in a purple robe.
and sent him back to Pilate.

¹² And though Herod and Pilate
had been enemies before, they
were reconciled that same day.

| Lk 23:13-25 | Jn 18:39-19, 16ᵃ |

¹³ Pilate then | 19 ⁴ Pilate
                                           | came outside again

summoned the chief priests
and the leading men and the
people
¹⁴ 'You brought this man before
me'
he said | and said to them,
'as a political agitator.
Now | 'Look
                                           | I am going to bring him out to you
I have gone into the matter myself
in your presence | to let you see
and found no case against the man | that I find no case'.
in respect of all the charges
you bring against him.
¹⁵ Nor has Herod either, since he
has sent him back to us. As
you can see the man has done
nothing that deserves death,
¹⁶ so I shall have him flogged
and then let him go.'

(¹⁷ He was under obligation | ³⁹ 'But according to a custom
                                           | yours
to release | I should release
one man for them | one prisoner

Mt	Mk
16 Now there was at that time a notorious prisoner whose name was (Jesus) Barabbas.	**7** Now a man called Barabbas was then in prison with the rioters who had committed murder during the uprising. **8** When the crowd went up and began to ask Pilate the customary favour,
17 So when the crowd gathered, Pilate said to them, 'Which do you want me to release for you: (Jesus) Barabbas, or Jesus who is called Christ?'	**9** Pilate answered them, 'Do you want me to release for you the King of the Jews?'
18 For Pilate knew it was out of jealousy that they had handed him over. **19** Now as he was seated in the chair of judgement, his wife sent him a message, 'Have nothing to do with that man; I have been upset all day by a dream I had about him'. **20** The chief priests and the elders, however, had persuaded the crowd	**10** For he realised it was out of jealousy that the chief priests had handed Jesus over. **11** The chief priests, however, had incited the crowd
to demand the release of Barabbas and the execution of Jesus.	to demand that he should release Barabbas for them instead.

Lk   Jn

every feast day.)   at the Passover;

would you like me, then,
to release

the king of the Jews?'

18 But as one man
they howled,   **40** At this they shouted:
'Away with him!   'Not this man,' they said
Give us   'but
Barabbas!'   Barabbas'.

19 (This man had been thrown into   Barabbas was a brigand.
prison for causing a riot in
the city and for murder.)

19 **1** Pilate then had Jesus taken
away and scourged;
2 and after this, the soldiers
twisted some thorns
into a crown
and put it on his head,

Mt	Mk

²⁹ ... 'Hail, king of the Jews!' ... | ¹⁸ ... 'Hail, king of the Jews!' ...
³⁰ and struck him on the head ... | ¹⁹ They struck his head ...

²¹ So when the governor spoke	¹² Then Pilate spoke again.
and asked them, 'Which of the two do you want me to release for you?' they said, 'Barabbas'.	
²² 'But in that case,' Pilate said to them 'what am I to do with Jesus who is called Christ?'	'But in that case,' he said to them 'What am I to do with the man you call the king of the Jews?'
They all said, 'Let him be crucified!'	¹³ They shouted back, 'Crucify him!'
^{23a} 'Why?' he asked 'What harm has he done?'	^{14a} 'Why?' Pilate asked them 'What harm has he done?'

Lk   Jn

	and dressed him in a purple robe. ³ They kept coming up to him and saying, 'Hail, king of the Jews!'; and they slapped him in the face.
23 ¹³ Pilate then . . . ¹⁴ said . . . 'Now	⁴ Pilate came outside again and said to them, 'Look, I am going to bring him out to you
I have gone into the matter myself in your presence and found no case against the man'.	to let you see that I find no case'. ⁵ Jesus then came out wearing the crown of thorns and the purple robe. Pilate said, 'Here is the man'.
²⁰ Pilate was anxious	¹² From that moment Pilate was anxious
to set Jesus free and addressed them again,	to set him free . . .

²¹ but they
shouted back,
'Crucify him! Crucify him!'
²² And for the third time
he spoke to them, 'Why?
What harm has this man done?

⁶ When they saw him
the chief priests and the guards
shouted,
'Crucify him! Crucify him!'

Pilate said,

'Take him yourselves and crucify
him:

I have found no case against him
that deserves death,
so I shall have him punished
and then let him go.'

I can find no case against him'.

⁷ 'We a have a Law,' the Jews
replied 'and according to
that Law he ought to die,

| Mt | Mk |

27 **12** But when he was accused
by the chief priests

15 **3** And the chief priests
brought many accusations against
him.

and the elders
he refused to answer at all.
13 Pilate then said to him,

4 Pilate questioned him again
'Have you no reply at all?
See

'Do you not hear
how many charges they have
brought against you?'

how many charges they are
bringing against you.'

23b But they   **14b** But they

Lk   Jn

because he has claimed to be
the Son of God.'
⁸ When Pilate heard him say
this his fears increased.
⁹ Re-entering the Praetorium,
he said to Jesus, 'Where
do you come from?'

But Jesus made no answer.
¹⁰ Pilate then said to him,
'Are you refusing to speak to me?

Surely you know I have power
to release you and I have
power to crucify you?'
¹¹ 'You would have no power
over me' replied Jesus 'if
it had not been given you
from above; that is why the
one who handed me over
to you has the greater guilt.'
¹² From that moment
23 ²⁰ Pilate was anxious to set   Pilate was anxious to set him free,
Jesus free . . .

but the Jews shouted, 'If
you set him free you are no
friend of Caesar's; anyone
who makes himself king is
defying Caesar'.
¹³ Hearing these words, Pilate
had Jesus brought out, and
seated himself on the chair
of judgement at a place called
the Pavement, in Hebrew Gabbatha.
¹⁴ It was Passover Preparation
Day,
about the sixth hour. 'Here
is your king,' said Pilate
to the Jews.
²³ But they   ¹⁵ They

Mt	Mk
shouted all the louder,	shouted all the louder,
'Let him be crucified!'	'Crucify him!'

24 Then Pilate saw that he was making no impression, that in fact a riot was imminent. So he took some water, washed his hands in front of the crowd and said, 'I am innocent of this man's blood. It is your concern.' ²⁵ And the people, to a man, shouted back, 'His blood be on us and on our children!'	
	¹⁵ So Pilate, anxious to placate the crowd,
²⁶ Then he released Barabbas for them.	released Barabbas for them
He ordered Jesus to be first scourged and then handed over to be crucified.	and, having ordered Jesus to be scourged, handed him over to be crucified.

MOCKING OF JESUS AS KING

Mt 27:27–31	Mk 15:16–20
²⁷ The governor's soldiers took Jesus with them into the Praetorium and collected the whole cohort round him.	¹⁶ The soldiers led them away to the inner part of the palace, that is, the Praetorium, and called the whole cohort together.

Lk   Jn

kept on shouting   shouted,*
at the top of their voices,
demanding
                                      'Take him away, take him away!
that he should be crucified.   Crucify him!'
And their shouts were growing
   louder.
                                      'Do you want me to crucify your
                                      king?' said Pilate. The chief
                                      priests answered, 'We have no
                                      king except Caesar'.

²⁴ Pilate   ¹⁶ᵃ So in the end Pilate

then gave his verdict:
their demand was to be granted.
²⁵ He released
the man they asked for,
who had been imprisoned
for rioting and murder,

and handed Jesus over to them   handed him over to them
                                      to be crucified.
to deal with as they pleased.

Lk   Jn

23 ¹¹ Then Herod, together with | 19 ² The soldiers . . .
his guards . . . |

Mt	Mk

<table>
<tr>
<td>

28 Then they stripped him
and made him wear
a scarlet cloak,
29 and having twisted some thorns
into a crown
they put this on his head

and placed a reed
in his right hand.
To make fun of him
they knelt to him,
saying,
'Hail, king of the Jews!'
30 And they spat on him
and took the reed
and struck him on the head with it.

31 And when they had finished
making fun of him,
they took off
the cloak
and dressed him in his own clothes
and led him away
to crucify him.
</td>
<td>

17 They dressed him up
in purple,
twisted some thorns
into a crown
and put it on him.

18 And they began saluting him,
'Hail, king of the Jews!'

19 They struck his head with a reed
and spat on him;
and they went down on their knees
to do him homage.
20 And when they had finished
making fun of him,
they took off
the purple
and dressed him in his own clothes.
They led him out
to crucify him.
</td>
</tr>
</table>

Lk   Jn

put
a rich cloak on him . . .

twisted some thorns
into a crown
and put it on his head,
and dressed him
in a purple robe.

and made fun of him . . .

[3] They kept coming up to him
and saying,
'Hail, king of the Jews!';

and they slapped him in the face.

After appearing before the Jewish authorities of the Sanhedrin, Jesus is now brought before the Roman governor Pilate. This scene is described by all four evangelists. Even John, who does not record the session of the Sanhedrin, reports the appearance before Pilate at considerable length. It will be best to study the four narratives one by one in order to bring out the particular message of each.

The narrative of Mark

Mark's narrative is the simplest and, despite an occasional clumsiness in presentation, the most detailed. He gives us the essentials, and in him we sense the turning-points of the drama better than we do in Matthew and Luke, who have omitted certain valuable details. Mark's presentation of the way in which the events unfold seems very plausible: two phases are to be discerned, separated by a dramatic reversal of events.

The first phase consists of a first encounter between Pilate and the Jewish leaders (Mk 15:2–5); then the crowd arrives and demands the customary pardoning of a prisoner for the Passover (Mk 15:6–7); lastly, the trial begins again, now in public with the crowd taking part, and ends with the sentence of death (Mk 15:8–15).

Before studying the trial itself we should take a brief look at the beginning of the chapter (Mk 15:1). *First thing in the morning, the chief priests together with the elders and scribes, in short the whole Sanhedrin, prepared a council. . . .** This second meeting of the Sanhedrin, on the Friday morning, is very brief in Mark and Matthew. All that is said of its discussions is: *They had Jesus bound and took him away and handed him over to Pilate* (Mk 15:1). As I explained in the preceding chapter, the session of the Sanhedrin in fact took place in the morning and not during the night. As for the discussions at this session, they are recorded by Mark as having taken place during the night (Mk 14:55–64). But we must now turn to the arrival at Pilate's palace.

* The wording has been slightly altered from the translation in the Jerusalem Bible.

In the first phase of the trial Pilate and the Jewish leaders confront one another. *Pilate questioned him, 'Are you the king of the Jews? 'It is you who say it', he answered. And the chief priests brought many accusations against him* (Mk 15:2–3). There is here already a slight awkwardness. Mark mentioned the accusations after the governor's question. Pilate cannot have thought up the notion that Jesus was the king of the Jews by himself, he must already have heard the accusations. Logically verse three ought to precede verse two, but in Mark's spontaneous style of writing this is of little importance.

From the beginning it is clear what is at stake in the debate: whether or not Jesus is the king of the Jews. It is with this that the trial will be concerned and with this that it will end, since the inscription on the cross will read: 'This is the king of the Jews'. It is clear that Roman power is going to condemn Jesus for political motives.

Pilate questioned him again, 'Have you no reply at all? See how many accusations they are bringing against you!' But to Pilate's amazement Jesus made no further reply (Mk 15:4–5). Jesus had at first replied, 'It is you who say it', which corresponds to an unenthusiastic affirmative, 'All right, I am a king, but in a different sense from the one you have in mind.' After this Jesus says nothing more. This total silence contrasts strongly with the speeches which he makes in John's gospel. Mark perhaps was thinking of the attitude of the Servant, the Lamb which is dumb before its shearers (Is 53:7).

After this first statement, which sets the trial in motion, there follows an interlude. *At festival time Pilate used to release a prisoner for them, anyone they asked for* (Mk 15:6). This is what is known as the privilege of Passover amnesty: each Passover the Roman governor used to release a prisoner. The gospels are the only evidence of such a custom. However, a somewhat similar case has been discovered in a Greek papyrus from Egypt (P.Fior.61, 59ss.); a prefect of Egypt says to the accused, 'You deserve to be scourged for the crimes you have committed, but I grant you to the crowd.' This gesture, though somewhat different, is comparable to Pilate's. But here it seems to be a special Palestinian custom – as John says, 'According to a custom *of yours*, I should release one prisoner'. This has the ring of truth; Passover was the anniversary of the deliverance from Egypt, the exodus from the land of bondage and the journey to the land of freedom. Every year, on the eve of this day, the Hebrews commemorated the great deliverance at a family meal and saw in it the pledge of further deliverance to come. It was therefore very suitable that a prisoner should be freed to mark the festival.

Now a man called Barabbas was then in prison with the rioters who had committed murder during the uprising (Mk 15:7). Mark says *the* uprising, taking it for granted that we know which uprising is meant. But we do not: all we know is that a terrorist has committed murder, is in prison and is called Barabbas. Barabbas is a Semitic, or more precisely Aramaic, name; 'Bar' means 'son' in both Aramaic and Syriac. Various etymologies have been suggested for it. It could be Bar Rabba, son of the master, son of the Rabbi. Or it could also be Bar Abba, son of his father, which is a way of naming someone whose actual name one does not know. This is an attractive solution: it would then be a kind of nickname.

When the crowd went up and began to ask Pilate the customary favour . . . (Mk 15:8). Notice first, 'The crowd went up' – the Praetorium then must be situated high up in the town. Notice also that the crowd asks for the customary favour, but without thinking of Jesus. We tend to imagine Jesus being taken to the Praetorium by the whole crowd and the leaders of the Jews, but this is not correct. It is only a delegation, comprising some chief priests and some Jewish leaders, that has come to rouse Pilate early in the morning. At this moment the crowd is busy about its own affairs and is not thinking about Jesus. Later it occurs to them to come and claim their Passover prisoner and they come up to the Praetorium, but still without Jesus or even Barabbas in mind.

The second phase of the trial begins with Pilate's words, '*Do you want me to release for you the king of the Jews*' (Mk 15:9). Pilate does not want to condemn Jesus and sees the Passover amnesty as an excellent way of getting out of the difficulty. The crowd is asking for a prisoner; 'Well,' says Pilate, 'there's this man who has just been brought before me; do you want me to release the king of the Jews?' Pilate hopes in this way to please the crowd as well as to extract himself from a tiresome situation, since, Mark goes on, *he realised it was out of jealousy that the chief priests had handed Jesus over* (Mk 15:10). Pilate understands the position of each party: the crowd is indifferent and has no interest in Jesus at this moment; the leaders are managing the whole plot, out of jealousy. In order to avoid giving in to the Jewish leaders, Pilate tries to get the crowd on his side by pardoning the prisoner. In this way the opponents of Jesus will have nothing further to say and their victim will be rescued from them. We must understand the psychological attitude of each of the parties involved: the Jewish leaders in charge of the affair want Jesus destroyed; the crowd is, like any crowd, of itself indifferent, it does not know what is going on and the release of any prisoner will do; Pilate is trying to bring the business to an end without having to condemn Jesus.

Pilate is sometimes represented as half Christian, impressed by Jesus, swayed by his spiritual stature and almost converted. This is too poetic a picture. He is to be seen simply as a Roman governor like so many others, who has enough sense to understand that Jesus is not dangerous, that the accusation brought against him is without foundation and that the poor man standing there so quietly and silently has done no harm. Besides, Pilate is glad to be able to stand up to the Jewish leaders, who pester him with unreasonable demands and against whom he wages a kind of perpetual cold war. He knows that they want this man condemned and he is going to do everything he can to avoid giving his consent. It is a mistake to put a halo round Pilate's head as is done in some apocryphal Christian writings. Neither is he the greatest criminal in the world. He is merely a Roman governor who had no thought of Jesus the day before, and who will perhaps no longer be thinking of him the day after. He sees clearly that the man is innocent, whatever the Jewish leaders may say, and tries to avoid taking a false step by making the crowd his allies against the leaders.

The chief priests, however, had incited the crowd to demand that he should release Barabbas for them instead (Mk 15:11). The Jewish leaders are unwilling to let Jesus escape; they stir up the crowd, suggesting Barabbas' name to them and saying, 'Set Jesus free? What are you thinking of? Ask for Barabbas, there's a man who has shown his mettle, leading the uprising and even assassinating someone! What's this Jesus done for you? And what can he do?' So the crowd – we know what crowds are – allows itself to be convinced and soon it is shouting for Barabbas to be released and Jesus condemned. The chief priests have succeeded in winning the crowd over and rousing it against Jesus.

And yet – and this must be emphasised even if it is not discernible here – the crowd was favourable to Jesus. Mark himself has shown this, a little earlier in his gospel. When Jesus expelled the vendors from the Temple (Mk 11:18), the chief priests were annoyed and wanted to put him to death, but they were afraid of him 'because the people were carried away by his teaching'. When Jesus questioned the scribes about the Son of David, Mark notes that 'the great majority of the people heard this with delight' (Mk 12:37). The leaders are angry at being attacked, the rabbis do not know what to reply, but the crowd, perhaps happy to see the powerful put at a disadvantage, willingly range themselves on Jesus' side. Later, when the leaders are preparing the plot against him and seeking to put him to death, they say, 'not during the festivities or there will be a disturbance among the people' (Mk 14:2), since they realise they cannot be certain of the crowd. The crowd, then, was favourable to Jesus rather than otherwise; nevertheless the chief priests succeeded in rousing it for Barabbas and against Jesus.

Pilate tries to get matters under control again, 'But in that case, what am I to do with the man you call the king of the Jews?' (Mk 15:12) The unfortunate Pilate is not very clever when he reminds them of a title which annoys them, 'the king of the Jews'. He succeeds only in rousing them further. *They shouted back, 'Crucify him!'* (Mk 15:13). The crowd has been skilfully manipulated, and, like all crowds, the less they understand why, the louder they shout.

Pilate continues to resist, *'Why? What harm has he done?' But they shouted all the louder, 'Crucify him!' So Pilate, anxious to placate the crowd, released Barabbas for them and, having ordered Jesus to be scourged, handed him over to be crucified* (Mk 15:14–15). Pilate ends by consenting. Although Mark does not go into details, we sense that Pilate is tired and can see no other way out: the crowd wants Jesus' death, so be it, let them have it! He releases the criminal Barabbas and hands Jesus over after having him scourged. We shall study the scene of the scourging later.

The narrative of Matthew

Matthew's narrative is very close to that of Mark, but he has omitted some useful details and the march of events becomes less clear. He has also inserted some additions[1].

In Matthew, as in Mark, Jesus is taken before the governor. Pilate questions him: *'Are you the king of the Jews?'* – *'It is you who say it.'* (Mt 27:11). The Jews accuse him, Jesus remains silent.

The first phase of the trial, in which the chief priests attack Jesus, is presented by Matthew in the same way as by Mark (Mt 27:12–14).

---

[1] Matthew 27:3–10 records the death of Judas. This deserves discussion by itself, but it is of minor importance and I have dealt with it elsewhere, see *Exégèse et Théologie*, Paris, 1951, pp. 340–59.

Then Matthew, still following Mark, recalls the Passover amnesty and the existence of Barabbas (Mt 27:15–16). It is worth noting that Matthew calls the latter *a notorious prisoner*. This helps us to understand why it is that the crowd so quickly takes sides with this man: he is a celebrated terrorist who has led an uprising and stood out against the Roman government.

Matthew does not say that the crowd goes up to ask for the Passover pardon, it seems as though they have been there since the beginning. So this precious detail in Mark's account has disappeared and with it a lively piece of description.

In Matthew's account Pilate very clumsily asks, '*Which do you want me to release for you: (Jesus) Barabbas or Jesus who is called Christ?*' (Mt 27:17). Pilate makes the mistake of mentioning the name of Barabbas and putting him on the same footing as Jesus. Plainly the crowd is going to choose the terrorist. In Mark, Pilate is much more skilful, keeping Barabbas' name out of it so that the crowd may forget him, but putting forward Jesus, whom the Jewish leaders have brought along, 'Take him; here's the prisoner I am releasing for you'.

There is one last awkwardness in Matthew's narrative, '*For Pilate knew it was out of jealousy that they had handed him over*' (Mt 27:18). Here 'they' refers to all the Jews, no longer merely the chief priests; in Mark it is the chief priests who are jealous, the crowd is on the whole favourable to Jesus. This detail is lost in Matthew.

On the other hand, Matthew's account includes three additions. The first is perhaps unauthentic: in some manuscripts Barabbas is called *Jesus Barabbas*. If this were genuine Jesus would be his first name, Barabbas his surname, and Pilate would have said, 'Which do you want me to release for you, Jesus Barabbas or Jesus Christ?' If the two men had the same name, Jesus, the parallelism would be more striking. This is not impossible, since Jesus was a common name. However, the manuscripts which support this addition are unreliable; it was perhaps added in the tradition on the grounds that the parallelism would strengthen the effect of the scene. At all events, the point is not very important.

Another note added by Matthew is the dream of Pilate's wife. *Now as he was seated in the chair of judgement, his wife sent him a message, 'Have nothing to do with that man; I have been upset all day by a dream I had about him*' (Mt 27:19). Matthew alone records this fact, and he does it discreetly. The apocryphal gospels give her name as

Procula, but Matthew does not tell us this. Historical details in Matthew alone are not absolutely reliable, and later tradition may be at work. In this instance, the theme of the judge's wife who asks her husband to spare a prisoner belongs to folklore; it is found again elsewhere, for example among the rabbis in Babylonia[1]. It could be that the story has found its way into Matthew through some other influence. But again, this is not of great importance either.

Matthew's last addition is more serious. *Then Pilate saw that he was making no impression, that in fact a riot was imminent. So he took some water, washed his hands in front of the crowd and said, 'I am innocent of this man's blood. It is your concern.' And the people, to a man, shouted back, 'His blood be on us and on our children!'* (Mt 27:24-5). This gesture of hand-washing is well known in the Bible, it expresses innocence of being mixed up in a crime. Both gesture and words have biblical precedents. The Deuteronomic Code lays down that the inhabitants of a town near which a murder has been committed are to wash their hands over a slaughtered heifer and say, 'Our hands did not shed this blood' (Dt 21:6). Similarly in the psalm which is recited at Mass, '*Lavabo*, I wash my hands' (Ps 26:6), this gesture is the natural expression of innocence.

The formula 'Let the blood be on the head of . . .' is also a biblical one. When Joab treacherously kills Abner, Saul's general, David says, 'I and my kingdom are innocent for ever before Yahweh of the blood of Abner son of Ner; may it fall on the head of Joab and on all his family!' (2 S 3:28-9; see also 2 S 1:16). What is surprising is that Pilate, the Roman governor, makes a biblical gesture. It is true that the symbolism of this gesture is spontaneous and could be universal. As for the words of the people, which Matthew alone gives, they are extremely forceful and involve the Jewish people in full responsibility for the death of Jesus. Matthew reveals the deeper meaning of the scene by means of a scriptural phrase of great power. It is not necessary that the Jews should have uttered these words just as they stand. As with many details of the gospels, especially if they stand alone or are late, we need not look for the exactness of a verbatim report; their truth consists in making clear the essential lesson of what happened. Here we are meant to understand that the Jewish crowd, despite the objections of the Roman governor, wanted

---

[1] Babylonian Talmud, Ta'an. 24b and Qid. 70b, quoted by STRACK-BILLERBECK, *Kommentar zum Neuen Testament aus Talmud und Midrasch*, vol. I, Munich, 1922, p. 1032.

Jesus to die. But even if we retain the culpability of the Jews, in the dialogue between Jews and Christians we must not take our stand on words like these alone, which create an abyss between us. It is true that injury has been done, but psychologically the memory of it may be so harsh and painful that it prevents any reconciliation. Today the Church bids us not to emphasise what divides us, but to see that good will and mutual understanding prevail. A phrase like this, true in itself, must be understood at the deeper level of Matthew's theology. And we must remind ourselves of other words uttered by Jesus, which restore the balance, 'They do not know what they are doing' (Lk 23:34). There is no doubt that the Jews acted against Jesus, but who can gauge the degree of a man's responsibility? When Peter reminds the Jews of Jerusalem, that they put Jesus to death, he goes on, 'Now I know, brothers, that neither you nor your leaders had any idea what you were really doing' (Ac 3:17; cf. 13:27). It is a question not of complete acquittal, but of ceasing to maintain an atmosphere of hatred which prevents any mutual understanding.

The narrative of Luke

Luke's outline is different: he abandons the distinction, brought out by Mark, between a first phase in which Pilate and the Jewish leaders are concerned, and a second in which the crowd takes part. Moreover, he supplements Mark, especially at the beginning, on the subject of the accusations. Mark and Matthew do not quote any concrete offence; the chief priests accuse Jesus, but what they accuse him of is not specified. How does Pilate know that Jesus calls himself the king of the Jews? Luke feels the need to be more precise about this.

They began their accusation by saying, 'We found this man inciting our people to revolt, opposing payment of the tribute to Caesar, and claiming to be Christ, a king' (Lk 23:2). Here are three charges of a kind that would rouse a Roman governor. Pilate does not care whether Jesus is the Messiah or not, but if this man is stirring up revolt he will have to intervene; similarly if he is stopping people paying the tribute or claiming to be a king. Luke uses the biography of Jesus skilfully to recall offences which the Jews could have presented to Pilate to stimulate his interest: Jesus is a revolutionary, Jesus opposes the tribute, Jesus claims to be king. The accusations are not entirely accurate, since Jesus did not oppose the paying of tribute to Caesar, on the contrary he said, 'Give back to Caesar what belongs to Caesar – and to God what belongs to God' (Mt 22:21). But the Jews did not scruple to modify his words in order to disturb the governor. In the same way, Luke brings out clearly how the Jews modulate from the theme of Christ to that of king: Christ is the messianic title in which they are interested, the religious title which was the subject of the trial before the Sanhedrin and which they refused to allow to Jesus; but in order to get the governor to take up the accusation they change it to king. The Christ is the Messiah king; and this ambivalence the Jews utilise in order to present the matter in a political light. Their scheming consists in this; they transform the religious themes, in which their own interest lies, into political ones which will capture the governor's attention. This is why the trial will end in a political sentence, death on a cross, and the charge that will be written up will be, 'King of the Jews'. The Jews had to manoeuvre like this to get the machine of the Roman power moving.

To Pilate's question, *'Are you the king of the Jews?'* Jesus replies, *'It is you who say it'*, as in Mark and Matthew (Lk 23:3). *Pilate then said to the chief priests and the crowd, 'I find no case against this man'.* (Lk 23:4). Notice this phrase, which is repeated three times (Lk 23:4; 23:14; 23:21). Similarly in John Pilate asserts three times, 'I find no case against him'. (This is one of the points of resemblance between Luke and John.) This declaration is important: the Roman governor, having examined Jesus, finds him not guilty! Luke underlines this fact for his readers in the Graeco-Roman world and for the eyes of the Roman authorities. Both the gospel and the Acts of the Apostles were written as an apologia, to show the Romans that they had nothing to fear from Christianity, either from Paul or from Jesus. In Acts, Luke recalls all the episodes where Paul appears before the Roman authorities without being found guilty. Similarly in the gospel, he takes care to show the public authorities of the Empire that the Christians have never plotted against it. This is why he is so careful to say in effect – your governor in Jerusalem had to try Jesus who was alleged to have claimed to be king, but after examining him he acknowledged three times that he found no case against him. Plainly, in order to be able to make this acknowledgement, Pilate must have talked to Jesus and conducted a brief enquiry. The texts of the gospels, according to which Jesus only replies, 'It is you who say it', are much abbreviated. We have to fill in the silence of the synoptic narratives.

Jesus before Herod

There follows an episode which is found only in Luke. The Jews continue to insist that Jesus '*is inflaming the people with his teaching all over Judaea; it has come all the way from Galilee where he started, down to here*' (Lk 23:5). Pilate then sees another possible solution to this difficult trial: he will send Jesus to Herod in order to try to extricate himself from the affair. Herod Antipas, one of the sons of Herod the Great, was the governor of Galilee; he used to go up to Jerusalem for the festivals. He did not stay in his father's palace since that was now the governor's, that is the Praetorium. When he came to Jerusalem as a pilgrim he stayed privately at the family residence of the Hasmonaeans, which was situated in the former Jewish quarter – now destroyed – of the present-day Old City, lower down than the Holy Sepulchre and dominating the valley of the Tyropoeon. Pilate knows that he is in Jerusalem for the Passover and sends Jesus to him.

Herod was delighted to see Jesus; . . . he . . . had been wanting for a long time to set eyes on him; moreover he was hoping to see some miracle worked by him (Lk 23:8). Herod sets to work questioning him; Jesus does not reply; the high priests continue to accuse him. Vexed and irritated, Herod derides him and, in order to make him a figure of fun, clothes him in a magnificent cloak, perhaps some striking item from his own wardrobe; then he sends him back to Pilate. *And though Herod and Pilate had been enemies before, they were reconciled that same day* (Lk 23:12).

This scene has been criticised by some scholars, who claim that it is not historical, but that Luke has invented it, taking Psalm 2 as his starting-point. This is the psalm quoted by Peter and John when they have been delivered from the Sanhedrin and are praying with the brethren (Ac 4:27). 'Why this uproar among the nations? . . . kings on earth rising in revolt, princes plotting against Yahweh?' (Ps 2:1). Peter and John comment on the psalm as follows: 'In this very city Herod and Pontius Pilate made an alliance with the pagan nations and the peoples of Israel, against your holy servant Jesus'. They see in Psalm 2 a prophetic announcement of the alliance of Pilate and Herod against Jesus. The first Christians, then, applied this text to the Herod–Pilate episode, but can one go on from this to say that they invented this transfer of Jesus to Herod in order to justify such an interpretation of the psalm? This, in my opinion, is putting the cart before the horse. The text of the psalm is too vague to give rise by itself to the invention of the episode. The appearance before Herod really took place and it was this fact which gave rise to the application of the psalm. The event preceded the application and not vice versa.

Moreover, Luke seems to have been well informed about the traditions concerning Herod, perhaps through Manaen, the tetrarch's childhood friend (Ac 13:1). Surely Luke was preparing us for this encounter between Jesus and Herod when, earlier, he added the words 'And Herod was anxious to see him' to the narrative of Mark (Lk 9:9). And in the following passage it sounds almost as though Jesus was making a kind of rendezvous in Jerusalem with the tetrarch: 'Just at this time some Pharisees came up. "Go away" they said. "Leave this place, because Herod means to kill you." He replied, "You may go and give that fox this message: Learn that today and tomorrow I cast out devils and on the third day attain my end. But for today and tomorrow and the next day I must go on, since it would not be right for a prophet to die outside Jerusalem" ' (Lk 13:31–3).

For the rest, this attempt to transfer Jesus to Herod is quite probable: analogous instances are found in law, for example where a magistrate may defer the case of a condemned man to a third party, to ask at least for another opinion.[1] Herod had no jurisdiction in Judaea, but he could be consulted. Pilate would have been happy if a Jewish ruler had taken the responsibility for condemning Jesus. On the other hand we know that relations between Pilate and Herod were strained. Herod enjoyed making complaints against the governor in Rome itself, where he had friends, so much so that Pilate was afraid of him and was trying to conciliate him. For Pilate to submit a case concerning his own subjects to Herod was a gesture of politeness which could only flatter him and improve their relations. All this is quite probable. Even if Luke did not receive a circumstantial account of the trial and has filled it with details drawn from the setting of the scene, I think that we have here an authentic fact, an interesting and unexpected incident in the trial. We shall see later that the mockery before Herod in the middle of the trial ties in very well with the maltreatment of Jesus before Pilate, which John records likewise in the middle of the trial.

---

[1] Cf. E. BICKERMANN, 'Utilitas Crucis. Observations sur les récits du procès de Jésus dans les Évangiles canoniques', in *Revue de l'Histoire des Religions*, CXII, 1935, pp. 169–241, esp. pp. 204–8.

When Jesus has been brought back from Herod, Pilate says to the crowd, '*I have found no case against this man in respect of all the charges you bring against him. Nor has Herod either ... I shall have him flogged and then let him go*' (Lk 23:14–16). For the last time Pilate tries to save Jesus by proposing to flog him and let him go. Since he has failed to get the crowd to demand Jesus' liberty under the Passover amnesty or to get Herod to side with him, he tries a third solution, that of a moderate punishment. 'Just to make you happy, I'll have him flogged, then let him go. Won't that be enough? Yet again Pilate's tactics are unsuccessful, the crowd insists, '*Away with him! Give us Barabbas!*' (Lk 23:18).[1] Just as in Mark and Matthew, the crowd clamours for Jesus' death and Barabbas' release. Pilate still stands firm, but the crowd shouts '*Crucify him!*' (Lk 23:21) For the third time Pilate declares, '*What harm has this man done? I have found no case against him that deserves death, so I shall have him punished and then let him go*' (Lk 23:22). But as the crowd continues to insist, he gives his verdict; *their demand was to be granted*, and *he handed Jesus over to them to deal with as they pleased* (Lk 23:24–5). Luke has chosen his words carefully: The Jews have 'demanded' Jesus, Pilate hands him over to their 'will', as the Greek has it. If Luke writes in this way, it is to emphasise that the governor did not give way willingly; it was not he who willed the death of Jesus, but the Jews who willed it, claimed it and obtained it.

The narrative of John

John leaves out certain features and details of the synoptics, but adds two facts. In the first place, we must notice the changes of scene: outside the Praetorium – inside the Praetorium. The Jews *did not go into the Praetorium themselves or they would be defiled and unable to eat the Passover* (Jn 18:28). That very evening. This is a valuable piece of information. It means that the Passover was celebrated on the Friday evening that year. So on the Thursday Jesus anticipated the Jewish Passover liturgically: the celebration was theologically that of a paschal meal, in the course of which he instituted the

---

[1] Verse 17 in our texts is omitted by some very good authorities; it is certainly spurious and has therefore not been reproduced here. It runs, 'He was under obligation to release one man for them every feast day.' It is an echo of the tradition found in Mark and Matthew, which an over-zealous copyist has thought fit to borrow for Luke.

Christian Passover of the Eucharist. But his real Passover, in the proper sense of the word, was celebrated on the cross and he himself was the Passover lamb. And this is no less wonderful.

The crowd, then, stays outside, Jesus is inside in the courtroom of the Praetorium, Pilate goes from one to the other; these changes of scene determine the whole dialogue. In John this dialogue is very detailed, made up of many more words than in the synoptics. It is somewhat theological, and through it John with his usual skill reveals the mainsprings of the action.

He explains first of all why Jesus was crucified and not stoned. The objection is familiar: if the Jews had killed Jesus they would have stoned him; therefore the crucifixion was the work of the Romans. John holds that it was because the Jews did not have the power to put anyone to death, and therefore got the Roman governor to execute Jesus in their stead, that Jesus died on the cross. The introduction (Jn 18:29–32) serves to demonstrate this. Pilate asks the Jews, *'What charge do you bring against this man?'* They replied *'If he were not a criminal, we should not be handing him over to you'.* Pilate said, *'Take him yourselves, and try him by your own law.'* Pilate is being ironical, and John likes irony. The Jews are annoyed and reply, *'We are not allowed to put a man to death'.* And John's revealing conclusion is: *This was to fulfil the words Jesus had spoken indicating the way he was going to die* (Jn 18:29–32). This much is clear: Jesus died on the cross because the Jews had not the power to put him to death, and the blow could only be struck by the Romans. This is a true historical fact, and of prime importance in establishing where the true responsibility lay.

John now embarks on a fresh, beautifully constructed section of dialogue (Jn 18:33–8). It is not a report taken down in shorthand, but a theological exposition in which John puts words into Pilate's mouth that he could not have uttered as they stand and, above all, makes Jesus say things which Pilate could not understand. He sets the debate in an area which makes sense to the Christian reader; he emphasises, as so often, the deeper meaning of what is going on, in this case the real meaning of the accusation concerning Jesus the king. The synoptics reported that when Jesus was accused of making himself out to be a king he replied in the affirmative. But this was all they said, and it left us in difficulties. Was this a serious offence? Were the Romans not right to be impatient? John is going to explain what kind of kingship is in question.

When Pilate asks, just as he does in the synoptics, '*Are you the king of the Jews?*', Jesus replies, '*Do you ask me this of your own accord or have others spoken to you about me?*' (Jn 18:24). This means: Have the Romans spotted Jesus as a dangerous agitator by themselves, or is it that the Jews have breathed the suspicion into their ear? *Pilate answered, 'Am I a Jew? It is your own people and the chief priests who have handed you over to me*' (Jn 18:35). Pilate asserts that he has nothing against Jesus personally, it is the Jews who have accused him. '*What have you done?*' Pilate asks. Jesus explains clearly, or rather John makes him explain for the Christian reader's benefit, what his kingdom is, 'I am a king but *mine is not a kingdom of this world*'. I am a king but not as you, Pilate, understand it. '*If my kingdom were of this world, my men would have fought to prevent my being surrendered to the Jews. But my kingdom is not of this kind*' (Jn 18:36). Obviously Pilate does not understand any of this. He tries again, '*So you are a king then*'. '*It is you who say it*', answered Jesus. '*Yes, I am a king. I was born for this, I came into the world for this: to bear witness to the truth; and all who are on the side of truth listen to my voice*' (Jn 18:37). The Johannine Christ is speaking to Christian readers; these words are above Pilate's comprehension. When Pilate, according to John, says, '*Truth? What is that?*' this shows clearly that the governor is baffled by Jesus' words. He is expecting a quite ordinary trial, thinking he has to do with an agitator, but the accused talks to him about a kingdom which is not of this world and about truth! *Then Pilate went out again to the Jews and said, 'I find no case against him*' (Jn 18:38). With this piece of dialogue, John explains the famous title 'King of the Jews' which was to be fixed to the cross and which the Jews exploited against the Christians by saying that Jesus was condemned for political reasons. But, as Jesus asserts before Pilate, it is a kingship which is not of this world and therefore does not threaten the Roman empire.

John then turns to the religious theme, the one which was decisive for the Jews. The crowd shouts, '*Crucify him! Crucify him!*' *Pilate said, 'Take him yourselves and crucify him: I can find no case against him*'. '*We have a Law*', *the Jews replied 'and according to that law he ought to die, because he has claimed to be the Son of God*' (Jn 19:7). At last the true motive is revealed. The offence of being 'King of the Jews' was made up, false, a mere pretext; the real offence is that Jesus claimed to be the Son of God. This the Jews now acknowledge. In this way John lays bare for us the main lines of the trial: the two matters at issue, the false political one and the real religious one. The offence of being 'King of the Jews' has no substance and cannot disturb the Roman governor. The real offence that the Jews have at heart is that 'he claimed to be the Son of God'. Pilate still does not understand. *When Pilate heard them say this his fears increased . . . he said to Jesus, 'Where do you come from?' But Jesus made no answer . . . 'Surely you know I have power to release you and I have power to crucify you?'* (Jn 19:9–10). Jesus replies with dignity, '*You would have no power over me, if it had not been given you from above*' (Jn 19:11). Jesus makes Pilate realise that he is nothing more than an instrument in this matter. And the governor, more than ever convinced that Jesus has done no harm, tries again to get him released.

In the verses which follow (Jn 19:12–16), John explains how Pilate only gave way out of fear. He realised that the kingship of Jesus was of a kind that constituted no threat to Rome; and as for the title 'Son of God' he was not merely unafraid of it, he did not even understand it. Then why did he surrender Jesus? John's answer is fear, intimidation. The synoptics only say that Pilate was anxious to placate the crowd: John reveals what the threat was. '*If you set him free you are no friend of Caesar's; anyone who makes himself king is defying Caesar*' (Jn 19:21). 'And you are working against Caesar if you protect Jesus'. Pilate realises that the affair is taking a serious turn, he is in danger of being denounced at Rome. The Jews are capable of bringing an accusation against him before Tiberius; his career is at stake. At that moment Pilate makes up his mind. He sits in the chair of judgement on the Lithostroton – either a stone pavement, or more probably a platform paved with coloured stones – in front of the Praetorium[1], and makes one last attempt,

---

[1] I have explained elsewhere my views on the siting of the Praetorium mentioned in the gospels, which I believe to have been not the Antonia to the north-west of the Temple, but the former palace of Herod to the west of the city; see 'Prétoire, Lithostroton et Gabbatha', in *Exégèse et Théologie*, I, pp. 316–39. Today I would insist more strongly on the more probable meaning of the word Lithostroton: a platform of coloured stone which stood in front of the palace. To the literary arguments which I brought forward in favour of Herod's palace, there should now be added the archaeological ones which militate against the Antonia: the pool of the Strouthion which lies within the Convent of Our Lady of Sion was still open to the sky at the time of the siege in A.D. 70 (cf. JOSEPHUS, *Wars*, V, 467) and the pavement which covers it (which has been claimed as the Lithostroton) dates probably from the time of Hadrian. In Jesus' day, the boundaries of the Antonia must have corresponded to the site of the present Moslem school, between the street and the esplanade of the Temple.

'*Here is your king*' (Jn 19:14). But the Jews will not have it, '*Crucify him! We have no king except Caesar*' (Jn 19:15).

So in the end *Pilate handed him over to them to be crucified* (Jn 19:16). *It was about the sixth hour*, says John, that is, midday, the hour when the preparations for the Passover began with the removal of all leavened bread. It was also the moment when preparations began for the ultimate Passover, with the crucifixion of the Lamb, Jesus.

The mockery and the scourging

We must go back to the scene of the Ecce Homo in the middle of the trial, with which we have not yet dealt (Jn 19:1–5). Pilate has Jesus scourged. The soldiers plait a crown of thorns and put it on his head. They salute him as 'king of the Jews' and slap him in the face. Then Pilate brings him out before the crowd, wearing a crown of thorns and says, '*Here is the man*'.

This scene bears a strong resemblance to the one reported by Mark and Matthew at the end of the trial. In their narratives, the soldiers take Jesus inside the Praetorium, crown him with thorns, clothe him in purple and mockingly salute him as 'King of the Jews'. This is evidently one and the same scene. But where is it to be placed, at the end of the trial where Mark and Matthew have it, or in the middle where John does?

The solution is, it seems, to distinguish between the scourging and the mocking. Scourging was the normal prelude to crucifixion. Death by crucifixion could be very slow, and so the unhappy creature was very severely scourged, even to the drawing of blood, in order to weaken him and thus make death quicker. Since scourging was the immediate prelude to crucifixion, I think Mark and Matthew are right to put it after the condemnation and just before setting out for Calvary. On the other hand, the middle of the trial is a better place for the mocking: Pilate displays Jesus to the crowd to excite their sympathy, saying, 'Here is the man', as though he meant, 'Surely that is enough. Let him go now.' This scene of mocking is supported by the one Luke records as taking place at Herod's palace. In the middle of the trial, according to Luke and John, Jesus is mocked and maltreated by Herod and Pilate; in my opinion this is the same event. Mocked and covered with a ludicrous cloak at Herod's palace, Jesus is still in this garb when he returns to Pilate. Doubtless, the governor's soldiery went one better than Herod's guards, and

Pilate, seeing the accused in this ridiculous get-up, took advantage of it to try to appease the crowd.

I suggest, then, that the mocking of Jesus as king should be placed in the middle of the trial, as Luke and John have it, and the scourging at the end of it, as reported by Mark and Matthew. These two brief scenes, somewhat alike in their content, will have been brought together; in the two traditions – Luke and John on the one hand, Mark and Matthew on the other – mocking and scourging were combined, now in the middle, now at the end of the trial, although historically they were distinct. Such displacements are fairly frequent in the gospel tradition and we need not be surprised. They are the price which has to be paid in any oral tradition, and in no way compromise the essential historical truth.

The four gospels have progressively revealed the underlying themes of the drama. What has emerged from our study is that the Christian view in the gospels is correct, that it was the Jews who were reponsible for Jesus' death and that they made use of the Roman powers to carry out their plan. But they were responsible only to the extent that blind leaders and an anonymous excited crowd can be. The Jews can be forgiven because they did not know what they were doing, as Jesus himself said. As for the Roman governor, he gave way out of cowardice; he was incapable of understanding the situation in all its dimensions and he was overtaken by events; he saw in Jesus only a man under sentence like so many others[1].

But it is essentially the Lord himself who interests us; he manifests such greatness in his simplicity; in that silence on which Mark insists, the silence of the lamb before its shearers; and in the measured and beautiful language attributed to him by John, in which he makes plain in what sense, theologically, he is 'King' and 'Son of God' and demonstrates how his case transcends these petty village proceedings. The Lord bears himself with surpassing dignity through all the indignities which he undergoes, the crown of thorns, the scourging and the sentence which he accepts without a word.

[1] Cf. P. BENOIT. 'Le Procès de Jésus,' in Exégèse et Théologie, I, pp. 281–9, where I have tried to assess the 'motives and responsibility in the condemnation of Jesus'.

7. The Ascent
of the Cross

THE WAY OF THE CROSS

Mt 27:32	Mk 15:21
³² On their way out,	
they came across a man from Cyrene, Simon by name,	²¹ They enlisted a passer-by, Simon of Cyrene, father of Alexander and Rufus, who was coming in from the country,
and enlisted him to carry his cross.	to carry his cross.

THE CRUCIFIXION

Mt 27:33–43	Mk 15:22–32^a
³³ When they had reached a place called Golgotha, that is, the place of the skull,	²² They brought Jesus to the place called Golgotha, which means the place of the skull.

Lk 23:26–32	Jn 19:16ᵇ–17ᵃ

Lk 23:26–32

²⁶ As they were leading him away
they seized on
a man,
Simon from Cyrene,

who was coming in from the
  country,
and made him shoulder the cross
and carry it

behind Jesus.
²⁷ Large numbers of people
followed him, and of women too,
who mourned and lamented for
him.
²⁸ But Jesus turned to them and
said, 'Daughters of Jerusalem,
do not weep for me; weep rather
for yourselves and for your
children.
²⁹ For the days will surely come
when people will say, 'Happy are
those who are barren, the wombs
that have never borne, the breasts
that have never suckled!'
³⁰ Then they will begin to *say
to the mountains, 'Fall on us!'*;
to the hills, 'Cover us!'
³¹ For if men use the green wood
like this, what will happen when
it is dry?'
³² Now with him they were also
leading out two other
criminals to be executed.

Jn 19:16ᵇ–17ᵃ

¹⁶ᵇ They then took charge of Jesus

and carrying his own cross

Lk 23:33–8

³³ When they reached
the place called

The skull,

Jn 19:17ᵇ–24

¹⁷ᵇ he went out of the city
to the place of

the skull,
or, as it was called in Hebrew,
  Golgotha,

Mt	Mk
34 *they gave* him wine to drink mixed with *gall*, which he tasted but refused to drink. **35a** When they had finished crucifying him, **38** At the same time two robbers were crucified with him, one on the right and one on the left.	**23** They offered him wine mixed with myrrh, but he refused it. **24a** Then they crucified him, . . . **27** And they crucified two robbers with him, one on his right and one on his left.
35b they *shared out* his *clothing* by *casting lots*,	**24b** and *shared out* his *clothing*, *casting lots* to decide what each should get.
36 and then sat down and stayed there keeping guard over him.	**25** It was the third hour when they crucified him.
37 Above his head was placed the charge against him it read: 'This is Jesus, the King of the Jews'.	**26** The inscription giving the charge against him read: 'The King of the Jews'.

Lk   Jn

they crucified him there   ¹⁸ where they crucified him
and

the two criminals also,   with two others.

one on the right,   one on
the other on the left.   either side
                                with Jesus in the middle.

³⁴ Jesus said, 'Father, forgive
them; they do not know what
they are doing.'

                                ²⁴ᵇ In this way the words of
                                scripture were fulfilled:

Then *they cast lots*   *They shared out*
to *share out*   *my clothing among them.*
his *clothing*   *They cast lots*
                                for my clothes.

³⁸ There was an inscription   ¹⁹ Pilate
above him:*   wrote out a notice
                                and had it fixed to the cross;

                                it ran:
'This is   'Jesus the Nazarene,
the King of the Jews'.   King of the Jews'.
                                ²⁰ This notice was read by many
                                of the Jews, because the place
                                where Jesus was crucified was
                                not far from the city, and
                                the writing was in Hebrew,
                                Latin and Greek.
                                ²¹ So the Jewish chief priests said
                                to Pilate, 'You should not
                                write "King of the Jews", but
                                "This man said: I am King of
                                of the Jews" '.
                                ²² Pilate answered, 'What I
                                have written, I have written'.

Mt	Mk
38 At the same time	27 And they crucified
two robbers were crucified with him, one on the right and one on the left.	two robbers with him, one on his right and one on his left.
	(28)
35b they *shared out* his *clothing* by casting lots	24b . . . and *shared out* his *clothing*, *casting lots* to decide what each should get.
39 The passers-by jeered at him; *they shook their heads* 40 and said, 'So you would destroy the Temple and rebuild it in three days! Then save yourself! If you are God's son, come down from the cross!' 41 The chief priests with the scribes and elders mocked him in the same way. 42 'He saved others;' they said 'he cannot save himself.	29 The passers-by jeered at him; *they shook their heads* and said, 'Aha! So you would destroy the Temple and rebuild it in three days! 30 Then save yourself: come down from the cross!' 31 The chief priests and the scribes mocked him among themselves in the same way. 'He saved others,' they said 'he cannot save himself. Let the Christ,
He is the King of Israel;	the king of Israel,

Lk   Jn

³³ᵇ . . . the two criminals also,   ¹⁸ᵇ . . . with two others,

one on the right,   one on
the other on the left.   either side
                                       with Jesus in the middle.

                                       ²³ When the soldiers had finished
                                       crucifying Jesus they took his
                                       clothing and divided it into
                                       four shares, one for each
                                       soldier. His undergarment was
                                       seamless, woven in one piece
                                       from neck to hem;
                                       ²⁴ so they said to one another
                                       'Instead of tearing it, let's throw
                                       dice to decide who is to have it.
                                       In this way the words of
³⁴ᵇ They *cast lots*   scripture were fulfilled:
to *share out*   *They shared out*
his *clothing*.   *my clothing among them.*
                                       They cast lots
                                       for my clothes.

                                       This is exactly what the
                                       soldiers did.

³⁵ The people stayed there
watching him.

As for the leaders,

they jeered at him.

'He saved others,'
they said
'let him save
himself
if he is
the Christ of God,
the Chosen One.'

Mt	Mk
let him come down from the cross now,	come down from the cross now, for us to see it
and we will believe in him. ⁴³ *He puts his trust in God;* now *let God rescue him if he* *wants him.* For he did say, "I am *the son of God*".'	and believe.'

27:48	15:36

Mt	Mk
	²⁶ The inscription giving
³⁷ Above his head was placed the charge against him; it read: 'This is Jesus, the King of the Jews'.	the charge against him read: 'The King of the Jews'.

THE TWO THIEVES

Mt 27:44	Mk 15:32ᵇ
⁴⁴ Even the robbers who were crucified with him taunted him in the same way.	³²ᵇ Even those who were crucified with him taunted him.

Lk   Jn

³⁶ The soldiers mocked him too,
and when they approached to offer
him vinegar they said,   19:29
³⁷ 'If you are the King of the
Jews, save yourself'.

                                        ¹⁹ Pilate
³⁸ There was an inscription   wrote out a notice
above him*   and had it fixed to the cross;

                                        it ran:
'This is   'Jesus the Nazarene,
the King of the Jews'.   King of the Jews'.

Lk 23:39–43

³⁹ One of the criminals
hanging there
abused him.
'Are you not the Christ?' he
said. 'Save yourself and us as
well.'
⁴⁰ But the other spoke up and
rebuked him. 'Have you no fear
of God at all?' he said. 'You
got the same sentence as he
did,
⁴¹ but in our case we deserved it:
we are paying for what we
did. But this man has
done nothing wrong.
⁴² Jesus,' he said 'remember
me when you come into your
kingdom.'
⁴³ 'Indeed, I promise you,' he
replied 'today you will be
with me in paradise.'

When we turn to the way of the cross and the crucifixion, we do not find any great legal problem or theological mystery to be examined, but we do find some very precious details to be meditated upon deeply: after the sentence Jesus is led out to execution. The evangelists do not give us as much detail as we would wish, but for those who know how to read them they are full of information about these crowning moments.

Simon of Cyrene

Jesus has been condemned by Pilate and then scourged, which was the legal preliminary to crucifixion. Then the soldiers lead him away and, say the three synoptics, *on their way out, they enlist a passer-by, Simon of Cyrene* (Mt 27:32; Mk 15:21; Lk 23:26). Cyrene is a country in North Africa, between Egypt and Tripolitania; a Jew from that part of the world was living in Jerusalem. He seems to have been known to Christians, since Mark informs us that he was *the father of Alexander and Rufus.* Mark gives their names, not because they are of any interest for the episode itself, but plainly because they were known to the Christian community[1].

This Simon is pressed into service; 'they enlisted him', Mark says. The Greek word used here comes from the Persian and is found again in French – *angarier quelqu'un* means to enrol in public service. The detachment of Roman soldiers sees this man passing and enlists him to help Jesus.

Who was coming in from the country (Mk 15:21), or from the fields. This small detail is of interest in a celebrated argument – is this the eve of the Passover or the feast day itself? If the synoptics are right, the Passover meal was held on the Thursday evening, and the festival itself is now in full swing. If John is right, the Passover has still to be celebrated this Friday evening. This man who is coming

[1] It is possible that Paul is alluding to the same Rufus in the epistle to the Romans (16:13). This somewhat rare Roman name could have been adopted by a Jew living in Rome, where Mark probably wrote his gospel. Paul and Mark would both have known him there. Details like these, which would have interested readers of those times, have the ring of authenticity.

back from the fields is a pawn in the struggle between the two views.
Those who maintain that the Passover has not yet begun have a
simple explanation why he is coming back from the fields: he has
been working there until the beginning of the Passover holiday. It is
more difficult for the others to explain why he is doing this at the
height of the feast day, but, as always in such cases, they have their
answers ready: he could have gone to look at his field without
actually doing any work; besides, he has hardly had time to do any,
scarcely the morning even – though that would surely be enough;
or lastly, he is coming back from the suburbs, from another house.
Personally, since I believe that John is right, I find it quite normal
that the man has been working in his field and is now coming back to
celebrate the feast of the Passover which is just about to begin.

The soldiers ask Simon to carry the cross, apparently because
Jesus, exhausted by his sufferings from the scourging, is too weak to
carry it himself. In the penalty of crucifixion, it was usual for the
condemned man to carry his own cross, either the whole of it or the
patibulum, the cross-beam which formed the top of the cross, the
upright remaining permanently fixed. However that may be, Simon
of Cyrene is enlisted to carry the cross, which means that he took
the whole burden. Although paintings usually represent Jesus as
carrying the cross and Simon as holding up the end of it, I think that
in fact Simon had the honour of carrying the whole crossbeam.

For what distance did Simon help Jesus? Matthew says 'on their
way out'; if this means out of the gate of the Praetorium, Jesus had
help for the whole distance; if it means out of a gate of the city,
Jesus carried his cross for a certain distance, then this man came to
his help at the moment that he came out into the country. If the
Praetorium stood on the site which has been traditional since the
Middle Ages, the way of the cross followed the course which we
revere today: if, as I think, it must have been situated at Herod's
palace, then it runs in almost the opposite direction. We must not
imagine that they left the city straightaway, whether by the North
Gate – which corresponds approximately to the site of the present
Damascus Gate – or by the gate which stood near Herod's palace.
That the condemned man should be led through the city as an
example was included in the punishment[1]. And it was the Roman

[1] Plautus says (Frag. *Carbonaria*, 2), 'Patibulum ferat per urbem', 'Let him
carry his cross through the city.' See also JOSEPHUS, *Ant.*, xx, 136, where Clau-
dius orders the tribune Celer to be dragged through the city of Jerusalem in
front of everybody, before being executed.

custom that the prisoner should be stripped naked, and hit and insulted during this passage through the city. According to the gospel, Jesus put on his clothes again, but he still had to pass through the city. He would have left Herod's palace, the present-day 'Tower of David', taken the present 'David Street' as far as the three parallel 'souks', followed these northwards and ended up at the gate which now stands in the Alexander Hospice. Going out by this gate, he would have been close to Calvary[1].

John says that Jesus was *carrying his own cross* (Jn 19:17) and makes no reference to Simon of Cyrene. This is not to deny the existence of Simon, which is well attested elsewhere, but he must have made the omission deliberately. He did so probably in order to combat a heresy which had arisen in his lifetime, Docetism. This heresy – the name of which is derived from the Greek word *dokein*, 'to seem' – holds that at the decisive moment of his sufferings Jesus vanished away and his place was taken by someone else. According to it, Jesus did not suffer on the cross, someone else was substituted for him, so much so that Jesus only 'seemed' to suffer and die. John, who knew of this heresy, is answering that Jesus himself carried his cross; he is rejecting the error of Docetism, not the fact that Simon came to Jesus' help.

The episode of Simon of Cyrene is genuine, and offers us an example to follow. When Luke writes, *'they made him shoulder the cross and carry it behind Jesus'* (Lk 23:26), it is obvious that he is thinking of the fulfilment of the words Jesus had spoken, 'Anyone who does not carry his cross and come after me cannot be my disciple' (Lk 14:27). Luke employs the same phraseology to show that in Simon of Cyrene we have a model of the Christian who takes on himself the cross of Christ and follows his Master.

The cross

Here we must go into further detail about the form of the cross. The gospel does not do so, but we know of this means of execution

---

[1] The traditional site of Calvary, consecrated by Constantine's basilica of the Holy Sepulchre, fits in well with the topography of Jerusalem in the time of Jesus; it lies outside an angle of the city wall not far from the Praetorium, but close to the city and beside an important road which led towards the sea in the west. Even if the first Christians lost sight of many of the places mentioned in the gospels, it would have been difficult for them to forget the greatest one of all, that of the death and resurrection of Christ. The fact that the Forum of Hadrian was established there would have helped to fix it in their memory. So the tradition which the Christian empire recovered and honoured at the beginning of the fourth century was well founded.

from the Romans. It was held generally to be the most terrible punishment after that of being burnt alive; it was also an ignominious one, being reserved for slaves and for those who were not Roman citizens. It could be a vertical stake, on which the condemned man was impaled or from which he was hung, head uppermost or head downwards as the case might be. It could also be a *furca*, a fork in which the head of the condemned was held; and sometimes when hung up in this way he was scourged until he died. Often it was a *patibulum*, a crossbeam at the top of a vertical stake, forming with it a simple T; or again our traditional cross, in which a piece of wood projected above the crossbeam. We learn from the gospel that the cross of Jesus was of the last type, since a notice was put above his head and this implies that there was a vertical projection at the top. The traditional form of our crucifixes, then, is justified.

On the way to the cross

On the way, Luke relates the encounter with the daughters of Jerusalem. No other detail concerning the way to the cross is vouched for by the gospel: the meeting with Mary, the meeting with Veronica, the three falls, which are recalled in our present-day devotion, are all derived from later traditions.

However, the meeting with Mary is very probable; she is seen later at the foot of the cross. Mary must have followed her son as close as possible, and it is known that a condemned man had the right to speak to his relatives. Luke does not tell us that Jesus spoke to Mary, but we are glad to believe he did.

The occasions when Jesus falls under the cross are also probable; and it is natural that Christian piety should have wished to be more explicit about them than the gospels.

As for the meeting with Veronica, it must be confessed that this story is less well authenticated. It appears in the fourth century as a combination of several legends. Originally she is the woman with an issue of blood mentioned in the gospel, and is identified in the West with Martha, in the East with a certain Berenice – hence Veronica, a form of the same name. According to the legend, this woman went to see Tiberius to bring charges against Pilate; after learning the facts, Tiberius condemned his governor, and was converted by seeing a picture of Christ which Veronica-Berenice had had painted! Sometimes, in the legends, the picture is painted on Tiberius' orders, sometimes the Lord, as he wipes his face, leaves the sacred imprint on the cloth. Nothing in all this has any authority from the gospel.

The encounter with the daughters of Jerusalem

Let us return to the data supplied by the gospel. According to Luke, *Large numbers of people followed him, and of women too* (Lk 23:27). Luke is fond of crowds and of their devotion, and especially that of women. He is tender-hearted and sensitive to the devotion and the attentions of the women who surround Jesus, and he recalls them several times in his gospel. Here he describes the women of Jerusalem who beat their breasts and lament over Jesus. Their presence is likely, since we know from Jewish writings[1] that eminent women used to take on themselves the task of preparing a spiced wine for the condemned man – this will be mentioned later – which dulled his senses and alleviated his sufferings. We are not told that they brought this drink themselves, but they prepared it and could have offered it themselves. These compassionate women come to help Jesus and to weep over him; they are not necessarily disciples, but they are devout and sympathetic.

Jesus says to them, '*Daughters of Jerusalem, do not weep for me; weep rather for yourselves and for your children. For the days will surely come when people will say, "Happy are those who are barren, the wombs that have never borne, the breasts that never have suckled". Then they will begin to say to the mountains, "Fall on us!"; to the hills, "Cover us!" For if men use the green wood like this, what will happen when it is dry?*' (Lk 23:28-31). This long speech takes up some phrases from the Old Testament and from the gospel.

The address to the hills, 'Fall on us, cover us', comes from the prophet Hosea (Ho 10:8) and will be taken up again in Revelation (Rv 6:16). The phrase, 'Happy are those who are barren, the wombs that have never borne' closely resembles the apocalyptic discourse as reported by Luke (Lk 21:23). It is not impossible that Luke has expanded Jesus' words to the women by borrowing from elsewhere.

But the beginning and the end (Lk 23:28 and 31) are wholly suitable to the context, despite the proverbial form of the last verse. We know of this kind of proverbial utterance among the Jews; here

[1] Cf. STRACK-BILLERBECK, *Kommentar zum Neuen Testament aus Talmud und Midrasch*, I, Munich, 1922, p. 1037.

are some examples – If the fire falls on the cedars, what will happen
to the hyssop on the wall? If Leviathan (a sea-monster to the Jews)
is caught with a hook, what will happen to the fish in shallower
water? If the hook falls into a torrent of running water, what will
happen to the water in cisterns? Each of these proverbs, like the
one here, contrasts power and weakness. Jewish proverbs exist which
are even closer, in which the figure of two kinds of wood is used –
When two sticks are dry and the third green, the dry kindle the
green. If the fire gets a hold on the damp wood, what will happen to
the dry? (but this last proverb dates only from the tenth century).
The proverb which Jesus is quoting here can also be compared with
two Old Testament texts, a prophecy of Ezekiel – 'I am about to
kindle a fire in you that will burn up every green tree as well as every
dry one' (Ezk 21:3), and a proverb – 'if here on earth the virtuous
man gets his due, how much more the wicked, how much the sinner!'
(Pr 11:31). The contrast is instinctive; if the just man is afflicted like
this, what will it be like for the sinner? We know also the saying
attributed to a Rabbi of the second century B.C. who was being led
to the cross and on the way was insulted by a wicked nephew, 'If
such things happen to those who do His will, what will it be like for
those who offend Him?'

In this way Jesus, by using a saying which can be understood by
anyone, brings out the truth of the situation: since his condemnation
is unjust, the mourning should not be for him but for those who are
really guilty – for you, Israel, and for your children, you poor women.
They are words of censure perhaps, but they are also full of compassion. Jesus is soon to say, 'Forgive them!' Here he intimates that
it is not himself but those who have condemned him who deserve
to be pitied.

It is here that Luke, who has an eye for effects, informs us that
there were two criminals with Jesus. The robbers make a more
abrupt appearance in the other gospels.

Calvary – Golgotha

They arrived at Calvary, known as *Golgotha*. 'Goulgoultha' is the
Aramaic form of the Hebrew 'Goulgoleth' which means 'skull'. The
Greek has eliminated one of the two 'l's in the Aramaic original –
hence Golgotha – and the Syriac the other, Gougoultha. The word
means 'skull', in Latin *Calvarium* – hence Calvary.

How did the place come by this name? It has been suggested that condemned men were beheaded there. A legend also exists that the skull of Adam was found there; the chapel of Adam in the Holy Sepulchre gets its name from this belief. According to this, Christ's blood flowed down on to Adam's skull – hence the skull which is often represented at the foot of the cross. The legend obviously is false; St Jerome was already indignant at hearing it preached at Calvary to an applauding crowd. But though from the historical point of view the legend may be a fabrication, from the theological point of view it contains a magnificent truth – it is the blood of Christ, the New Adam, which has cleansed the First Adam.

To return to topography: obviously it was not this Christian legend which led to this spot being called 'the place of the skull' in Jesus' time. There is a last explanation, proposed by Père Vincent. in the days when place-names were still well remembered he heard an old man who lived in the neighbourhood of the Holy Sepulchre call this place the 'Ras', that is, 'the Head'. And in fact there is a prominent rocky knoll there which could have given rise to the name, 'the skull'.

In more recent times, General Gordon, as good a soldier as he was a bad archaeologist, thought he had discovered the 'Skull' in the rocky knoll which stands near the grounds of the Dominican Priory. Looked at with the eye of faith and good will, this knoll has in it caves which suggest eyes, and it is possible to imagine that it might represent a skull. In which case, the knoll would be Calvary, the Holy Sepulchre would be a neighbouring tomb (the Garden Tomb) and the Dominican church would become the Church of the Holy Sepulchre! All this is quite fantastic and totally without foundation. There is a Byzantine cemetery there; the tomb which can be seen has three niches and a cross quartered with Alpha and Omega; it connects underground with the Byzantine cemetery of St Stephen. The old gate still exists, walled up. The whole arrangement is characteristic of a Jewish cemetery, brought back into use in Byzantine times; it has nothing to do with the tomb of the Lord.

Jesus has reached Calvary. Mark says, to give the Greek word its full force, *they carry Jesus* (Mk 15:22). Mark uses this word when he is describing someone who finds difficulty in moving by himself; they carried to Jesus the sick (Mk 1:32), a paralytic (Mk 2:3), a deaf-mute (Mk 7:32), a blind man (Mk 8:22), an epileptic child (Mk 9:17). In each case the person in question is carried, or at least led by the hand like someone who cannot walk by himself any longer. If Mark uses the word deliberately here it is to suggest that Jesus is in a state of total exhaustion and has to be helped, to be taken by the hand, and led to the top of this little knoll.

At this point, according to Mark, *they offered him wine mixed with myrrh* (Mk 15:23). This is very likely: wine mixed with myrrh was an intoxicating drink which was given to the condemned so that they might lose consciousness and suffer less. The Book of Proverbs gives this advice; 'Procure strong drink for a man about to perish, wine for the heart that is full of bitterness: let him drink and forget his misfortune, and remember his misery no more' (Pr 31:6). It was the custom, out of pity for the unhappy man, to dull his senses. But Jesus does not accept the wine. He wishes to bear the suffering sent by his Father consciously and to the full.

Matthew speaks of wine mixed with gall, which is less probable. Myrrh is a kind of incense which gives a spicy fragrance to the wine and makes it more intoxicating; gall is more difficult to understand. It is most likely that Matthew is writing as a theologian here. He has in mind one of the many psalms used to interpret the passion, where the unhappy psalmist complains that he has been given gall and vinegar to drink (Ps 69:22). A little further on Matthew mentions the vinegar (27:48); here (27:34) he substitutes gall for myrrh.

The crucifixion

When they had finished crucifying him (Mt 27:35) – *Then they crucified him* (Mk 15:24) – *They crucified him there* (Lk 23:33). The evangelists indicate this moment of greatest suffering in only the briefest manner. What do we know about crucifixion?

There were two ways of fixing the limbs of the condemned man to the cross, with ropes or with nails. Our texts here do not indicate which was used, but in the narratives of the resurrection Luke and John mentions the mark of nails, and it has been the constant Christian tradition that Jesus was nailed to the cross. In the epistle to the Colossians, when Paul compares Jesus to the bond which the Jewish law brandished in the face of the sinner and which Jesus cancelled with his death, he says that this bond was 'nailed' to the cross in his person (Col 2:14). Ignatius, in his epistle to the community at Smyrna, the gospel according to Peter (an apocryphal work from the second century), Barnabas, Melito, Justin, Irenaeus,

Clement of Alexandria and Tertullian – all these early Fathers refer
to nails. This is a very strong tradition. There is only one difficulty:
the evangelists do not quote 'They have pierced my hands and feet'
from Psalm 22:16, which would be so fitting here. But in fact this
verse of the psalm is obscure and its meaning varies according to the
text one is using, Hebrew, Greek, Latin or Syriac, so that its application here would not be so obvious to the ancient writers as one
might have supposed. In fact it only begins to be used in this way
with Justin in the second century.

The exact place of the nails is not made clear either. The general
impression is that they cannot have been driven through the palms,
since, under the weight of the body, the nails would immediately have
torn through them; they must have been driven through the bone
of the wrist. The shroud of Turin, of doubtful authenticity for all
its beauty, does represent the nails as having been driven through in
this way.

However, even this precaution was not enough to ensure that a
human body would stay hanging for several hours. So it appears
that a piece of wood was placed between the legs to take the weight
of the body. The Fathers mention this seat[1], Justin appears to compare Jesus on the cross to a judge sitting on his throne[2], and Augustine
likens him to a Master teaching from his doctoral chair[3].

Lastly, there seems to have been a support under the feet to prevent
the body collapsing. We know this in particular from the Palatine
drawing, a caricature made by a pagan in the third century to deride
a Christian companion[4]; it is a figure of Christ on the cross with an
ass's head and the inscription, 'Alexamenos worships God'. Although
this is a piece of mockery, it is an interesting document; it shows the
cross in the form described here and furnished with a stick or small
board. A support of this kind seems probable, and is often shown in
our crucifixes.

Was Jesus completely naked when he was crucified? This was the
norm among the Romans and the Fathers often thought it had been
so; Augustine, among others, compares the nakedness of Christ to
that of Noah[5]. However, in Palestine the Romans probably avoided

---

[1] JUSTIN, *Dialogue*, 91, 2; IRENAEUS, *Adv. Haer*, II, 24, 4; TERTULLIAN, *Ad
Nationes*, 1, 12.
[2] *I Apology*, 35, 6.
[3] *Commentary on St John*, 119, 2.
[4] Cf. DAREMBERG and SAGLIO, *Dictionnaire des antiquités grecques et romaines*,
I, 1575, fig. 2084.
[5] *Contra Faustum*, 12, 23.

offending Jewish delicacy, which was very sensitive in this matter. Jewish law insisted that the condemned should have a cloth round their loins, in front for a man, in front and behind for a woman. The evangelists have already told us that Jesus was given back his clothing for the walk to the cross, so it is probable that the soldiers let Jesus keep a piece of cloth round his hips on the cross, and in fact the Palatine sketch seems to show the crucified Christ wearing a small tunic.

The two robbers

Luke and John now tell us that two criminals were crucified at the same time, one on the right, one on the left and Jesus in the middle. Mark and Matthew only mention this later, but this is the more logical place to bring them in. Is this historically true or not?

Certain critics ask this question in view of a passage of Isaiah (53:12), where the prophet is describing the sufferings of the Servant of Yahweh: 'He was numbered among the sinners'. Jesus applied this to himself after the Supper, 'I tell you these words of scripture have to be fulfilled in me: "*He let himself be taken for a criminal*" ' (Lk 22:37). Some critics think that the robbers were invented for the text to be fulfilled; but I disagree. To begin with, if it were so, the text would have been quoted to show that it had been fulfilled. It is not. Admittedly it is found in a few manuscripts (in Mark 15:28), but it is a spurious addition and is lacking in the best manuscripts. And secondly, the expression 'numbered among sinners' is very vague and quite insufficient to justify the invention of the two robbers.

It is also objected that Jewish law did not allow two condemnations or two executions on the same day; but this is only the theory of the Mishnaic law which was elaborated in Jewish schools after the fall of Jerusalem, when such executions were no longer the practice. In fact the history of the Jews in this period records crucifixions carried out by the hundred, on the orders of Alexander Jannaeus, for example, one of the Hasmonaean kings, and after him on the orders of various Roman governors[1]. There is, then,

---

[1] Cf. JOSEPHUS, *Ant.*, XIII, 380 (Alexander Jannaeus); *Ant.* XVII, 295 and *Wars*, II, 75 (Quintilius Varus); *Ant.* XX, 129 and *Wars*, II, 241 (Ummidius Quadratus); *Wars*, II. 306 (Gessius Florus).

no difficulty in accepting the fact that two criminals who were awaiting execution were put to death at the same time as Jesus; the authorities would have wanted to be done with them too before the Passover[1].

Luke alone preserves some very precious words of Jesus at this point. While he is being crucified, Jesus says, *'Father, forgive them; they do not know what they are doing'* (Lk 23:34). This verse is omitted by some important authorities, such as Vaticanus, Codex Bezae, some uncials, some manuscripts of the Old Latin and some Coptic and Syriac versions. This is enough to disturb certain critics. Nevertheless it must be retained as authentic since it is supported by the Fathers from very early times, in fact from the beginning of the second century – which is as early as we can get – by Hegesippus, Tatian and Irenaeus; in the third and fourth centuries it is attested by Origen, the Clementine Homilies, the Acts of Pilate, Eusebius, Athanasius, Gregory of Nyssa, Basil, Diodorus, Chrysostom, Hilary and Augustine.

Besides, it is unlikely that this verse was added later, since there is no reason why it should be found only in Luke and not in Mark or Matthew. Luke preserved this saying because it reflected his own leanings. He was a gentle and compassionate man and he was glad to record a saying of the Lord which had impressed him deeply; Jesus, even as he is crucified, asks his Father to pity and to pardon them[2]. Later, the words got left out, either accidentally in some very early manuscript, or deliberately – some copyist perhaps was shocked to find Jesus pardoning the Jews.

It is the Jews whom Jesus has in mind, not only the Romans. He is thinking of those who are really guilty and asking that they be pardoned. In a later and more anti-semitic period, the leniency of these words was found shocking and they were suppressed. But we should retain them as part of a useful dialectic; the Jews are guilty but they are to be forgiven because they did not really know what they were doing.

---

[1] If the existence and death of these two criminals is to be regarded as historical the same cannot be said for their names. These are not given in the gospels but legend offers various ones: the one on the right is called Zoathan, Joathas, Dismas, Titus; the one on the left, Chammatha, Camma, Maggatros, Gistas, Dumachus. These have no historical value at all.

[2] In the Acts of the Apostles, Luke again tells the Jews, in the words of Peter and of Paul, that they acted in ignorance (Ac 3:17; 13:27). He also makes Stephen say as he dies in imitation of his Master, 'Lord, do not hold this sin against them' (Ac 7:60).

The clothing

The soldiers share out Jesus' clothing and draw lots for what each is to get; the synoptics report this very briefly (Mk 15:24; Mt 27:35; Lk 23:34).

Psalm 22 immediately comes to mind; it is one of those which is most readily applicable to the passion: 'They divide my garments among them and cast lots for my clothes' (Ps 22:18). The context too is significant, the preceding verses contain the expressions, 'I can count every one of my bones' and 'A pack of dogs surround me'. This psalm served to describe the passion; the evangelists are certainly thinking of it here. But – and this must be stressed again – they are not inventing this detail in order to be able to apply the psalm, they are preserving this one detail out of many others which they have passed over, because those others have no echo in the scriptures. The evangelists have a preference for recording details which fulfil the scriptures, using the very phrases of the Old Testament to bring the prophecy home at once to Christian readers. The sharing out of the clothing is highly probable since it was the custom to grant the effects of the condemned to the executioners.

John gives us more details of this, doubtless in order to show the fulfilment of scripture. *They divided it into four shares, one for each soldier* (Jn 19:23). Jesus was guarded by four soldiers, just as Peter was later when he was imprisoned in Jerusalem; this squad was called a *tetradion* (Ac 12:4). *His undergarment was seamless, woven in one piece from neck to hem*, which they did not want to tear and so drew lots for it. *In this way the words of scripture were fulfilled: They shared out my clothing among them, they cast lots for my clothes* (Jn 19:24). John is making a point here, perhaps even a little artificially. According to the parallelism of the Hebrew psalm, there is no distinction between clothing and clothes, the two words are synonymous as they are in English. John seems to have read into them the two different items of dress that Jesus must have been wearing, according to the Greek usage of the times – a *chiton*, the tunic worn underneath, and a *himation*, a kind of cloak worn over it like the *abaye* which Arabs wear over their dress. John makes it very clear that one of these garments was divided and the other drawn for by lot. Such precision suggests that John has some symbolism in mind, since, when he goes into details, it is usually for the sake of their deeper significance. But it is not clear what his intention is here. The seamless undergarment has sometimes been interpreted as the Church which is one and indivisible. But such thinking belongs to a later age; it makes its appearance with St Cyprian at a time when the unity of the Church was threatened. Although this is a fine theological application of the text, we cannot be certain that it corresponds to what John had in mind. He is perhaps alluding to Joseph's coat, a woven coat with long sleeves, which his brothers dipped in blood to persuade Jacob that he was dead (Gen 37:23–33), or perhaps to the high priest's robe, which is said to have been woven in one piece and which Philo compares to the world with its four elements. Is it then the garment of the Logos, which makes the whole universe one? We have to be careful not to look for too far-fetched a symbolism in it or we shall go beyond John's own intentions.

The time of the crucifixion

It was the third hour when they crucified him, Mark tells us (Mk 15:25). The third hour corresponds to our nine in the morning. According to John it was midday when sentence was passed on Jesus (Jn 19:24). How are we to reconcile these contradictory statements? The attempt to do so has been going on for a long time, but some of the explanations are very far-fetched. Some do violence to the text, making Mark refer to the sentence and John to the crucifixion, whereas in fact it is the other way round. Others, for example Augustine, claim that Mark means that Jesus was crucified 'with the tongue', i.e. sentenced to death; still others believe that the manuscripts are incorrect.

It is better to acknowledge the fact that each evangelist is following his own plan. The sixth hour, midday, of John has a liturgical meaning, it is the moment when the Passover began; Jesus therefore was sentenced at the beginning of the Jewish Passover. Mark uses a simpler reckoning, in periods of three hours, as the Romans did: the meeting of the Sanhedrin takes place at dawn, that is, the first hour (Mk 15:1); at the third hour, the crucifixion; at the sixth, the darkness; at the ninth, Jesus dies. His division of time is schematic. Since Mark and John each have their own way of reckoning, it may be that we have to give up the idea of choosing between them altogether. John's seems the more likely: the morning was taken up with the meeting of the Sanhedrin, the trial before Pilate, then before Herod, then before Pilate again; midday is not too late to place the passing of sentence, and in this case the crucifixion cannot have taken place until about one in the afternoon.

The inscription on the cross

As regards the title on the cross, the basic agreement of the four evangelists is very striking. All report the same central expression, *'The King of the Jews'*. But there are minor variants. Mark gives those words alone (Mk 15:26). Matthew adds to them, *'This is Jesus, the King of the Jews'* (Mt 27:37) – Luke, *'This is the King of the Jews'* (Lk 23:38) – and John further, *'Jesus the Nazarene, King of the Jews'* (Jn 19:19). The title attributed to Jesus is common to all four and seems absolutely historical.

It was customary among the Romans to put the reason for condemnation above the head of the condemned. So it is probable that Pilate had done this, and in my view the reason why Jesus was condemned, in spite of some slight differences between the evangelists, was essentially the allegation that he claimed to be the king of the Jews. We have seen this already, in the account of the trial; this was the charge the Jews presented to the Romans, even though it was not their own; to them it was the claim to be Christ, the Son of God, which was intolerable. Pilate understood well enough that this political charge was only a pretext, and that Jesus was not really a political agitator, but out of cowardice he gave way and accepted this charge as being the only one he could present to the emperor in his records: 'he claimed to be the king of the Jews'.

John tells us further, and this is very likely, that *the writing was in Hebrew, Latin and Greek* (Jn 19:20). The inscription was written first in Hebrew (or in Aramaic, which comes to the same thing, since in those days the word meant either); it was the language of the country, whereas Latin was the language of the government and Greek was the main common language. The Romans spoke Latin among themselves, but not to the Palestinians, who did not understand it; in default of Hebrew or Aramaic, which they themselves did not know, they spoke Greek. The language common to the people and the administration was Greek, and this has been confirmed recently by documents discovered in the desert of Judaea; deeds, contracts etc., valid for the Jews, are written in Greek. As with English in the Arab countries today, a lot of people had to know some Greek; Jesus and his apostles must have had a certain knowledge of a language that was so widely spoken.

This notice was read by many of the Jews, because the place where Jesus was crucified was not far from the city (Jn 19:20). This is true of the present Golgotha. In those times the city wall went from the Khan of the Copts under the Lutheran church, turned to pass underneath the Alexander Hospice, followed the course of the Souk ez-Zeit and came down the present-day Way of the Cross. Calvary, therefore, was outside but close to the city, in an angle of the walls and near one of the gates. Anyone who left the city on the road down to the sea would pass this rocky knoll and see those who had been crucified there. The Roman custom was to crucify people outside a city but close enough for everyone to see[1].

Pilate did not come to watch the execution. The Jews go to see him at his palace and protest, *'You should not write, "King of the Jews", but "This man said: I am the King of the Jews"'*. Pilate answered, *'What I have written, I have written'* (Jn 19:21-2). Pilate in his reply employs a semitic turn of speech (two perfects) rather than a Greek one (aorist and perfect), and this is somewhat surprising. However that may be, Pilate does not want to hear anything more about the affair: I have made enough concessions already, I handed him over to you; now leave me alone, I have written what I meant to, there is no need to go over things again.

The attitude of the bystanders

What is the attitude of those who are present at the crucifixion of Jesus: the crowd, the Jewish leaders, the robbers?

The passers-by jeered at him; they shook their heads and said, 'Aha! So you would destroy the Temple and rebuild it in three days! Then save yourself: come down from the cross!' (Mk 15:29–30 and Mt 27:39–40). Mark and Matthew are making use of psalms or other texts of scripture such as the following: 'All who pass your way . . . whistle and shake their heads' (Lm 2:15); 'Every passer-by will be appalled at it [the ruins of Jerusalem] and shake his head' (Jr 18:16); 'All who see me jeer at me, they toss their heads and sneer' (Ps 22:7). This gesture is common in the Bible; shaking the head expresses indignation or scorn. The synoptics have taken over this traditional expression intentionally, but this does not make the facts any the less probable.

The passers-by are made by the evangelists to use the words of Jesus about the Temple which were recalled at the trial, words which

[1] Cf. CICERO, *In Verrem*, v, 66.

were a kind of synthesis of his unheard-of claim to be able to destroy
the Temple and rebuild it in three days. The crowd reminds him of
this on the cross. The 'Aha' of Mark is not the equivalent of 'Alas',
but an ironical exclamation, a piece of mockery. '*Save yourself*' is an
allusion to all the cures performed by Jesus to save people and
restore them to health; now it is up to him to save himself. These
insults have the ring of truth even if the evangelists have formulated
them in ways that recall the Old Testament and the gospel.

The chief priests and the scribes, to whom Matthew adds the
elders, jeer at him in almost identical terms, '*He saved others, he
cannot save himself. Let the Christ, the king of Israel, come down
from the cross now, for us to see it and believe*' (Mk 15:31–2). The
Jewish leaders say 'the king of Israel' and not 'the king of the Jews'.
This change is significant, for by using the expression 'king of
Israel', which has a religious meaning, they give away the fact that they
do not believe in the political charge. Jesus claimed to be the Messiah
and it is for this that they jeer at him. Luke gives it a more precise
sense, '*the Christ of God, the Chosen One*' (Lk 23:35). 'The Chosen
One' is a title of the Servant of Yahweh (Is 42:1), and it is implied
by the words of the voice from heaven at Christ's baptism, 'This is
my Son, the Beloved; my favour rests on him' (Mt 3:17). At the
transfiguration, Luke makes a similar modulation of the quotation
from Isaiah, 'This is my Son, the Chosen One; listen to him' (Lk 9:35)

'*For us to see it and believe*'. These words of Mark's are curious,
since they exactly reproduce words already spoken to Jesus by the
Jews, 'What sign then will you give for us to see it and believe?'
(Jn 6:30). They are asking Jesus to perform a miracle for them, and
this he will not do, he has performed so many already which have
been of no use. Any extra miracle would now be useless; in his hour
he must die.

Here Matthew adds a quotation from Psalm 22 (v. 8). '*He puts
his trust in God; now let God rescue him if he wants him*' (Mt 27:43).
The last words of this verse, '*For he did say, "I am the Son of God"* '
are an allusion to the beginning of the Book of Wisdom. This book
presents the virtuous man persecuted by the wicked, who say of him:
'He claims to have knowledge of God, and calls himself a son of the
Lord. Before us he stands, a reproof to our way of thinking, . . . In
his opinion we are counterfeit; . . . he boasts of having God for his
father. Let us see if what he says is true, let us observe what kind of
end he himself will have. If the virtuous man is God's son, God will

take his part and rescue him from the clutches of his enemies . . . Let us condemn him to a shameful death since he will be looked after – we have his word for it' (Ws 2:13–20). This description of the devout and virtuous man, the Holy One of Israel, is quasi-prophetic. Matthew very rightly sees in it a figure of the persecuted Jesus and uses it to convey the insults of his enemies. The outrages done to the virtuous man are now eminently realised in Jesus, put to death by the wicked.

Luke alone relates that the Roman soldiers joined in the jeering. Using the detail about the vinegar, which comes later in Mark and Matthew, he composes a general picture of the scene; after the insults of the Jews (Lk 23:35), he describes those of the Romans (23:36–8), and then those of the robbers – a kind of synthesis (23:39). It is skilfully composed, but no less plausible for that; the soldiers would have lent their support and acted as a kind of chorus to the Jews.

As for the two robbers, Mark and Matthew simply say that they taunted Jesus. Luke is more detailed; one taunts him, the other begs a favour. These differences between the synoptics need to be reconciled. It might be that Mark and Matthew are merely speaking in general terms, but it is equally open to us to believe that Luke has chosen the two robbers as types or incarnations of the two attitudes which lie behind the passion. The bad robber stands for the Jews and their insults, '*Are you not the Christ? Save yourself and us as well*'. This represents the religious motive, the opposition to Jesus as Christ. The good robber typifies the Romans and re-states the political motive to show that it has no validity, '*Have you no fear of God at all? You got the same sentence as he did, but in our case we deserved it . . . But this man has done nothing wrong*' (Lk 23:40–1). These are much the same words as Pilate has used; the good robber is thinking of Jesus as king, '*Remember me when you come into your kingdom*' (Lk 23:42).

Without denying that the robbers may have said these things, we are at liberty to think that Luke is skilfully reminding us of the way in which the trial was polarised, between, on the one side, the Jewish people who reject Jesus as Christ and, on the other, the pagans who see nothing dangerous in Christ's kingship and understand that he is not culpable.

Jesus replies, '*Indeed, I promise you, today you will be with me in Paradise*' (Lk 23:43). 'Paradise' is a Persian word which means 'garden' and has long been used to indicate the place of immortality. What does Jesus mean here? Does he mean, as some people have claimed, that the ascension is to take place immediately, even before the resurrection? Is paradise to be opened before the Easter resurrection? Surely not. It is sufficient to take it to mean life with God, into which the robber is to enter, accompanying Jesus, from the moment of his death. He is not to go to hell, far from God, but is to be already with Jesus, as the poor man Lazarus was carried away to the bosom of Abraham (Lk 16:23). 'As soon as you die you'll be all right' is roughly what Jesus means.

We should be wrong if we insisted on chronological adjustments. There is a great difference between the time of mankind, in which Jesus took flesh here below, and the time of God in his conduct of the history of salvation. In the same way that Jesus ascended into heaven at the moment of his resurrection and waited some time before showing himself to men, so, here, the immediate entry of the robber into paradise does not prevent his having, like all the saints of the Old Testament, to wait for heaven to be opened by the risen Jesus. For him, as for all those who ask pardon of the Lord at the moment of death, the assurance is that of being near him after death, in the garden of God, waiting for the final resurrection.

8. The Death of Jesus

Mt 27: 45–56	Mk 15: 33–41
27 ⁵⁵ And many women were there, watching from a distance . . . Among them were	15 ⁴⁰ There were some women watching from a distance. Among them were
Mary of Magdala, Mary the mother of James and Joseph, and the mother of Zebedee's sons.	Mary of Magdala, Mary who was the mother of James the younger and Joset, and Salome.
⁴⁵ From the sixth hour	³³ When the sixth hour came
there was darkness over all the land until the ninth hour.	there was darkness over the whole land until the ninth hour.
v. 51	v. 38
⁴⁶ And about the ninth hour, Jesus cried out in a loud voice, '*Eli, Eli, lama sabachthani?*' that is, '*My God, my God, why have you deserted me?*' ⁴⁷ When some of those who stood there heard this, they said, 'The man is calling on Elijah',	³⁴ And at the ninth hour Jesus cried out in a loud voice, '*Eloi, Eloi, lama sabachthani?*' which means, '*My God, my God, why have you deserted me?*' ³⁵ When some of those who stood by heard this, they said, 'Listen, he is calling on Elijah'.

Lk 23: 44–49   Jn 19: 25–30

²⁵ Near the cross of Jesus

23 ⁴⁹ All *his friends*
stood   stood
at a distance;
so also did the women . . .

his mother
and his mother's sister,
Mary the wife of Clopas,
and Mary of Magdala.

²⁶ Seeing his mother and the
disciple he loved standing
near her, Jesus said to his
mother, 'Woman, this is your
son'.
²⁷ Then to the disciple he said,
'This is your mother'. And
from that moment the
disciple made a place for
her in his home.

⁴⁴ It was now about
the sixth hour   19:14
and, with the sun eclipsed,
a darkness came
over the whole land
until the ninth hour.
⁴⁵ The veil of the Temple
was torn right down the middle;

²⁸ After this, Jesus knew that

Mt   Mk

⁴⁸ and one of them quickly   ³⁶ Someone
ran   ran
to get a sponge   and soaked a sponge
which he dipped in *vinegar*   in *vinegar*
and, putting it   and, putting it
on a reed,   on a reed,
gave it him *to drink.*   *gave* it him *to drink*
⁴⁹ 'Wait!'
said the rest of them,   saying,
'and see if Elijah   'Wait and see if Elijah
will come to save him.'   will come to take him down'.

⁵⁰ But Jesus, again   ³⁷ But Jesus
crying out   gave
in a loud voice,   a loud cry

yielded up his spirit.

                                        and breathed his last.
⁵¹ At that,   ³⁸ And
the veil of the Temple   the veil of the Temple
was torn in two   was torn in two
from top to bottom;   from top to bottom.
the earth quaked;
the rocks were split;
⁵² the tombs opened and the
bodies of many holy men rose
from the dead,
⁵³ and these, after his resurrection,
came out of the tombs,
entered the Holy City and
appeared to a number
of people.
⁵⁴Meanwhile the centurion,   ³⁹ The centurion,
                                        who was standing in front of him,
together with the others
guarding Jesus,
had seen   had seen

Lk   Jn

everything had now been
completed, and to fulfil the
scripture perfectly he said
'*I am thirsty*'.
²⁹ A jar full of vinegar stood
there,

23:6

so putting a sponge
soaked in the vinegar

on a hyssop stick,
they held it up to his mouth.

³⁰ After Jesus had taken the
vinegar

⁴⁶ and when Jesus
had cried out
in a loud voice,
he said,   he said,
                                      'It is accomplished';
                                      and bowing his head

'Father, *into your hands
I commit my spirit*'.   he gave up his spirit.
with these words
he breathed his last.

23:45

⁴⁷ When the centurion

saw

Mt	Mk

<table>
<tr><td></td><td>how he had died,</td></tr>
</table>

the earthquake and all that was taking place, and they were terrified	
and said, 'In truth this was a son of God'.	and he said, 'In truth this man was a son of God'.
⁵⁵ And many women were there, watching from a distance, the same women who had followed Jesus from Galilee and looked after him.	⁴⁰ There were some women watching from a distance.
⁵⁶ Among them were	Among them were
Mary of Magdala, Mary the mother of James and Joseph, and the mother of Zebedee's sons.	Mary of Magdala, Mary who was the mother of James the younger and Joset, and Salome.
	⁴¹ These used to follow him and look after him when he was in Galilee. And there were many other women there who had come up to Jerusalem with him.

Lk   Jn

what had taken place,

he gave praise to God
and said,
'This was
a great and good man'.
  ⁴⁸ And when all the people who
had gathered for the spectacle
saw what had happened,
they went home beating
their breasts.
  ⁴⁹ All *his friends*   19 ²⁵ Near the cross of Jesus
stood   stood
at a distance;
so also did the women

who had accompanied him

from Galilee,

and they saw all this happen.

                                              his mother,
                                              and his mother's sister,
                                              Mary the wife to Clopas,
                                              and Mary of Magdala.

We come now to the last moments of the Passion, the final words of Jesus on the cross, his death, and the phenomena which accompany it.

The holy women at the foot of the cross

Although the synoptics do not mention them until after Jesus' death, this is the best place to consider the holy women, since it will enable to us to set the words of Jesus to his mother beside the other words he uttered while he was dying.

Among the friends standing in a group at some distance from the cross are the women who have followed Jesus from Galilee; they have accompanied and looked after him with love and devotion as he wandered from place to place, and have even come all the way up to Jerusalem. They are not all easy to identify because the evangelists differ about their names.

There is no difficulty about *Mary of Magdala*, since she is named by all; she is distinguished from the rest by the name of a small village on Lake Tiberias which must have been her home. This woman, from whom Jesus had driven seven demons (Lk 8:2), was one of those most attached to him. From the gospels it seems she was a sinner but was rewarded with being the first to see and hear Jesus after his resurrection. She is certainly to be distinguished from the sinful woman who wept over Jesus' feet (Lk 7:36–50), and even more certainly from Mary of Bethany, the sister of Martha and Lazarus.

After her, another woman is mentioned by name, *Mary the mother of James and Joseph* (Mt 27:56) or *Mary the mother of James the younger and Joset* (Mk 15:40), which comes to the same thing in practice. James and Joseph are called 'brothers of Jesus' (Mk 6:3 and Mt 13:55); they were probably cousins, but the mention of their mother may have been meant to indicate the degree of relationship.

A third woman is also mentioned, *the mother of Zebedee's sons*, according to Matthew; *Salome*, according to Mark. This is probably the same person, a woman called Salome, the wife of Zebedee and mother of James the elder and John.

To learn more about these women we have to have recourse to the fourth gospel. John seems to mention four women, *his mother*, that is Jesus' mother, *his mother's sister*, that is a sister of the Blessed Virgin, *Mary, the wife of Clopas* and lastly *Mary of Magdala* (Jn 19:25). We know already about Mary of Magdala, and there is obviously no difficulty about Mary, Jesus' mother. But some scholars have asked whether 'Mary, the wife of Clopas' and 'his mother's sister' are one and the same person, or two different people. Most probably it is a question of two different people; it would be astonishing if the sister of the Blessed Virgin were called Mary as well. Surely 'his mother's sister' is Salome, the wife of Zebedee, mentioned here by the synoptics. In this case James and John are cousins of Jesus on his mother's side. And on the other hand, 'Mary the wife of Clopas', mentioned in the fourth gospel, is surely Mary, the mother of James and Joset, spoken of by Mark and Matthew. It is thought that Clopas was Joseph's brother; it would then follow that Clopas' wife was Joseph's sister-in-law and his children would be cousins of Jesus on their father's side, their father being the brother of Jesus' legal father. The results which we arrive at in this way are possible but not certain since we cannot be certain of the identifications we have made. Père Lagrange proposed them in one of his commentaries[1], but proposed a different set in another commentary[2]. There is no point in delaying longer over this matter, which is, after all, secondary in comparison with our main task.

The holy women will be present when Jesus is taken down from the cross and buried, and at the visit to the tomb on Easter morning.

Jesus and his mother

The next two verses of John are very important. *Seeing his mother and the disciple he loved standing near her, Jesus said to his mother, 'Woman, this is your son'. Then to the disciple he said, 'This is your mother'. And from that moment the disciple made a place for her in his home* (Jn 19:26-7). These words seem to convey more than merely the anxiety of a loving son to provide Mary with support in her loneliness after he has gone, they hint at a deeper meaning. But we should not neglect their surface meaning either, since it provides a strong argument against those who claim that Mary had other children after Jesus. This is widely held among Protestants; but if Jesus had had brothers who were also born of Mary, there would have been no need at all to confide her to the care of the beloved disciple.

Nevertheless. this is indeed more than a gesture of filial love. The Fathers of the Church, Chrysostom, Cyril of Alexandria, Augustine, hardly saw beyond this. But ever since the twelfth century with the

[1] *Comm. Jean*, 4th ed., p. 493.   [2] *Comm. Marc*, 4th ed., p. 93.

Abbot Rupert, and especially since Denys the Carthusian in the fif-
teenth, exegetes and theologians have seen in it the institution of the
spiritual motherhood of Mary. The disciple whom Jesus loves is not a
mere individual, but the representative of all the disciples of Christ;
in his person they are entrusted to Mary and she is made their mother.

We should notice that Jesus says first of all, 'Woman, this is your
son'; he speaks first to Mary, not John. If he had merely wanted to
entrust his mother to someone, he would have said, 'John, here is
your mother, look after her' and then to Mary, 'Mother, go with
him'. Jesus instead begins with Mary; she is chosen for and receives
a mission, to adopt this disciple as her son, and through him all
Jesus' disciples. All true disciples of Christ, those who do his will,
who follow his precepts and love him, are represented symbolically
by the beloved disciple and they are all entrusted by Jesus to his
mother as her children. This theological interpretation is becoming
more and more widely accepted among Catholics; and since the
Church regards it as one of the foundations of the doctrine of Mary's
spiritual motherhood, it will be useful to set it against its scriptural
background in order to understand it as fully as possible.

Scholars point out that it is complementary to the episode at
Cana, and they are no doubt right. At that moment too Jesus
addressed his mother as 'Woman'; used like this, the word is not
contemptuous but respectful, a mark of distinction; it emphasises the
role of wife and mother. At Cana Jesus says to her in front of the
disciples, 'Woman, why turn to me? My hour has not come yet',
as though he were making a rendezvous. Now his hour has come,
that hour which, for John, means the Passion. So Jesus repeats the
word, 'Woman, this is your son', to indicate that Mary is to assume a
role which she could not have done up to that moment.

Are we to go further still and see in Mary the second Eve? Some
exegetes think so; John, they say, is alluding in this passage to the
beginning of Genesis, the scene where Eve, after the Fall, receives
both her punishment and the promise that from her descendants
will come a woman who will overcome the serpent. Did John have
this text in mind and make Mary the counterpart to Eve? Throughout John's gospel Satan is shown as the enemy whom Jesus is to
overcome through the triumph of the cross; but there is no clear
suggestion here that John intended a reference to our first mother
in the earthly paradise.

However, there is another and closer figure, that of the Church as

mother, of which Mary is the most striking personification. This
involves a profound piece of typology which I can only sketch briefly
here. Mary is the historical realisation of the 'daughter of Sion'
of the old prophets. In the Old Testament, the 'daughter of Sion'
personifies the messianic community, the chosen people, and
especially the faithful remnant that returned to Jerusalem after the
Exile; she holds in her bosom the 'Poor', that is, the devout and
humble people who were waiting for salvation. And it was in these
circles of modest fervent people that God prepared for the coming
of the Messiah; they were the cradle of the Christian Church.
Zechariah and Elizabeth, Joseph and Mary, and Jesus himself,
came from among them, and the Good News of Jesus is addressed
principally to them. In the Infancy narrative, Luke sees in Mary the
perfect example of these pure and humble souls who were waiting
for salvation and who received it. The annunciation and the Magnificat clearly present her in this light; Mary is that daughter of Sion
foretold by the prophets, who rejoices because God is with her[1];
God comes to her and takes her as his bride, giving her a child,
the Messiah King. In the Magnificat, the daughter of Sion praises
the greatness of God, who pulls down the mighty and raises the
humble; the canticle could find no better place than in the mouth of
Mary. Luke is not the only one to suggest this typology. First John,
then the primitive Church, saw in Mary the fulfilment and the personification of the Church, she that brings forth the messianic people.
The Mother of Jesus brings forth in him and with him that whole
new people that is to spring from his resurrection; all these children
Mary carries in her womb as she once carried Jesus.

In Revelation (Rv 12), the vision of the woman adorned with the
sun, standing on the moon, with the stars about her head, is not only
Mary; it is in the first place the Church, which brings forth the
Messiah in agony and whom God himself protects from the attacks
of the Dragon in the desert; but it is also Mary, who represents that
community of holy people, the Church.

With several exegetes I think that here, at this solemn moment,
we are being shown the birth of the Church; the Church is born of
Jesus on the cross, of his pierced heart and at this moment Mary is
given the duty of caring for the Church. From the time when, by
conceiving and bearing him, Mary became the mother of Jesus, she
had in principle been given this duty; at the moment when Jesus

[1] The words of the angel in Luke 1:28 echo Zp 3:14–15; Zc 9:9; Jl 2:21 and 27.

by his death in agony on the cross definitively brings the Church into being, she is there fulfilling her task of mother. It is in this way that we may speak of her as co-redemptress. But we must be careful what we mean by the word; we cannot say that Mary saved the human race; Jesus is the only saviour, and Mary can only act in virtue of her Son. Yet in the birth-pangs of the Church, in the agony of the cross, Jesus was not alone. As man, sensitive and suffering, he needed a helper and his mother stood beside the cross. She helped to accept and offer everything to God; like a mother, she shared in the birth of the Church.

In my opinion it is incorrect to speak of Mary as 'Virgin Priest'; she is not a priest. Jesus is the one and only Priest and all other priests are his sacramental representatives. But Mary is the mother of that Priest and she alone can fill that role. She helped her Son to consummate his sacrifice. Thus all the graces which come to us from Jesus – and they come from him alone since he is the one source of salvation – come through the hands of Mary. Mary, in glory beside her Son, collaborates with him in distributing these graces, just as in her role of mother, a role at once humble and exalted, she had collaborated with him in the winning of grace[1].

'Woman, this is your son', 'Son, this is your mother' – movingly simple as these words are, we see now something of what was concealed in them.

The last words of Jesus

According to Mark and Matthew, *at the ninth hour* (that is, about three o'clock in the afternoon) *Jesus cried out in a loud voice, 'Eloi, Eloi, lama sabachthani', which means, 'My God, my God, why have you deserted me?'* (Mk 15:34 and Mt 27:46). 'He cried out in a loud voice' – this scriptural formula is not to be taken too literally, it is used habitually to introduce a solemn utterance. Here too it is not a question of an inarticulate cry, since Mark and Matthew give both the actual Aramaic words and their translation. There are slight variations: 'Eloi' is a more Aramaic, 'Eli' a more Hebrew form; Matthew's 'lema'* is more Aramaic than Mark's 'lama'. The phrase as recorded by Matthew seems closer to what Jesus would have said

[1] Of course, salvation comes from Jesus alone, and Mary is saved by him like the rest of us. But in her position as the mother chosen by God, she shared in the work of salvation in a unique way and already at that moment received the duty of caring for all the children of God, all of us.
* As found in the Greek and La Bible de Jerusalem (1961), though not in *The Jerusalem Bible* or the Authorised Version. [Ed.]

and provides a better explanation of why it was misunderstood as
the name of the prophet Elijah. It is possible, as a recent scholar has
pointed out[1], that in those days the expression 'My God' was
pronounced 'Eliya' – this suffix is found in the manuscripts from the
Dead Sea – and this would make the misunderstanding of those who
heard it even more intelligible. However this may be, it is striking
that the evangelists have transcribed the actual Aramaic words,
as they did with other expressions of the Lord that impressed them
deeply, 'Ephphata', 'Rabbuni', 'Abba'. They have kept these words
in the form in which Jesus uttered them and they must surely be
authentic. The evangelists must have found it deeply disturbing that
Jesus should have been deserted by his Father.

From the beginning, Christian exegetes have given a great deal of
attention to these words and several suggestions have been put forward to explain this desertion by God. Some of the Fathers, especially
the Latin Fathers, saw it as metaphorical – Jesus is speaking in the
name of sinful humanity, it is as though in his person God had
abandoned sinners. This was the opinion of Origen, Athanasius,
Gregory Nazianzen, Cyril of Alexandria and Augustine. The Latin
Fathers were particularly embarrassed by the fact that Psalm 22
continues 'verba delictorum meorum' whereas the Hebrew says
'my groans'. Jesus could not have spoken of *his* sins, it must therefore be sinful humanity which is speaking through him. But is it
possible to say that even the sinner is deserted by God?

Eusebius and Epiphanius suggest a second and more subtle explanation; it is the human nature of Jesus speaking to the divine nature,
reproaching the Word for his coming temporary abandonment of the
human nature in the tomb. But this is hardly satisfying either; even in
death the human nature, body and soul, remains united to the Word.

A last interpretation, which is more literal and much simpler, is
that defended by Tertullian, Theodoret, Ambrose, Jerome, St
Thomas, the Middle Ages and many modern exegetes: Jesus experiences in his human consciousness the sense that he has really
been abandoned by his Father. So long as we understand what we
are talking about, this is profoundly true. It is *not* despair, whatever
those may think who, like André Gide, claim that Jesus died in
despair and use these words to back their claim. Certainly we should
not be afraid of taking Christ's distress seriously; but distress is the

[1] A. GUILLAUME, 'Mt 27:46 in the Light of the Dead Sea Scroll of Isaiah', in
Palestine Exploration Quarterly, LXXXIII, 1951, pp. 78–80.

word we should use, not despair. Despair presupposes the loss of
confidence in God, distress implies only an enormous sadness and
desolation. Jesus, obedient to his Father, chose to experience human
death in all its tragic intensity. His Father did not abandon him to
everlasting loss, but to whatever sin and evil could do. At Gethsemane Jesus asked that death might pass him by, but in the end
bowed to his Father's will; on the cross, he refuses the cup of spiced
wine in order to experience and drink the cup of human death to
the dregs. The pain of human death, the great tragedy for each and
every one of us, consists precisely in this sense of abandonment; you
are deserted by all and find yourself alone face to face with God your
judge. Jesus, who represents all men, feels himself deserted by God,
he allows himself to experience this annihilation, this total suffering;
before God he feels himself to be covered with the world's sin and
his terrible distress comes from this. God has abandoned him to the
hands of sinners, of Romans and Jews.

We should not then be afraid to admit Jesus' distress and we
should certainly not make his sufferings out to be merely apparent,
as though he did not really suffer because he knew what the outcome
was to be. We must not empty this mystery of substance by toning
it down. Jesus, the Son of God, lived as man in the fullest sense of
the word, and willingly experienced the full tragedy of human death.

The real distress of Jesus makes it legitimate for us to say this, but
we must also take note of an important point: the phrase itself comes
from scripture, it is the first verse of that Psalm 22 which has already
contributed so many features to the narrative of the Passion. When
Jesus utters these words he is not making them up himself, but showing that the scripture is fulfilled in him, that it is his cry of desolation
which the psalmist announced. Furthermore, although the psalm begins in anguish it finishes in a mood of confidence. For the readers
of those times, whether Jew or Christian, to quote a text was sufficient
to recall also what followed it. They knew the scriptures by heart,
and the opening of the psalm would be enough to remind them
of the whole of it. And the last third of the psalm expresses the even-
tual confidence of the sufferer: 'Then I shall proclaim your name to
my brothers, praise you in full assembly ... For he has not despised
or disdained the poor man in his poverty ... but has answered him
when he calls' (Ps 22:22–4). In this way Jesus conveys that distress is
followed by salvation and suffering by triumph. He hallows our cries
of distress with his own cry, but his trust in God remains unbroken.

These words must be authentic since the first Christians would never have invented anything so harsh and so tragic. They throw a great light on Jesus' sufferings and bring him very close to us in our own experience of desolation.

On hearing this cry, the bystanders thought that he was calling on Elijah. 'Eli', which means 'My God', sounds somewhat like Elijah; they believe, or pretend to believe, that he is appealing to Elijah. Elijah was especially the prophet of the eschatological age, and the Jews held that he came to the assistance of the dying. Like Enoch, according to the Bible (Gn 5:24), Elijah went up to heaven without dying, he was taken up by a chariot of fire from beside the Jordan (2 K 2:11). Tradition also held that he was to return at the last times, as Malachi had foretold (Ml 3:23). Jesus himself had said that Elijah had returned in the person of John the Baptist. So some of the bystanders said, 'Listen, he is calling on Elijah' (Mk 15:35).

Someone ran and soaked a sponge in vinegar and, putting it on a reed, gave it to him to drink, saying 'Wait and see if Elijah will come to take him down' (Mk 15:36). The translation is deliberately colloquial, in order to reproduce the tone of the speakers. There seems to be some jeering and malice in this – if he is calling on Elijah, we must give him some vinegar and prolong his life. The Romans did, in fact, give vinegar to the condemned to bring them back to consciousness and make them suffer longer; they even used to pour it on their wounds to revive them. In Mark's account, then, the bystanders are mocking and cruel; don't let him die, Elijah's coming.

Matthew's text (Mt 27:48–9) creates a different impression; one of the bystanders, in a gesture of pity, fetches a sponge to quench Jesus' thirst with vinegar[1]. It is the rest who say, *'Wait and see if Elijah will come to save him'* (Mt 27:49). In Mark, the speaker is the same man who gives him the vinegar, the gesture is mixed with mockery. In Matthew, it is inspired by compassion and a desire to alleviate Jesus' suffering.

Despite these slight variations, the two texts share a common basis which is very likely to be true, even though it fulfils a passage from one of the two great psalms of the Passion: 'When I was thirsty they gave me vinegar to drink' (Ps 69:21). Matthew has already

[1] This is not pure vinegar, but the refreshing drink called *posca* which the Romans used. The Roman squad which crucified Jesus had a container of *posca* to refresh themselves. When Jesus cries out one of the soldiers gives him a drink from it.

alluded to gall – mixed with the wine instead of myrrh – at the beginning of the Passion; here he refers to the vinegar. I do not think that the episode has been invented for the sake of applying the psalm, it is in itself very likely to have happened.

John's narrative is couched in a somewhat different form. Since he is interested in showing how Jesus fulfilled the scriptures, he underlines this, *Jesus knew that everything had now been completed, and to fulfil the scripture perfectly he said, 'I am thirsty'* (Jn 19:28). John has in mind the psalm, 'When I was thirsty they gave me vinegar to drink' (Ps 69:21). Jesus himself uses his thirst, in itself only too real and only too appalling, to fulfil the scripture which foretold his suffering. According to John, the sponge soaked in vinegar was put on a hyssop stick. This is odd, since hyssop is a small flexible plant and it could hardly be used to hold up a sponge to a man who was raised so high. It is not easy to see what is meant, and some commentators suggest that the hyssop itself was fixed to the end of a reed, others that there is a corruption in the text and that instead of 'hyssōpō' we should read 'hyssō', a javelin; in which case, the soldiers fixed the vinegar-soaked sponge on to a javelin. However, even this ingenious theory has its difficulties; on the one hand it would be a very technical word for John to use, and on the other the javelin was the weapon of legionaries whereas in Jerusalem at that time there were only auxiliary troops. Whatever solution we adopt, and it is not easy to find one, we should not forget that a branch of hyssop appears in the liturgy where it is used to apply the blood of the Passover lamb (Ex 12:22); so its appearance is very fitting when Jesus dies on the cross as the new Passover Lamb. John alone adds, *'After Jesus had taken the vinegar'* (Jn 19:30). Jesus drinks it in order to fulfil the scripture, although he has refused the spiced wine.

We come now to Jesus' last words. Mark and Matthew do not actually quote any words: *Jesus gave a loud cry* (Mk 15:37), *Jesus, again crying out in a loud voice* (Mt 27:50). Luke uses a similar phrase, *When Jesus had cried out in a loud voice* (Lk 23:46). We are not to read any extra tragic significance into this phrase or to think of it as some extraordinary phenomenon, like those who see it as a sign of despair or others who see in it a proof that Jesus still had all his strength. It is in fact a stereotyped expression which is often found, for example, when Paul speaks to the cripple at Lystra (Ac 14:10), when the governor, Festus, addresses Paul (Ac 26:24), when the sick are healed by Jesus and praise God (Lk 17:15 and 19:37), when Jesus calls out to Lazarus (Jn 11:43). In none of these cases does the expression suggest an extraordinary cry, and we must interpret the language of the gospels according to the actual usage of their times[1]. Jesus therefore does not give a more than human cry, he utters in a loud voice words which Luke and John will tell us.

Luke records the words, '*Father, into your hands I commit my spirit*', John, '*It is accomplished*' (Lk 23:46 and Jn 19:30). We do not have to choose between these two utterances, both are entirely credible. The one recorded by John gives expression to Jesus' clear intention to fulfil the scripture. The Greek word translated 'accomplish' is used technically with this meaning. 'Everything is accomplished', I have carried out my Father's will, completed the plan he announced in the scriptures. From the beginning of the Passion Jesus had voluntarily undergone everything that was foreseen, the sharing of his clothing, the vinegar . . . Jesus, like a good workman at the end of the day, is saying, 'My work is done, I can go'.

The words recorded by Luke are not less fine, 'Into your hands I commit my spirit'. They have more psychological resonance, coming from one of the psalms – '*In manus tuas commendo spiritum meum*' (Ps 31:5). This psalm was recommended by the rabbis as part of the evening prayer and is one which we use at Compline. It is in the evening that man commits himself to God, and in the evening of his life, at death, he does the same. It is very likely, then, that Jesus uttered this in the evening of his life.

It is impossible for us to decide whether Jesus actually uttered one and not the other, or which he uttered first. We have to take the gospels as they are, each with its own traditions and its own plausibility, and be grateful, even if we do not see any way to combine them and have to forgo the hope of doing so. All these different words, guaranteed by the inspiration of the sacred writers, have their part in giving us different aspects and glimpses of the depths of Jesus' soul. The total distress of his abandonment to the powers of evil is followed by the confidence of the worker who has done his work well, 'It is accomplished', and who says to his Father, 'I commit my spirit to you, I leave it to you now to bring about the rest, the resurrection'.

And with these words *he breathed his last*, according to Mark and

---

[1] It would be naïve to insist that every word should carry its full etymological sense. Thus, in English, 'astonished' would mean 'struck by thunder', but to insist on this against its normal significance today would be nonsense.

Luke, *he yielded up his spirit*, according to Matthew, *he gave up his spirit*, according to John. They seem very brief expressions to indicate so profound a reality, but in a case like this, discretion or silence is far to be preferred. The four evangelists avoid all romanticism as they describe the end of the work by which Jesus definitively accomplishes man's salvation. John notes that he *bowed his head*, the detail of an eye-witness; but it is unnecessary to look for a symbolic meaning in this. Jesus bows his head like any dying man; after the last breath, his head falls forwards and those who see it realise that life has departed.

The phenomena accompanying Jesus' death

Jesus' death is gentle and confident, however tragic, but it is accompanied by various phenomena which the evangelists use to bring out its other and extraordinary dimension. Darkness covers the earth from the sixth to the ninth hour – from midday to three o'clock – the veil of the Temple is torn in two, the centurion admits that Jesus is the Son of God and (according to Matthew) some of the dead rise again.

Here we have to take into account the literary genre of these descriptions; let us say it once again, these are not photographic snapshots or on-the-spot reporting but narratives of a biblical character written with a theological intention. Without denying in principle the possibility of miraculous events, we have the right to ask why they have been told in this way and whether it was not the intention of the writers to recall certain biblical themes and show their realisation.

It is in fact quite normal in the Bible for a writer who wants to describe the Day of Yahweh, the great eschatological Day, to use images of cosmic phenomena, of a commotion of the earth which includes darkness and disturbances among the stars. The imagery is oriental; it uses clichés which are not meant to be taken literally, but to express some deeper idea, some spiritual reality. It will be enough to quote some passages from the prophets to indicate these literary themes on which the evangelists were brought up. For example, from Zephaniah – the opening of our *Dies Irae* – 'A day of wrath, that day, a day of distress and agony, a day of ruin and of devastation, a day of darkness and gloom, a day of cloud and blackness' (Zp 1:15). Joel also describes the Day of Yahweh, 'As they come on, the earth quakes, the skies tremble, sun and moon grow dark, the stars lose their brilliance' (Jl 2:10). And further on, 'I will display

portents in heaven and on earth, blood and fire and columns of
smoke. The sun will be turned into darkness, and the moon into
blood' (Jl 3:3–4). More valuable still, and closer to the text of the
gospels, is this from Amos: 'That day I will make the sun go down
at noon, and darken the earth in broad daylight. I am going to turn
your feasts into funerals, all your singing into lamentation; I will
have your loins all in sackcloth, your heads all shaved. I will make
it a mourning like the mourning for an only son, as long as it lasts
it will be like a day of bitterness' (Am 8:9–10). Amos mentions
another feature which recalls the tearing of the Temple veil: 'I saw
the Lord standing at the side of the altar. "Strike the capitals" he
said "and let the roof tumble down!"' Already, several verses
earlier, Amos had written, 'Is this not the reason for the earthquakes?'
Thus in Amos the earth quakes, the sky darkens while it is still day,
disasters happen in the Temple, and lastly the dead are drawn out
of Sheol, 'Should they burrow their way down to Sheol, my hand
shall haul them out' (Am 9:2).

There is, then, an habitual style in which the biblical authors describe the Day of Yahweh. But, for the evangelists, the day on which
Jesus died is the Day of Yahweh, the great day of wrath and the
opening of the eschatological era. So it is perfectly natural for them to
use the traditional images of prophetic language to depict it themselves.

In his own apocalyptic discourse Jesus had already announced
the end of Jerusalem or the end of the world, in terms of this same
cosmic imagery. To understand it properly we have to allow for the
oriental love of paradox, and this is not always easy for westerners.
The following are some examples of this literary form, drawn from
what was said by the Jews of the death of famous rabbis[1]:
'When R. Acha died, the stars became visible at midday . . . When
R. Hanan died, statues fell down . . . When R. Hanina died, Lake
Tiberias burst open . . . When R. Ishaq died, the thresholds of
seventy houses in Galilee broke . . . When R. Shemuel died, the
cedars in Israel were uprooted . . . a shaft of fire fell from heaven
and formed a partition between his bier and the funeral procession,
and for three hours there was thunder and lightning in the world.'
With parallels like these in mind, we can examine the various
phenomena described in the gospels and, without exaggerating the
element of the marvellous, look instead for the theological significance of each.

[1] Palestinian Talmud, Aboda Zara, 3, 42c, 1.

The darkness

This cannot be a true eclipse, at the time of the Passover full moon, since eclipses of the sun only take place at the new moon. Luke in fact does not say that it was; the word *eklipontos* means simply that the sun disappeared. Failing an eclipse, we may perhaps imagine that the sky was overcast as happens not infrequently in spring – the black sirocco, as Père Lagrange called it, days when the sun is grey and as pale as the moon and the atmosphere is disturbed. God could have caused one of these dark sandstorms and the Christians would quite legitimately have seen it as the realisation of the darkness announced by the prophets as a feature of the Day of Yahweh. Some exegetes have suggested that there was an eruption among the volcanos of the Jebel Hauran, but this is going too far.

The tearing of the veil of the Temple

This event is not to be taken too literally either. Père Lagrange observes that a strong gust of wind can tear down a tent; this is possible, although the veil of the Temple was heavier than a Bedouin tent.

We must go straight for the symbolism and decide what the gospels mean by the event, since they are not interested in anecdote for its own sake. The veil is a symbol which stands for the barrier which kept pagans away from the Jewish religion. The veil in question is probably that of the Holy Place, rather than that of the Holy of Holies; it hid the interior of the Temple from people in the outer court, above all from pagans; and by excluding them it protected the private mystery of the religion, the intimate presence of Yahweh inside the Temple. For the veil to be torn meant that the privacy and exclusiveness were abolished, and so Jewish worship ceased to be the privilege of a single people and access to it became open to all, even to Gentiles. Such is the deeper meaning of this phenomenon.

This can be developed even more precisely, in regard to Jesus himself. The epistle to the Hebrews makes use of the same symbolism to tell us that Jesus has given us 'the right to enter the [heavenly] sanctuary, by a new way which he has opened for us . . . through the curtain that is to say, his body' (Heb 10:19–20). Thus the veil of the Temple is Christ's own body, murdered and dead, and it is through his death that he has entered the heavenly sanctuary to perform from then on the liturgy of the heavenly High Priest.

A profound theology, then, is hidden in this detail from the gospels. It has been recorded in order to teach Christians that through Christ's death the system of Jewish worship has been abolished and religion has become universal and that he himself, the first to penetrate into the sanctuary of heaven, has opened the way to salvation for all men.

The centurion's admission

This fact is quite credible. The centurion is on duty, carrying out his orders. According to Mark, he is deeply impressed by Jesus' death: *The centurion, who was standing in front of him, had seen how he had died, and he said, 'In truth this man was a son of God'* (Mk 15:39). He has seen many condemned men die, but this death is like no other. The centurion cannot have meant 'Son of God' in the sense in which we with our developed Christian faith understand it; even less than the high priest could this pagan have understood what was, not without difficulty, to be defined by the Council of Nicaea. It is possible that he used it in a metaphorical sense – a holy man, a friend of God. But it is also quite possible that it was Mark (and Matthew following him) who gave the phrase its Christian overtones. The form recorded by Luke sounds more probable, *'This was a great and good man'* (Lk 23:47), that is a just man, an innocent man. According to Matthew it was not the death of Jesus that impressed the centurion but the earthquake, a heavenly or preternatural event, in which God was involved.

In any case, the evangelists are not particularly interested in the centurion himself, whose name they do not give[1]; for them he is a symbol of the pagan world, the representative of Rome. Since Pilate has stayed in his palace, this officer represents the empire at the foot of the cross, and through his words the empire acknowledges Jesus to be a son of God, to be at least an innocent man. At the moment when the veil of the Temple is torn and the Jewish religion is to be laid open to all, the pagan world declares that this death was praiseworthy and that this man was truly a saint. The access of the pagans to salvation is dawning.

The resurrection of some of the dead

Only Matthew records this event. Just before this he has said, *the earth quaked, the rocks were split* (Mt 27:51). This is a traditional

[1] In tradition he is called Longinus and his chapel is shown at the Holy Sepulchre. But the name is merely derived from the Greek for a lance, *lonche*.

description of the Day of Yahweh. In the Byzantine epoch, when one wanted to paint a resurrection or a Trinity, the model was already given, complete with characters, composition, colours etc. Allowing for obvious differences, we can say that the same rule holds good in the Bible. When one wanted to describe the Day of Yahweh, the terms were already given: darkness, earthquake, the dimming of the stars. Matthew stems from this tradition. There is nothing to prevent us imagining that there was a real earthquake, but we do not have to believe that the cleft in the rock which is displayed at Golgotha resulted from it.

What follows is much more strange. *The tombs opened and the bodies of many men rose from the dead, and these, after his resurrection, came out of the tombs, entered the Holy City and appeared to a number of people* (Mt 27:52–3). It is difficult to make out what is meant by this curious episode. The critics agree that these holy men are personages from the Old Testament, patriarchs like Abraham, Isaac, Jacob and David. But what kind of a return to life is meant? Some of the Fathers thought it was a return to the life of this world, followed by another death. According to them it was a miracle, a sign of power, like other resurrections in the gospel, for example that of Lazarus. But the context does not bear out this interpretation; it is difficult to imagine Abraham coming out of the tomb, wandering round Jerusalem for two or three days and then dying again later. This way of looking at things is so odd that it forces us to try to find something other than a temporary resurrection here.

Most of the Fathers, and modern theologians, think that we must see this as the eschatological resurrection, the realisation of the prophetic announcements that at the end of the age the dead will rise again. The holy men of the Old Testament could not enter heaven until Jesus had opened it to them and had to wait in that provisional state called limbo. Once salvation was won, it is part of our faith that limbo was opened up and the dead of the Old Testament entered Paradise; true enough, they were without their bodies, but they did arrive at that state of happiness reserved for souls while waiting for the final resurrection. Plainly, this is what Matthew is telling us here; the holy men of the Old Testament are associated with the resurrection of Christ and enter the eschatological era with him. They appear in the Holy City, but by this is not necessarily meant the earthly Jerusalem; it is rather the Holy City

of heaven, the heavenly Jerusalem as it is called in the epistle to the
Hebrews (Heb 11:10; 12:22–3; 13:14) and in Revelation (Rv 3:12;
21:2–10; 22:19). This passage of Matthew is a piece of theology
rather than historical in substance, as many of the Fathers realised[1].
It is a rich, imaginative statement of the doctrine of the descent into
hell, that doctrine which is included in the creed and from which we
learn that Jesus descended into hell not to fight against the devil,
over whom he had already triumphed through the crucifixion, but
to open the gates for the souls he had delivered. All those who were
waiting under the first phase of the plan of salvation are freed from
Sheol by Christ and brought with him into paradise. Matthew's few
phrases, then, convey this doctrine; the Old Testament dead do not
rise again in the sense in which we would use the word – in this sense
they will not rise until the end of time – but from now on they are
associated with the glory of the risen Christ and enter the Holy City.

Such are the events which accompany the Lord's death and mark
the coming of the Day of Yahweh, of that new era which begins with
the death of Jesus. The age of the world dominated by Satan has, in
principle, come to an end. With Jesus there begins a new age which
will shine out in a day-and-a-half's time at his resurrection, but in
fact in Jesus himself it is already definitely established.

For us Christians this age is both already here and still to come;
we are already united to the Lord and, by grace and faith, we already
live in the eschatological age with the glorified Christ; and yet at the
same time part of us still lives in the world of sin, the world of the Old
Adam. Each of us has to quit that old world and tread again the
way of the cross as Jesus did; in that lies the whole of Christian
living. We know that the Master trod this road for us, that he gave
human death a meaning, a redemptive value; this is the reason for
our confidence, we know that everything is already won. It remains
for us to die, of course; it is our greatest task and we are preparing
for it all our life long. Death is the supreme sacrifice, the total gift of
ourselves by which we pass from this world to the other. Everything
about it that was tragic and barren has become fruitful and even
easy, since Christ has died for us.

---

[1] The details of this passage are highly unlikely if they are taken literally;
the bodies of the holy men rise from the dead on Good Friday, but they wait
until Easter Sunday, after the resurrection of Christ, to come out of the tombs!
They leave the tomb only after Christ's resurrection because they cannot enter
paradise before him, but they are delivered from limbo from the moment that
Jesus triumphs over death.

9. The Burial

THE WOUND FROM THE LANCE

Mt   Mk

THE BURIAL

Mt 27: 57–61	Mk 15: 42–7
[57] When it was evening,	[42] It was now evening, and since it was Preparation Day (that is, the vigil of the sabbath), [43] there came
there came a rich man of Arimathaea, called Joseph,	Joseph of Arimathaea, a prominent member of the council,

Lk	Jn 19: 31–7
	[31] It was Preparation Day, and to prevent the bodies remaining on the cross during the sabbath – since that sabbath was a day of special solemnity – the Jews asked Pilate to have the legs broken and the bodies taken away. [32] Consequently the soldiers came and broke the legs of the first man who had been crucified with him and then of the other. [33] When they came to Jesus, they found he was already dead, and so instead of breaking his legs [34] One of the soldiers pierced his side with a lance; and immediately there came out blood and water. [35] This is the evidence of one who saw it – trustworthy evidence, and he knows he speaks the truth – and he gives it so that you may believe as well. [36] Because all this happened to fulfil the words of scripture: *Not one bone of his will be broken*; [37] and again, in another place, scripture says: *They will look on the one whom they have pierced.*

Lk 23: 50–6	Jn 19: 38–42
	[38] After this,
[50] Then a member of the council arrived, an upright and virtuous man	
named Joseph.	Joseph of Arimathaea,
[51] He had not consented to what the others had planned and carried out.	

Mt	Mk
	who himself lived in the hope
	of seeing the kingdom of God,
who had himself become	
a disciple of Jesus.	
	and he boldly
58 This man went to Pilate	went to Pilate
and asked for	and asked for
the body of Jesus.	the body of Jesus.
Pilate thereupon	44 Pilate, astonished that he

who himself lived in the hope
of seeing the kingdom of God,

who had himself become
a disciple of Jesus.

and he boldly
58 This man went to Pilate
went to Pilate
and asked for
and asked for

the body of Jesus.
the body of Jesus.
Pilate thereupon
44 Pilate, astonished that he
should have died so soon,
summoned the centurion and
enquired if he was already
dead.
45 Having been assured of this
by the centurion,
ordered it to be handed over.
he granted the corpse to Joseph

59 So
46 who bought a shroud,
took Jesus down from the cross,
Joseph took the body,
wrapped it
wrapped him
in a clean shroud
in the shroud

60 and put it in his own
and laid him in a
new
tomb
tomb
which he had hewn
which had been hewn
out of the rock.
out of the rock.

He then rolled
He then rolled
a large stone
a stone

Lk   Jn

He came from Arimathaea,
a Jewish town,
and he lived in the hope
of seeing the kingdom of God.

who was
a disciple of Jesus –
though a secret one
because he was afraid of the Jews –

⁵² This man went to Pilate
and asked for

asked Pilate
to let him remove

the body of Jesus.   the body of Jesus.
                                          Pilate

gave permission,
so they came and took it away.
³⁹ Nicodemus came as well – the
same one who had first come to
Jesus at night-time – and he
brought a mixture of myrrh
and aloes, weighing about a
hundred pounds.

⁵³ He then
took it down,

⁴⁰ They took the body of Jesus
wrapped it   and wrapped it
in a shroud

with the spices in linen cloths,
following the Jewish burial custom.
⁴¹ At the place where he had been
crucified there was a garden,
and in this garden

and put him in a

a new
tomb   tomb
which was hewn

in stone
in which no one   in which no one
had yet been laid.   had yet been buried.

Mt	Mk
across the entrance of the tomb and went away.	against the entrance to the tomb.

<table>
<tr>
<td>

⁶¹ Now Mary of Magdala
and the other Mary
were there,
</td>
<td>

⁴⁷ Mary of Magdala
and Mary the mother of Joset
</td>
</tr>
</table>

Mt	Mk

sitting
opposite the sepulchre.

were watching and took note

of where he was laid.

THE GUARD AT THE TOMB

Mt 27:62–6

[62] Next day, that is, when Preparation Day was over, the chief priests and the Pharisees went in a body to Pilate

[63] and said to him, 'Your Excellency, we recall that this impostor said, while he was still alive, 'After three days I shall rise again'.

[64] Therefore give the order to have the sepulchre kept secure until the third day, for fear his disciples come and steal him away and tell the people, 'He has risen from the dead'. This last piece of fraud would be worse than what went before.'

[65] 'You may have your guard' said Pilate to them. 'Go and make all as secure as you know how.'

[66] So they went and made the sepulchre secure, putting seals on the stone and mounting a guard.

Lk   Jn

⁵⁴ It was Preparation Day

and the sabbath was imminent.

⁴² Since it was the Jewish Day of
Preparation

and the tomb was near at hand,
they laid Jesus there.

⁵⁵ Meanwhile the women who
had come from Galilee with
Jesus were following behind.
They took note

of the tomb
and of the position of the body.
⁵⁶ Then they returned and
prepared spices and ointments.
And on the sabbath day they
rested, as the Law required.

The burial of Jesus is described in all four gospels. The historical character of these texts has been especially under fire from the critics, since those who wish to deny the resurrection have to destroy the proofs adduced by the gospels, that is, the empty tomb and the appearances. I shall discuss the appearances later on, but as regards the empty tomb, one of the arguments consists in maintaining that Jesus was never buried, or that he was buried in two successive tombs and that subsequently a mistake was made as to which he rested in. To understand and refute these objections we shall have first to consider carefully what the texts tell us.

The narrative of Mark

It was now evening, and since it was Preparation Day (that is, the vigil of the sabbath), there came Joseph of Arimathaea, a prominent member of the council . . . (Mk 15:42–3). It is the evening of the crucifixion. The Greek word translated 'Preparation' means the eve of the sabbath, the *erev shabbat* of the Jews, which has the special meaning of 'preparation' for the sabbath, as Mark explains for the benefit of readers who are unfamiliar with this expression peculiar to Judaism. Joseph is a native of Arimathaea, a village known to us from the Bible[1]. He is plainly a historical person, well known to the Christian community, and a member of the council, that is, the Sanhedrin. The Sanhedrin was composed of chief priests, scribes and prominent landowners, and doubtless it is to this last category that Joseph belongs. At any rate he is a man of sufficient standing to be able to approach Pilate. *Who himself lived in the hope of seeing the kingdom of God*, Mark tells us, though this does not necessarily mean that he had been a disciple of Jesus; he is rather one of those devout souls who long for salvation and are ready to receive the Good News. Doubtless he was well disposed towards Jesus.

---

[1] Arimathaea is usually identified as the Arab village of Rentis, to the west of Aboud. Other sites have been suggested by scholars, but Rentis remains the most probable.

And he boldly went to Pilate and asked for the body of Jesus (Mk
15:43). It needed courage to go and see the governor after the
harassing morning Pilate had spent struggling (not very hard, it
must be admitted) with the Jews to try to save Jesus. If he ended by
giving in, he was not proud of it. Moreover, he had been upset by
the Jews who wanted to have the title over the cross changed and had
sent them away without granting their request. Was it possible to
approach him again? Joseph had good reason to be afraid that he
would be unwelcome.

However, Pilate listened to him and was *astonished that he should
have died so soon* (Mk 15:44). Crucifixion did not bring death
quickly; only loss of blood did that. If the scourging had not been
too bloody and the sufferer was not nailed up, or if, although nailed,
his blood clotted quickly, he might remain on his cross, groaning
and screaming, for two or three days. This the Romans well knew,
so Pilate was astonished. In fact the two robbers were still alive, but
Jesus was dead, doubtless because he had lost a great deal of blood
through the scourging, and also because God willed that he should
die at the appointed hour, when his sacrifice was completed.

Pilate *summoned the centurion and enquired if he was already dead.
Having been assured of this by the centurion* – who had been at the
cross – *he granted the corpse to Joseph* (Mk 15:44–5). Notice the
word 'granted', Pilate makes a present of the body. This seems to
have been the normal practice; we know, however, that Verres, the
proconsul so often attacked by Cicero, made money out of everything, and was not afraid to sell the corpses of those who had been
executed.[1] Pilate gives the body to Joseph.

*Who bought a shroud, took Jesus down from the cross, wrapped him
in the shroud* (Mk 15:46). Mark speaks of a shroud, in Greek *sindon*,
that is, a large sheet. This detail is to be retained; John uses a
different word. It is of interest for the problem of the way in which
Jesus was buried and of the Holy Shroud. The synoptics mention
only a shroud in which the body is rolled, there is no question of linen
cloths and spices.

And laid him in a tomb which had been hewn out of the rock (Mk
15:46). This is the method of burial practised throughout Palestine;
Mark notes the fact for the sake of Christians in other lands who
perhaps are unfamiliar with the customs of Jerusalem. In other lands
the dead are either buried in the ground or placed in monuments,

[1] Cf. CICERO, *In Verrem*, v, 45–51.

pyramids, towers or tombs erected for the purpose, but in Jerusalem, which is built on rock, it is easy to hew a burial chamber out of the rock. This chamber, which became the Holy Sepulchre, disappeared, only after a thousand years, at the hands of a mad caliph who had it destroyed, but even now traces of it remain in the rock underneath the Holy Sepulchre. *He then rolled a stone against the entrance to the tomb* (Mk 15:46). Ancient tombs closed by a stone are still to be seen in Jerusalem today: the tomb of Helen of Adiabene, the so-called 'Tomb of the Kings', is a very fine example; there used to be a round stone of this kind at St Stephen's, but all that remains is the groove in which it was rolled. This method of closing a tomb was not universal, but it was relatively frequent.

When Joseph has completed the burial we are not told that he goes away, but Mark notes that *Mary of Magdala and Mary the mother of Joset were watching and took note of where he was laid* (Mk 15:47). These are women he has already mentioned by name. They do not do anything by themselves, but they have been watching carefully, since they want to come back.

The narrative of Matthew

Matthew's narrative differs little from Mark's; as usual, he is less rich in detail, but adds certain touches that he feels necessary for spiritual or theological reasons.

When it was evening – Matthew does not tell us that it was the eve of the sabbath – *there came a rich man of Arimathaea called Joseph* (Mt 27:57). Matthew calls him a rich man, perhaps because he was so in reality, perhaps because prominent people usually are, perhaps, lastly, because of a text from Isaiah which the first Christians could have applied to Jesus, 'They gave him a grave with the wicked, a tomb with the rich' (Is 53:9). This passage, which is difficult to interpret, comes from the Servant songs. It is possible that the first Christians, wishing to find all prophecies fulfilled in Jesus, saw in Joseph the rich man spoken of by Isaiah. Matthew is more exact than Mark about Joseph, *who had himself become a disciple of Jesus* (Mt 27:57). Now, instead of a devout Jew waiting for the Kingdom, Joseph has become a disciple; he is already a Christian.

This man went to Pilate and asked him for the body of Jesus. Pilate thereupon ordered it to be handed over (Mt 27:58). The text resembles Mark's except that some telling details have been left out.

So Joseph took the body, wrapped it in a clean shroud (Mt 27:59).
Out of respect for the sacred body of the Lord, Matthew is anxious
to tell us that it was wrapped in a clean shroud. He does not mind
emphasising what might seem obvious. So too with the 'new' tomb.
And put it in his own new tomb which he had hewn out of the rock
(Mt 27:60). This detail is of interest, not only for the respect for
Jesus which it indicates, but also because it explains how Jesus after
his execution could be buried in a tomb; we shall come back to this
point presently. Matthew also informs us that the tomb belonged to
Joseph, which Mark did not; from him we might have inferred that
Jesus was put in a tomb which was found there by chance. Matthew
explains the situation: Joseph possesses a tomb close by the cross,
so it is natural for him to take charge of the situation. It is a fine
gesture of reverence, love and honour towards Jesus.

*He then rolled a large stone across the entrance of the tomb and
went away* (Mt 27:60). Matthew tells us at this point that the stone
is a large one, a detail which it is useful to know for the events of
Sunday morning. Mark leaves it till then to tell us that the women
were wondering how to remove a stone that was so big.

*Now Mary of Magdala and the other Mary were there, sitting
opposite the sepulchre* (Mt 27:61). These women are present at the
burial and watch it.

The narrative of Luke

*Then a member of the council arrived, an upright and virtuous man
named Joseph* (Lk 23:50). This is a good example of the way Luke
likes to emphasise moral and spiritual qualities. Mark told us that
Joseph was a prominent man, Matthew that he was rich, Luke is
interested in his soul. A devout man himself, he notes that Joseph
was good, virtuous (*agathos*), an upright man who kept the Law.
This is the way in which Luke does justice to the people he presents
in his narrative; Zechariah (Lk 1:6) and Simeon (Lk 2:25) are likewise given a generous character.

*He had not consented to what the others had planned and carried
out* (Lk 23:51). Luke here gives us a necessary piece of explanation.
In the light of Mark and Matthew alone, it would be quite in order
to ask how a member of the Sanhedrin could be favourable to Jesus –
surely the Sanhedrin as a whole had condemned him to death? Luke
forestalls this objection by telling us that not all the members were

in agreement with the decision; some courageous ones either voted against the death penalty or at least abstained from voting. Joseph was one of these; so perhaps were Nicodemus and a few others.

He came from Arimathaea, a Jewish town, and he lived in the hope of seeing the kingdom of God (Lk 23:51). Like Mark, Luke does not say he was a disciple, simply a devout man. The next two verses are of no special interest (Lk 23:52-3). Like Matthew, Luke notes that the tomb was new, *a tomb which was hewn in stone in which no one had yet been laid.*

It is at the end of his account that Luke tells us the exact time of day in order to explain what has just happened. *It was Preparation Day and the sabbath was imminent* (Lk 23:54). The Greek word translated 'was imminent' is the occasion of some difficulty; normally it is used of the dawn, 'began to shine', but the Jewish sabbath began in the evening. It hardly seems possible to say that the sabbath began to shine just as night was falling. But perhaps we have to admit that the word was used in a wider sense, meaning the beginning of a period in which the light would soon shine. Or again, as several ingenious exegetes have suggested, it may refer to a light other than daylight, such as the light of Venus, which begins to shine at sunset and announces the coming of night. Or lastly it may, as Père Lagrange suggested, be an allusion to the lights which the Jews lit for the sabbath; in a town full of devout Jews, these candles, which are lit on the Friday evening, give a general illumination.

Meanwhile the women who had come from Galilee with Jesus were following behind. They took note of the tomb and of the position of the body (Lk 23:55). The holy women watch not only where but how Jesus is buried. We get the impression, even more clearly than from reading Mark, that they want to come back and need to know how to find him.

Then they returned and prepared spices and ointments (Lk 23:56). This piece of information is found in neither Mark or Matthew. The women are already thinking of bringing spices and ointments and go off to get them ready. We are not told that they buy them; from dusk on Friday the sabbath has begun and the bazaars are closed; we must suppose therefore that they had these things at home, which is, after all, quite possible. However that may be, Luke tells us that *on the sabbath day they rested, as the Law required* (Lk 23:56). This explains why they do not go back to the tomb until Sunday morning.

The narrative of John

John's account is complex and rather different from that of the synoptics. It falls into three parts (as a literary analysis shows): first a wholly original section to which there is nothing corresponding in Mark, Matthew or Luke (Jn 19:31–7); then the action taken by Joseph of Arimathaea, a passage which closely resembles the parallel passages in the synoptics (Jn 19:38); and lastly a third section in which Nicodemus comes on the scene, a passage which has many resemblances to the synoptics but some differences as well (Jn 19:39–42).

We will start with the first section, which is recorded only by John, and try to discover its value and deeper meaning.

It was Preparation Day, and to prevent the bodies remaining on the cross during the sabbath – since that sabbath was a day of special solemnity – the Jews asked . . . (Jn 19:31). Mark had already mentioned the Day of Preparation, but without explaining why. John explains things for us: the fact that it is the eve of the sabbath means that the bodies must be taken down from the cross or else the corpses of the condemned will pollute the holy day of the sabbath. The Book of Deuteronomy demanded as much, without even referring to the sabbath 'If a man guilty of a capital offence is put to death and you hang him on a tree, his body must not remain on the tree overnight; you must bury him the same day, for one who has been hanged is accursed of God, and you must not defile the land that Yahweh your God gives you for an inheritance' (Dt 21:22–3). A man hanged on a cross is accursed; Paul later is to use this same powerful text to tell the Galatians that Christ underwent the curse of the Law, 'by being cursed for our sake' (Ga 3:13). For the Jews a man who is executed is impure; if his body remains exposed all night and the following day, it defiles the land of Israel. It must be buried by the evening, the more so if the following day is a sabbath, and even more so if, as John tells us, *that sabbath was a day of special solemnity*. Solemnity reaches a peak when the sabbath is the day of the Passover festival. When the day of Passover falls on a sabbath, it becomes an absolutely exceptional feastday; so the Jews cannot contemplate the bodies being left on the cross until then and they ask the governor to have them buried. This request of theirs may shock us when we remember that this 'impure' corpse was the Lord Jesus Christ; but Jesus himself was willing to undergo total indignity before coming to his resurrection: he is simply got rid of, buried.

The Jews asked Pilate to have the legs broken and the bodies taken away (Jn 19:31). Notice that it is the Jews who are asking; John does not mention Joseph of Arimathaea yet. Some critics use this detail to distinguish two different burials and try to explain the empty tomb in this way, i.e. that there was a tomb which was not empty. The Jews ask that the legs of the condemned be broken. They evidently suppose that the bodies are still living; the breaking of the legs will bring things to an end and then the bodies can be taken away.

Consequently the soldiers came and broke the legs of the first man who had been crucified with him and then of the other. When they came to Jesus, they found he was already dead – like Pilate, the soldiers are astonished that he is already dead – *and so instead of breaking his legs* – this painful action was unnecessary – *one of the soldiers pierced his side with a lance; and immediately there came out blood and water* (Jn 19:32–4). The soldier acts in a way that is not necessary; out of curiosity he wants to make sure that Jesus is dead. These facts are quite credible; the breaking of the legs, the omission of this in Jesus' case because he was dead, the thrust from the lance, the flow of blood and water, are all perfectly plausible. Medical experts tell us that, in the case of those crucified, some blood remains in the heart and a serous liquid accumulates round it, as a result of the body hanging, so that a thrust from a lance might release a liquid which looked like water.

However plausible these details may be from a physiological point of view, and however moving, this is not the reason why John mentions them. He is writing about Jesus, and he sees a profound theological meaning in the fact, as the following verse gives us to understand. *This is the evidence of one who saw it – trustworthy evidence, and he knows he speaks the truth – and he gives it so that you may believe as well.* This is a very solemn testimony. But who is meant by 'he' in the different phrases? 'He' who saw it and gives evidence is plainly the evangelist. Why, then, does he not use the first person and say, 'I saw it, I am giving evidence'? Is this a recognised manner of speaking among semitic people? Is the third person used out of discretion or humility? Such humility would seem affected rather than convincing.

There is another possible explanation: it is not John speaking but those of his disciples who edited the gospel. The fourth gospel has a long literary history, and it is possible that it reached its final form only towards the end of the first century, after the death of St John. There is another indication of this at the end of the gospel (Jn 21:23). What we have here would be the disciples of John speaking about their master – he who saw it has given evidence and we tell you his evidence is truthful – and in this case the use of the third person 'he' becomes quite normal.

Another question arises – who is the 'he' who 'knows he speaks the truth'*? This is Jesus Christ. In his first epistle, John frequently calls on the testimony of Christ, referring to him as 'he'. It is a mark of respect; there is no need to use the name 'Jesus', it is sufficient to say 'he'. The Pythagoreans did the same in regard to their master.[1] So here, the disciples of John are not only bearing witness on behalf of their master, but they are calling the Lord Jesus as a witness, so that the reader may believe what he is being told.

The blood and the water

What is it that is so profound about this detail recorded by John? John sees in it the fulfilment of two texts of scripture: 'Not one bone of his will be broken' and 'They will look on the one whom they have pierced'.

The first text comes from the Book of Exodus (Ex 12:46) and from the Book of Numbers (Nb 9:12). The passage describes the rite of the Passover and concerns the Passover lamb: 'It is to be eaten in one house alone, out of which not a single morsel of the flesh is to be taken; nor must you break any bone of it.' Whatever the origin of the Passover rite may have been, it forbade the breaking of the Passover victim's bones. Now the soldiers did not break Jesus' legs; and John sees in this simple detail a sign that Jesus is the Passover lamb. In this way he allies himself with the profound theology of St Paul, who says, writing to the Corinthians, 'Christ, our passover, has been sacrificed' (1 Co 5:7). The Book of Revelation contains the

---

* Trans. note – The first 'he' in this phrase, and in the examples from the first epistle about to be quoted, represents the Greek pronoun *ekeinos*, a fact which can be conveyed in French by using *celui-là*.

[1] Here are some texts from the first epistle of St John – 'when the one who claims to be living in him is living the same kind of life as He lived.' (1 Jn 2, 6). 'Surely everyone who entertains this hope must purify himself, must try to be as pure as Him' (1 Jn 3, 3). 'Now you know that he appeared in order to abolish sin, and that in him there is no sin' (1 Jn 3, 5). [Note that these texts taken from *La Bible de Jérusalem*, being translated direct from the Greek, show slight variations from *The Jerusalem Bible*. Ed.]

same teaching, 'Then I saw . . . a Lamb that seemed to have been sacrificed' (Rv 5:6, 12). This identification of Jesus with the Passover lamb is profoundly true, it is the essential meaning of the Eucharist: Jesus takes the place of the Jewish Passover, he was sacrificed on the cross at the moment when the Jews were sacrificing the lambs.

The second text comes from the prophet Zechariah: 'They will look on the one whom they have pierced' (Zc 12:10). Exegetes do not know how to explain this difficult text and propose various solutions. Some look to the Servant in Isaiah to provide an explanation: a mysterious personage is to be pierced, and this will cause mourning like the mourning for an only son: all Israel will lament over him and beat their breasts. Other see in it an allusion to the death of King Josiah at Megiddo in Galilee, when he tried to bar the way to Pharaoh Neco; this killing of an heir of David on the field of battle suggested the mysterious future death of another descendant of David. Others translate the Hebrew text differently: the original does not mention a man who has been pierced; instead God says, 'They will look on me whom they have insulted'. In this passage God complains that he has been scorned in the person of his messenger; he calls himself the shepherd who is sold for thirty pieces of silver (Zc 11:12).

Whatever the original meaning of Zechariah's text, it is certain that the first Christians saw a new and deeper meaning in it and applied it to the piercing of Jesus on the cross. This application is found again in the Book of Revelation: 'It is he *who is coming on the clouds*; everyone will see him, even *those who pierced him*, and *all the races of the earth will mourn over him*' (Rev 1:7).

In the thrust of the lance John sees the fulfilment of a prophecy; but also he plainly perceives a mystery in the blood and water that flow from the side of Christ. What is the symbolism here? We do not know with certainty. The Fathers hesitated; many of them thought of the mystery of redemption, since the blood, in John as in the whole of the New Testament, is the expression of the price which Jesus paid for sin. As for the water, this could refer to baptism, or even the sacraments in general (for some have found in it hints of both Eucharist and baptism). Others of the Fathers thought it meant the Church issuing from the side of Christ. For other critics, it is simply grace, the Spirit issuing from Christ; earlier, in John, Jesus had applied to himself the words of scripture, 'From his breast shall flow fountains of living water' (Jn 7:38-9). Throughout the

Bible and in John, water is a symbol of the Spirit, of wisdom, of grace, or of divine life; thus streams of living water flow from the body of the dead Christ.

These various interpretations are fundamentally one, for the sacraments are the spiritual life which flows from Christ and it is the Church that lives by them. We can contemplate them all together, in a greater whole, and recognise with John the profound symbolism of the water and blood which really issued from the side of Christ; fountains of living water – grace and the sacraments – flowed and continue to flow from the Christ who died for us. And we should not forget the three witnesses mentioned in John's first epistle, 'the water, the blood and the Spirit' (1 Jn 5:6).

This theme of the water and the blood has some curious echoes in Judaism. A rabbinic 'haggadah'[1] reports that when Moses struck the rock twice with his rod he made blood and water flow from it at the same time. This is a late and curious tradition, but the similarity is interesting. It is very unlikely that the rabbinic writings were imitating the gospel. Their text has a quite different meaning: the blood which issues from the rock symbolises the punishment which Moses has earned by uttering harsh words against the Israelites. However, even if the application is different, the fact remains that blood and water issue from Moses' rock. Now in Moses, who led the chosen people through the desert, the first Christians saw a type of Christ; Paul says, 'The rock was Christ' (1 Co 10:4). Writing to the Corinthians about the sacraments, Paul treats the crossing of the Red Sea, the water in the desert, the quails and the manna as foreshadowing the sacraments of the New Testament. So, if the Christians on the one hand likened Jesus to the rock of Moses, and if the Jews on the other said that water and blood issued from this rock, it is difficult not to feel that there is a profound analogy in the use which John makes of the idea here. Without taking it any further, it is at least interesting to note this common stock of imagery and symbolism[2].

---

[1] *Exodus Rabba*, 3 (70a).
[2] The theme of the water and the blood also corresponds to an ancient and over-simplified conception of physiology. Another rabbinic midrash, *Leviticus Rabba*, 15 (115c), contains the information that man is made half of water, half of blood: if he is virtuous, the two elements are in equilibrium; if he is sinful, one element is dominant: if this element is water he becomes dropsical; if it is blood he becomes leprous. This ancient physiology lends itself to a lot of different applications; we see one of them in the case of Moses and the rock, but St John's is immeasurably finer.

John's symbolism is a profound and beautiful application of a fact he actually observed about the body of the Lord Jesus. The whole passage is characteristic of John, who has a gift for setting down actual concrete facts and then drawing magnificent theological symbols from them.

The appearance of Nicodemus

In the following verse we return to a narrative very similar to that of the synoptics, in which John merely summarises the course of events. *After this, Joseph of Arimathaea, who was a disciple of Jesus* – as Matthew also says – *though a secret one because he was afraid of the Jews* – *asked Pilate to let him remove the body of Jesus. Pilate gave permission, so they came and took it away* (Jn 19:38). The attitude of Joseph is to be noted since it closely resembles that of Nicodemus when he came to find Jesus (Jn 3:2). However, the main problem posed by this summary of the synoptic narratives is how to reconcile this approach made by Joseph with that made by the Jews and reported a little earlier by John (Jn 19:31).

Moreover a third episode follows in which Nicodemus appears (Jn 19:39–42). John has already mentioned him, as he reminds us here, *Nicodemus came as well* – *the same one who had first come to Jesus at night-time* – *and he brought a mixture of myrrh and aloes, weighing about a hundred pounds* (Jn 19:39). This is something new; the synoptics have made no mention of spices or embalming. Myrrh and aloes are perfumes, scented wood that can be used for embalming a corpse. A hundred pounds is equal to something over 70 lbs in modern terms. This is an astonishing amount; it could be explained as the liberality of a rich and generous man, but it could also be that this round number, 100, conceals some symbolism – not long before Jesus had been anointed with a pound of nard (Jn 12:3); here it is multiplied a hundredfold.

They took the body of Jesus and wrapped it with the spices in linen cloths, following the Jewish burial custom (Jn 19:40). The Greek word translated 'linen cloths' can also mean 'bands', but the former is preferred by some exegetes who – in the interests of the Holy Shroud of Turin – are anxious to make John's words fit the 'shroud' of the synoptics. But this will be discussed later. In addition, John refers to 'the Jewish custom'. In actual fact, there is no clear evidence that the Jews buried people in this way; we know that they used to anoint the corpse with oil, but spices do not seem to be presupposed by the rabbinic sources. However, John is well informed, and it is possible that he is giving us genuine information.

At the place where he was crucified there was a garden, and in this garden a new tomb in which no one had yet been buried (Jn 19:41). The garden is a new, but perfectly plausible, feature; someone has had a tomb made in a garden on the edge of the town near the walls. No one who knows Jerusalem and its surroundings will find this difficult to understand. Like Matthew, John specifies that it is a new one. John here seems to be taking up and completing what Matthew and Luke have told us.

Since it was the Jewish Day of Preparation and the tomb was near at hand, they laid Jesus there (Jn 19:42). This last detail adds nothing to the synoptics.

Such is John's narrative. It gives us useful information but it also raises two questions which will have to be examined. The first concerns the relation between the approach of the Jews to Pilate and that of Joseph, and the second, how to reconcile the spices brought by Joseph and the spices which, according to the synoptic account, the holy women are going to bring on Sunday morning.

It is possible to say that the approach of the Jews and that of Joseph do not contradict one another. Joseph is one of the Jews and, when the group have asked for the bodies to be taken down, he decides to take further action by himself: the task of burying Jesus in his own tomb. This is possible, though John does not say the tomb was Joseph's.

In fact, it is better to recognise that two traditions have been juxtaposed. The words 'After this' in verse 38 look like a literary device to join them. John has composed his account by putting two parallel narratives end to end; in one, the approach is made by the Jews without its being said exactly by whom; in the other, Joseph is named. This slight problem will occur again later.

But in regard to the embalming a choice has definitely to be made. If Nicodemus really used that mass of spices why do the women still want to embalm the body on Sunday morning? According to the synoptics, Joseph did not have time to use any spices; perhaps the women promised themselves that they would come back on Sunday morning and bring some. But according to John, there was no need, a hundred pounds of spices had already been used.

A first answer might perhaps be found in feminine devotion; yes, some spices have been applied, but we want to bring out own offering to the Lord, our own spices! But there are other serious difficulties in the synoptic narrative, notably that of the stone which would be so difficult for the women to remove. Mark reports that they raised this question among themselves, 'Who will roll away the stone for us?'. But why did they not think of this before they started out? Again, they believed Jesus to be dead (they knew nothing yet of the resurrection); is it likely that after thirty-six hours they would want to take a corpse out of its grave? And further, if Matthew is right about the guard and the seals put on the stone, how could the women hope to get into the tomb?

We are brought to the point where we have to choose between John and the synoptics. As in the case of the Passover, we have to decide which is right, since the Holy Spirit has permitted the traditions to disagree. Myself, I would decide for John; he seems to have been a witness, he gives the name of Nicodemus, and the spices are not improbable. But then what are we to make of the synoptic narratives? In fact, it is only Mark and Luke that need to be considered. Matthew does not mention spices, he has described the guard and the sealed tomb, and so he cannot attribute to the women any intention of entering the tomb. He says that the women go to the tomb on Sunday morning simply to 'see', just as we return to a friend's grave to put flowers on it and pray there. Matthew says no more than this and it is all quite plausible. As for Mark and Luke, what could have happened is that without knowing John's tradition they wanted to provide a reason for the women's visit and imagined that they went there to take spices. They would be making a suggestion rather than recording a real memory and their suggestion would have the advantage of emphasising the honour done to Jesus' body.

The internal difficulties of John's narrative can be convincingly explained by the existence in his text of three fragments which have been juxtaposed – the request of the Jews and the fact that Jesus' bones were not broken, come from his own personal tradition (Jn 19:31–7), then a passage about Joseph of Arimathaea (Jn 19:38), and lastly the entrance of Nicodemus, which has some individual features as well as some resemblances to the synoptics (Jn 19:39–42). This concern to complete his narrative with the help of information taken from the synoptics can be found in other passages of John's gospel; such additions made for a closer agreement between the gospels[1].

The guard over the tomb

This is an addition made by Matthew alone. *Next day, that is, when Preparation Day was over, the chief priests and the Pharisees went in a body to Pilate and said to him, 'Your Excellency, we recall that this impostor said, while he was still alive, "After three days I shall rise again".* *Therefore give the order to have the sepulchre kept secure until the third day, for fear his disciples come and steal him away and tell the people, "He has risen from the dead". This last piece of fraud would be worse than what went before.' 'You may have your guard' said Pilate to them. 'Go and make all as secure as you know how.' So they went and made the sepulchre secure, putting seals on the stone and mounting a guard* (Mt 27:62–6).

The Greek text reads, 'You have a guard', and this may be understood in two ways. Either it means, 'Here is one, I give you one', in which case it is composed of Roman soldiers. Or, 'You have a Jewish guard, the Temple soldiers, use them', in which case it is the Jews who provide the guard and seal the tomb.

This episode has its sequel further on, when the stone is found to have been rolled away and the guards have to tell lies (Mt 28:11–15), but it gives rise to several objections. It is hardly likely that the Jews would wait until the day after the burial before mounting a guard; if the disciples had wanted to steal the body, the first night would have been the best time to do so; would they have waited two or three days to take it away? Again, the following day was a sabbath, could devout men approach Pilate on the day of rest? Lastly, it is surely strange that the Pharisees thought of the resurrection of Jesus while no such thought crossed the minds of the disciples. Neither Mark, nor Luke, nor John, mention such a guard. For all these reasons, Matthew's information on this point has often been questioned.

The corresponding narrative after the resurrection gives us the clue. The episode of the guard belongs to polemic: the story is still current among the Jews that the body of Jesus was stolen away

---

[1] We shall find a very similar method of composition further on when we come to the discovery of the empty tomb and the appearance to Mary Magdalene (Jn 20): this passage includes a fragment proper to the Johannine tradition, a fragment of Johannine tradition fused with the synoptic tradition, and between the two a verse taken from the synoptics. This confirms the literary analysis I have made of the present passage.

(Mt 28:15). Matthew echoes disputes that were going on between Jews and Christians thirty or forty years after the actual events. The Jews accused the Christians of having stolen the body of their Master in order to stimulate belief in his resurrection, and Matthew is writing to refute this calumny. It is therefore a late tradition, though this does not necessarily imply that it was invented. We must merely be careful not to attach too much importance to the details, which we have shown to be improbable.

The historical value of the burial narratives

Here it is useful to emphasise the essential historical value of these narratives. Whatever the truth may be about certain details, we can assert with absolute confidence that Jesus was buried. This might seem to be self-evident, but there are certain critics who, wanting to deny the resurrection and its proof, the empty tomb, claim that Jesus was not buried, or that he was buried in an unknown tomb.

Certain of them, for example Loisy and Guignebert, assert that Jesus' body was left lying on the ground or was thrown into the 'common grave for criminals'. This is contradicted not only by the gospel narratives but also by some precious texts of St Paul: about the year 57 A.D. Paul is writing to the Corinthians and he repeats an ancient tradition; 'I taught you what I had been taught myself, namely that Christ died for our sins, in accordance with the scriptures; that he was buried; and that he was raised to life . . .' (1 Co 15:3–4). This ancient tradition confirms the gospel narratives.

In the Acts of the Apostles, Peter's discourse after Pentecost starts from the psalm, 'You will not allow your holy one to experience corruption' (Ps 16:10); Peter says that David, the author of the psalm, has indeed experienced corruption and his tomb can be seen to this day; David therefore must have been speaking of someone else, that is, the Messiah (Ac 2:27–31). This line of argument seems to presuppose that the tomb of Christ is also known but is empty.

Jewish custom itself also absolutely forbids us to believe that Jesus was deprived of burial. The Jews had so great a respect for the body and such scrupulousness about the purity of the land of Israel that they would never have left the corpse of a criminal lying on the ground. Jewish writings make it plain that the executed were well and truly buried[1]; there were two vaults reserved for this near the

[1] MISHNA, *Sanhedrin*, 6, 5f; and its Gemara in the Babylonian Talmud, 47a.

place of execution, one for those who had been stoned or burnt, the other for those who had been strangled or beheaded. No one wanted to dishonour them; if they were not buried in family vaults, it was because their bodies were impure and accursed and must not be allowed to defile the bodies of good men by their contact. If there happened to be a new tomb, as yet unoccupied, nothing prevented its being used; this is what is interesting, in Jesus' case, about the 'new' tomb, 'in which no one had yet been laid'. There was no legal objection whatsoever to putting the body of the crucified man there. The Jews were so little intent on dishonouring the bodies of the executed that once death had done its work and the body, as though purified by punishment, was dried up, it became pure again and the bones were collected and taken back to the family vault. The historian Josephus tells us precisely this in the *Jewish Wars* (IV, 317): the Jews have such respect for the body that 'they take down even those who have been condemned and crucified and bury them before sunset'. Josephus is here describing a Jewish law without a thought of the gospel[1]. It is inconceivable therefore that Jesus was left unburied.

Some critics, convinced by this evidence, take up another position; certainly Jesus was buried, but not by Joseph of Arimathaea. This is the opinion of Goguel, for example[1]. Jesus was buried by the Jews, as St John says; he was buried, by his enemies, who put him in a common grave or in an unknown tomb. Later, the Christians, humiliated by this anonymous burial at his enemies' hand, invented Joseph of Arimathaea and the story of a burial carried out by his friends. They did this to strengthen their own piety. For Goguel, the first Christians believed in the resurrection of Christ only in regard to his soul; it was later that they imagined that he had risen in the flesh. But then they had to make up this story of a devout man who had placed Jesus in a tomb which was both well known and could be shown to be empty. In reality, according to Goguel, the tomb in which Jesus had been placed by his Jewish enemies was completely unknown, and the discovery of the empty tomb is therefore impossible.

[1] Those who claim that Jesus was not buried refer to the words of a bishop of Ephesus, in 536, who in a flight of fancy in one of his sermons says that Jesus was cast out naked and without a tomb; the same text, however, immediately goes on to say that Joseph of Arimathaea came to bury him. In other words this was a piece of rhetoric, not a historical tradition.
[1] *La foi en la résurrection de Jésus dans le christianisme primitif*, Paris, 1933, pp. 121–55.

One powerful, and even decisive, answer to this lies in the person of Joseph of Arimathaea. He is certainly historical; we know his position and his birthplace; he makes himself felt, in the gospel narratives, as a man of flesh and blood. If the Christians, after it was all over, had made up a story of burial by friendly hands, they would have attributed it to Peter or James or some other character from the gospels. Where, if not in real life, did they find this Joseph of Arimathaea, who is not mentioned anywhere else? His existence is a valuable historical detail which was, and had to be, accepted by all four evangelists, and of itself it guarantees the truth of the burial of Jesus. As I have shown earlier, it is wholly plausible that this influential man was able to approach Pilate and obtain permission for the burial. Perhaps it is an exaggeration to call him a disciple; the change from Mark and Luke, for whom he is a prominent man who lives in the hope of seeing the kingdom of God, to Matthew and John, for whom he has become a disciple, betrays the growth of tradition. It is possible that the Christians embellished him and made him out to be more of a Christian than he actually was; there are analogous cases in the gospel, and Pilate is later almost turned into a saint. But, stripped of accretions, Joseph remains a prominent and upright Jew, who refused to condemn Jesus and, after the Passion, showed his respect for this Man by burying him in an honourable way.

Other critics accept the burial by Joseph but find ways of making the discovery of the empty tomb impossible. For G. Baldensperger,[1] for example, there were two burials: first, immediately after his death, the Jews bury Jesus in an unknown common grave with the others who had been crucified; evening comes and Joseph gets from Pilate permission, not to bury, but to transfer Jesus. He goes and takes the body from the common grave and carries it off to a more honourable tomb, his own. The women have seen only the first burial, and when they return on Sunday morning they are astounded to find it empty. They do not know that Joseph has taken the body elsewhere – so our whole faith is based on an enormous illusion!

A reconstruction like this has no basis in fact and smacks rather of a novel. Baldensperger admits that there was a long interval between the first burial and Joseph's. In actual fact, Jesus died about three or four o'clock, his body must have been taken down about

---

[1] 'Le tombeau vide', in *Revue d'Histoire et de Philosophie Religieuses*, XII, 1932, pp. 413–43; XIII, 1933, pp. 105–44; XIV, 1934, pp. 97–125.

half past five or six, and so there is no room for more than one burial. Again, he bases his theory on an odd piece of philology. The gospel narratives employ two different words to designate the tomb: *mnema* and *taphos*. These are in fact synonymous, despite their different etymologies, just as the words 'tomb' and 'sepulchre' are. Mark and Matthew use them for the sake of variety, just as we would ourselves, but Baldensperger wants them to be indications of two distinct burials, one in a *mnemeion*, the other in a *taphos*. Moreover, he finds the stone rolled in front of the door unacceptable; for him, a door and a stone which is rolled across are two incompatible ways of closing something; one tomb therefore had a door, the other a stone; the evangelists mixed them both together. In fact, Baldensperger knows nothing about Palestinian tombs, where the door means an opening in front of which a stone is rolled. His knowledge is bookish and unreal, and the romance he offers us cannot shake the solidly based narrative of the gospel.

Finally, we need to explain why the holy women could not share in the burial but only stand by and watch. It is sometimes objected that if they had been there it would have fallen to them to bury him. But the answer is that it was not normally the business of women to bury someone, let alone in such circumstances. What could a handful of poor, unknown Galilean women have done for a criminal crucified by the public authority and guarded by a captain and his squad? Even if they had wanted to, the disciples themselves could have done nothing. It had to be a senator who would take on the job of going and asking the governor. The holy women watched but could do nothing by themselves. This is all perfectly plausible. Joseph of Arimathaea deserves our recognition and admiration, and the burial carried out in the presence of the women is a datum of historical value. It makes a solid foundation on which we can establish the truth of the fact that the tomb was found to be empty by the women, by Peter and by John.

10. The Empty Tomb

THE WOMEN AT THE TOMB

Mt 28:1–8	Mk 16:1–8
After the sabbath,	[1] When the sabbath was over, Mary of Magdala, Mary the mother of James, and Salome, bought spices with which to go and anoint him.
and towards dawn on the first day of the week,	[2] And very early in the morning on the first day of the week
Mary of Magdala and the other Mary went to visit the sepulchre.	they went to the tomb, just as the sun was rising.
	[3] They had been saying to one another, 'Who will roll away the stone for us from the entrance to the tomb?'
[2] And all at once there was a violent earthquake, for the angel of the Lord, descending from heaven, came and	[4] But when they looked they could see that the stone – which was very big – had already been rolled back.
rolled away the stone	[5] On entering the tomb
	they saw a young man in a white robe
and sat on it. [3] His face was like lightning, his robe white as snow. [4] The guards	seated on the right-hand side,

Lk 24:1–11   Jn 20:1

¹ On the first day   ¹ It was very early
of the week,   on the first day
                                        of the week
                                        and still dark,
at the first sign of dawn,

                                        when Mary of Magdala

they went to the tomb   came to the tomb.

with the spices they had prepared.

² They found   She saw
that the stone   that the stone

had been rolled away   had been moved away
from the tomb,   from the tomb
³ but on entering   20 ¹¹ᵇ . . . she stooped
                                           to look inside

discovered that the body
of the Lord Jesus was not there.
⁴ As they stood there
not knowing what to think,

                                           ¹² and saw
two men   two angels
in brilliant clothes   in white
suddenly appeared at their side.
                                           sitting . . .

Mt	Mk
were so shaken, so frightened of him, that they were like dead men.	and they were struck with amazement.
[5] But the angel spoke; and he said to the women, 'There is no need for you to be afraid. I know you are looking for Jesus, who was crucified.	[6] But he said to them, 'There is no need for alarm. You are looking for Jesus of Nazareth, who was crucified:
	he has risen, he is not here.
[6] He is not here,	
for he has risen, as he said he would.	
Come and see the place where he lay,	See, here is the place where they laid him.
[7] then go quickly and tell his disciples,	[7] But you must go and tell his disciples and Peter,
"He has risen from the dead and now he is going before you to Galilee; it is there you will see him". Now I have told you.'	"He is going before you to Galilee; it is there you will see him, just as he told you".'
[8] Filled with awe and great joy the women came	[8] And the women came out

Lk	Jn
[5] Terrified,	
the women lowered their eyes.	
But the two men said to them,	[13] They said, 'Woman, why are you weeping?'
'Why look	
among the dead for someone who is still alive?	
[6] He is not here;	'They have taken my Lord away' she replied
he has risen	
	'and I don't know
	where they have put him.' . . . [17] Jesus said to her, . . . 'But go and find the brothers, and tell them:
Remember what he told you when he was still	
in Galilee:	
[7] that the Son of Man had to be handed over into the power of sinful men and be crucified, and rise again on the third day?'	
	I am ascending to my Father and your Father, to my God and your God.'
[8] And they remembered his words.	
[9] When the women returned	[18] So Mary of Magdala went

Mt	Mk
quickly	and ran away
away from the tomb	from the tomb
	because they were frightened
	out of their wits;
	and they said nothing to a soul,
	for they were afraid . . .
and ran	
to tell	
the disciples.	

PETER AND THE OTHER DISCIPLE AT THE TOMB

Mt	Mk

Lk   Jn

from the tomb

they told all this to the Eleven and to all the others.	and told the disciples
	that she had seen the Lord and that he had said these things to her.

[10] The women were Mary of Magdala, Joanna, and Mary the mother of James. The other women with them also told the apostles, [11] but this story of theirs seemed pure nonsense, and they did not believe them.

Lk   Jn 20:2–10

[2] and [Mary of Magdala] came running to Simon Peter and the other disciple, the one Jesus loved. 'They have taken the Lord out of the tomb' she said 'and we don't know where they have put him.'

[12] Peter, however,

went running to the tomb.

[3] So Peter set out with the other disciple to go to the tomb. [4] They ran together, but the other disciple, running faster than Peter, reached the tomb first;

He bent down and saw the binding cloths but nothing else;

[5] he bent down and saw the linen cloths lying on the ground,

but did not go in. [6] Simon Peter who was following

Mt   Mk

CHRIST APPEARS TO MARY OF MAGDALA

Mt   Mk

16:9–10

Lk   Jn

now came up, went right into
the tomb, saw the linen cloths
on the ground,
⁷ and also the cloth that had
been over his head; this was
not with the linen cloths but
rolled up in a place by itself.
⁸ Then the other disciple who
had reached the tomb first
also went in; he saw and he
believed.
⁹ Till this moment they had failed
to understand the teaching of
scripture, that he must rise
from the dead.

he then went back home,   ¹⁰ The disciples then went home
amazed at what had happened.   again.

Lk   Jn 20:11–18

¹¹ Meanwhile Mary stayed outside
near the tomb, weeping. Then,
still weeping, she stooped to look
inside,
¹² and saw two angels in white
sitting where the body of Jesus had
been, one at the head, the other
at the feet.
¹³ They said, 'Woman, why are
you weeping?' 'They have taken
my Lord away' she replied
'and I don't know where they
have put him.'
¹⁴ As she said this she turned
round and saw Jesus standing
there, though she did not
recognise him.
¹⁵ Jesus said, 'Woman, why are
you weeping? Who are you
looking for?' Supposing him
to be the gardener, she said, 'Sir,
if you have taken him away,
tell me where you have put him,

CHRIST APPEARS TO THE WOMEN

Mt 28:9–10   Mt

⁹ And there, coming to meet them,
was Jesus. 'Greetings' he said.
And the women came up to him
and, falling down before him,
clasped his feet.
¹⁰ Then
Jesus said to them,
'Do not be afraid;

go and
tell my brothers

that they must leave
for Galilee;
they will see me there'.

28 ⁵ But the angel spoke;
and he said to the women,
'There is no need for you to be
afraid . . .
⁷ then go quickly
and tell his disciples,

'He has risen from the dead
and now he is going before you

to Galilee;
it is there you will see him."
Now I have told you.'

Lk	Jn
	and I will go and remove him'.
	¹⁶ Jesus said, 'Mary!' She knew him then and said to him in Hebrew, 'Rabbuni!' – which means Master.
	¹⁷ Jesus said to her, 'Do not cling
	¹⁷ to me, because I have not yet ascended to the Father. But go and find the brothers, and tell them: I am ascending to my Father and your Father, to my God and your God.'
	¹⁸ So Mary of Magdala went and told the disciples that she had seen the Lord and that he had said these things to her.

Mk	Jn
	20 ¹⁷ Jesus said to her,
	'Do not cling to me . . .
16 ⁶ But he said to them, 'There is no need for alarm . . .	
⁷ But you must go and tell his disciples and Peter,	But go and find the brothers and tell them:
"He is going before you	I am ascending
to Galilee; It is there you will see him, just as he told you".'	to my Father and your Father . . .'

THE BRIBED SOLDIERS

Mt 28:11-15   Mk

[11] While they were on their way,
some of the guard went off into the city
to tell the chief priests all that had
happened.
[12] These held a meeting with the elders and,
after some discussion, handed a
considerable sum of money to the
soldiers
[13] with these instructions, 'This is
what you must say, "His disciples
came during the night and stole him
away while we were asleep".
[14] And should the governor come
to hear of this, we undertake to
put things right with him and
to see that you do not get into
trouble.'
[15] The soldiers took the money and
carried out their instructions,
and to this day that is the
story among the Jews.

Lk   Jn

To study the discovery of the empty tomb, we shall begin by taking the synoptics together and examining them in detail; we shall then examine John's account.

The holy women at the tomb

At what moment do the women go to the tomb? *On the first day of the week* (Lk 24:1), says Luke; *when the sabbath was over* (Mk 16:1), says Mark; *after the sabbath* (Mt 28:1), says Matthew; we take this to be Sunday morning. It cannot be on the Saturday evening after sunset since the evangelists give us the exact time: *towards dawn on the first day of the week* (Mt 18:1); *at the first sign of dawn* (Lk 24:1); *very early in the morning* (Mk 16:2); so it is early morning when the women come. They do not start out the moment the sabbath day has legally come to an end, but wait for the approach of daylight.

The evangelists give their names again: *Mary of Magdala*, always given first, who plays the chief part; then *the other Mary* according to Matthew, or *Mary the mother of James* according to Mark, who is the same Mary the mother of James and Joset who has been spoken of before; and Mark adds *Salome* to those two.

Marks tells us that they *bought spices with which to go and anoint him* (Mk 16:1). Luke does not mention this here, since according to him they had already prepared spices on Friday evening. And Matthew says nothing about it because he has put a guard at the entrance and does not envisage the women entering the sealed tomb at all. As I have indicated in the preceding chapter (pp. 225), his presentation is the most plausible; according to him they *went to visit the sepulchre*, as devout women do go to the grave of someone they love, to shed tears and pray there.

According to Mark and Luke, the women come with the avowed intention of embalming Jesus. *They had been saying to one another, 'Who will roll away the stone for us from the entrance to the tomb?'* (Mk 16:3). It is a little late for them to think of this: or perhaps it is Mark who introduced the difficulty too late and rather awkwardly.

All the same this remark is not without effect; the women's disquiet prepares the way for the miracle of the tomb which has opened of itself and without human intervention. *But when they looked they could see that the stone – which was very big – had already been rolled back* (Mk 16:4). Here is another example of Mark's spontaneous, impromptu style. He tells us how big the stone is at the moment when it matters; the size of the stone which has been rolled away by a divine hand impresses on us the power of the divine intervention. Luke also says, *They found that the stone had been rolled away from the tomb* (Lk 24:2).

Matthew offers us a more complete story. *And all at once there was a violent earthquake, for the angel of the Lord, descending from heaven, came and rolled away the stone and sat on it. His face was like lightning, his robe as white as snow. The guards were so shaken, so frightened of him, that they were like dead men* (Mt 28:2–4). Matthew adopts again the literary genre that he has already used at the moment of Christ's death. There, he introduced a previous earthquake and other marvels – such as the resurrection of the dead – more spectacular than those in Mark and Luke. This exaggeration, the earthquake and the dazzlingly white angel, is very much in the style of the Old Testament. Matthew is illustrating in imaginative language a reality which of itself is transcendent and inexpressible – that the body of Jesus, repossessed by the Holy Spirit, leaves the completely closed tomb and enters into the glory of his Father. This is a real event but it transcends experience. The entry of Christ into the eschatological world of God is beyond the grasp of our human senses and it is unthinkable that anyone should try to describe it; all that men can ascertain are the external effects, the empty tomb and the appearance. It is to suggest this indescribable mystery that Matthew has recourse to powerful images in which the laws of nature seem to have been turned upside down. The presentation is poetic and profoundly true; it is the best way of expressing a genuine supernatural event.

Besides, when we compare Matthew with certain other writings, his discretion is remarkable. At this very point, one manuscript of the Old Latin translation of Mark's gospel has a much livelier description: 'Suddenly, at the third hour, there was darkness over the whole earth, and angels descended from heaven, and springing up [?] into the brilliance of the living God, they ascended together with him, and suddenly there was light.' The text is not clear, but we gather that there is a miraculous intervention of angels who descend from and return to heaven. The gospel of Peter, an apocryphal writing from the second century, tries to describe the phenomenon of the resurrection in the grand manner. It introduces two figures whose heads are as high as the heavens, and who are plainly angels; these two descend from heaven to the tomb; then a voice thunders, coming from the tomb, and the two figures come out framing a third and even taller figure, whose head is higher than the heavens. This attempt to describe how Christ rises from death and enters into glory is presumptuous and in doubtful taste. Compared with such pretentious descriptions we can appreciate Matthew's discretion; he uses a biblical manner and cosmic imagery to describe a basic fact: the entry of Christ into the kingdom of God.

The empty tomb

On entering the tomb they saw a young man in a white robe seated on the right-hand side, and they were struck with amazement (Mk 16:5). This young man, plainly an angel, is clothed in white (as angels always are) and is sitting on the right, which is the nobler side. As usual the marvellous strikes the women with amazement. We recognise the usual biblical setting for a manifestation of the divine: the angel is a reflection of the majesty of God and serves as his messenger.

Luke is slightly different. On entering [they] discovered that the body of the Lord Jesus was not there. As they stood there not knowing what to think, two men in brilliant clothing suddenly appeared at their side (Lk 24:3–4). One angel or two? It hardly matters, since neither Mark nor Luke saw them. Similarly at Jericho, were there one or two blind men? These slight variations in tradition are of no importance. These men are obviously angels, and the women are afraid.

The angel, or angels, speak to the frightened women. But he said to them, 'There is no need for alarm. You are looking for Jesus of Nazareth, who was crucified: he has risen, he is not here. See, here is the place where they laid him' (Mk 16:6). In this very simple way the resurrection is announced. Matthew's text is almost identical: 'There is no need for you to be afraid'. He has added 'for you' to distinguish them from the guards who were shaking and half-dead with fear. The soldiers might well be afraid since they were enemies, but the women have nothing to fear. 'I know you are looking for

Jesus, who was crucified' – Matthew does not say 'of Nazareth' but it comes to the same thing – '*He is not here, for he has risen, as he said he would. Come and see the place where he lay*' (Mt 28:5–6). The account is substantially the same as Mark's.

. Then the angel gives the women an errand. '*But you must go and tell his disciples and Peter, "He is going before you to Galilee; it is there you will see him, just as he told you*" ' (Mk 16:7). The Greek word *proagein* can mean 'to go before, precede' or even 'to lead'; so here it can be understood as either 'Jesus is going to lead you back to Galilee just as he used formerly to lead you from Judaea to Galilee' or 'Jesus is going before you and you will find him there'. Whichever we adopt, Mark is indicating that there will be a meeting in Galilee. We shall see later the difficulties raised by this.

Matthew says substantially the same as Mark again. '*Then go quickly and tell his disciples, "He has risen from the dead and now he is going before you to Galilee; it is there you will see him". Now I have told you.*'

But Luke records the message of the angels in a somewhat different form. *Terrified, the women lowered their eyes. But the two men said to them, 'Why look among the dead for someone who is still alive?*' (Lk 24:5). Here we find a theological statement very characteristic of Luke, who in speaking of the resurrection is fond of applying the Pauline antithesis of death and life. He makes the two disciples on the way to Emmaus say, 'Some women from our group . . . came back to tell us they had seen a vision of angels who declared he was alive' (Lk 24:22–3). This idea of the *living Jesus* is found again in the Acts of the Apostles when Paul in his discussions with the Jews asserts that Jesus is alive (Ac 25:19).

Still more worthy of note is the description of the women lowering their eyes to the ground and being reproached by the angel for looking among the dead: don't turn to the earth where the dead are, look upwards where the living are; lift up your eyes, leave off this unhappy searching below for someone who is above. The opposite is to happen at the ascension: when Jesus has just ascended to heaven and the disciples are still looking up to the sky, the angel says, 'Don't look up to heaven any longer, Jesus has gone and is not coming back till the Parousia' (Ac 1:11). Jesus has already told them to go back to Jerusalem to receive the Holy Spirit, since the apostles still have work to do on earth. From the theological point of view these two scenes are complementary. It is a mistake for men to be always one step behind, sometimes clinging to the earth when Jesus has risen, sometimes wanting to keep their eyes fixed on the heavens when they have to live and work here below.

'*Remember what he told you when he was still in Galilee: that the Son of Man had to be handed over into the power of sinful men and be crucified, and rise again on the third day?*' *And they remembered his words* (Lk 24:6–8). Luke has kept the word Galilee, but changed the sense. According to Mark and Matthew, the angel announces a rendezvous in Galilee, which is where most of the appearances are to take place. But in Luke all the appearances happen in Judaea, at Emmaus, in Jerusalem, on the Mount of Olives; this is why he alters the phrase so as to avoid mentioning a rendezvous in Galilee. By using the past tense, he makes it refer to predictions which Jesus made when he was in Galilee. Luke is a skilful writer and knows how to get himself out of a difficulty gracefully.

How does the scene end? According to Mark, *the women came out and ran away from the tomb because they were frightened out of their wits; and they said nothing to a soul, for they were afraid* . . . (Mk 16:8). The poor women are so frightened that they do not carry out the errand they have been given. But it is not the Jews they are afraid of. They are seized with fear in the face of a miracle.

According to Matthew, it is the opposite: they are filled with joy. *Filled with awe and great joy, the women came quickly away from the tomb and ran to tell the disciples* (Mt 28:8). They are on their way to tell them, when they meet Jesus.

Luke's account is different again: *they told all this to the Eleven and to all the others.* And he then gives their names, *Mary of Magdala, Joanna and Mary the mother of James. The other women with them also told the apostles, but this story of theirs seemed pure nonsense, and they did not believe them* (Lk 24:9–11). We see then that the women's message for the apostles is handled differently by each of the three synoptics: in Mark they keep their mouths shut and do not dare to speak; in Matthew, they are full of joy and eager to tell everything; in Luke, they give their message but are not listened to.

A more serious difficulty is that Mark's narrative ends abruptly at this point. It is true that our present editions of his gospel tell us the sequel, but this sequel is not from the same hand, and today everyone acknowledges that the conclusion has been added later. There are even different conclusions to be found in the manuscripts. The way in which Mark's gospel came to an end seemed surprising, and it was felt that a suitable conclusion ought to be added. The ending which has been accepted into the Church's canon has authority and must be regarded as inspired by the Holy Spirit, but it is not the authentic work of Mark.

What is the explanation of this? Did Mark write a conclusion which was lost, perhaps on a sheet of manuscript which got torn off and disappeared? Was the conclusion deliberately suppressed, and if so by whom? The critics are divided. For some, it seems impossible that the book should have ended so abruptly; Mark must have written an ending which recorded the appearances in Galilee as the angel had foretold them, and for some reason of which we are ignorant this ending must have been suppressed. For others, no portion of the text has been lost: Mark chose to end his gospel without describing the appearances, perhaps because he envisaged writing a second book. One critic has even suggested that at the beginning of the Acts of the Apostles Luke is using a source which is to be identified as Mark's second book; but this is guesswork. For myself, for reasons which I will go into later (pp. 260f), I have the impression that Mark decided to end his gospel at this point without mentioning the appearances. He felt it sufficient to have announced the fact of the resurrection in the angel's words, and so his gospel ends quite satisfactorily on the affirmation that Jesus has risen from the dead.

Before taking Luke's verse 12, it will be best to study what John tells us, with which that verse is closely linked.

The narrative of John: the discovery of the empty tomb[1]

As in the account of the burial, John here gives us three fragments juxtaposed: the discovery of the empty tomb by Peter and John (Jn 20:1–10), the appearance of the angels to Mary of Magdala (Jn 20:11–14a), the appearance of Jesus to Mary of Magdala (Jn 20:14b–18). Again, it seems to me, we have a case where there are three different strata in the tradition.

It was very early on the first day of the week and still dark, when Mary of Magdala came to the tomb (Jn 20:1). This is very like the synoptics, but Mary of Magdala is alone, or at least the only one named. *She saw that the stone had been moved away from the tomb*

---

[1] Cf. P. BENOIT, 'Marie-Madeleine et les Disciples au Tombeau selon Jn 20: 1–18' in *Judentum, Urchristentum, Kirche* (Festschrift für Joachim Jeremias, Beiheft 26 zur ZNW), Berlin, 1960, pp. 141–52.

(Jn 20:1). Here the narrative differs from the synoptics: Mary neither goes nor looks in, but runs to warn Peter. We have to be careful not to take all the gospels together as is so often done, but to read John by himself. No angels appear to her at this point; that is to come later. For the moment, as soon as she sees that the stone has been removed, she rushes off to Peter without stopping to go closer to the tomb.

And came running to Simon Peter and the other disciple, the one Jesus loved. 'They have taken the Lord out of the tomb' she said 'and we don't know where they have put him' (Jn 20:2). Mary plays the part of a messenger, bringing the apostles the news that the tomb is empty. She has not seen Jesus or the angels; she realises that the tomb is empty and jumps to the conclusion that he must have been taken away; she has no thought yet of the resurrection. Panic-stricken, she goes looking for the chief of the apostles to tell him this new development which she feels must be serious. Her use of the first person plural betrays the fact that she is not alone; John is thus in agreement with the synoptics. Peter, startled, goes off in his turn.

Peter set out with the other disciple to go to the tomb. They ran together, but the other disciple, running faster than Peter, reached the tomb first; he bent down and saw the linen cloths lying on the ground, but did not go in. Simon Peter who was following now came up, went right into the tomb, saw the linen cloths on the ground, and also the cloth that had been over his head; this was not with the linen cloths but rolled up in a place by itself. Then the other disciple who had reached the tomb first also went in; he saw and he believed. Till this moment they had failed to understand the teaching of scripture, that he must rise from the dead. The disciples then went home again (Jn 20:3–10).

The account is exact and lively. Two details are to be kept in mind. First, there is the disciple who runs faster and arrives at the tomb first, who waits for Peter and effaces himself in Peter's presence, and who then enters and believes. Secondly, the description of the various cloths, giving the impression that they have been carefully arranged. We know that John does not describe anything for the mere pleasure; what is his purpose here?

The two disciples

Every exegete agrees that there is a symbol or a hidden meaning here. Some hold that the coming of the two disciples symbolises the

Church and the Synagogue. The Synagogue runs and arrives first
without going in, while the Church arrives later but enters first into
the faith of Christ. But this is a very artificial interpretation and
bears little relation to the meaning of the narrative.

John's thought seems simpler. We find quite frequently in his
gospel the theme of rivalry between Peter and another disciple. This
combination of Peter and the 'other' occurs several times: Peter is
always shown as the leader, older and more venerable, but the other
is also important and surpasses Peter in certain respects. It is almost
as though we could hear John's disciples wanting to put their master,
if not above Peter, at least on the same level. They are proud of their
master's intuition.

Here are some of the facts: during the supper, the 'disciple whom
Jesus loved' is leaning on his breast and Peter has to question the
Lord through him. The disciple puts the question and transmits the
answer (Jn 13:23-6). Later, when the two of them arrive at Caiaphas'
palace, Peter does not go in, whereas the 'other', who knows the
high priest's household, succeeds in getting Peter in. So the chief
of the apostles needs his help (Jn 18:15-16). We shall come across
another instance of this rivalry, when Jesus tells Peter about his
martyrdom. Peter asks, 'What about him, Lord?', and Jesus answered, 'If I want him to stay behind till I come, what does it matter
to you? You are to follow me' (Jn 21:21). The same preoccupation
appears in all these passages, which is to put the leader of the
Johannine circle on the same level as Peter.

These parallels explain the way in which the present scene is
managed. Peter, the elder of the two, arrives last, but the 'other',
out of deference, has not gone in. It is for Peter, as the chief apostle,
to go in first. However, the 'other' has greater insight; from the
moment he enters he sees and believes. There is no mention of
Peter's believing. It is worth recalling here, too, a detail from the
miraculous draught of fishes – Jesus appears on the shore and the
disciples do not recognise him at first; when, however, the 'disciple
whom Jesus loved' says, 'It is the Lord', Peter immediately throws
himself into the water to go and meet him (Jn 21:7). The chief
of the apostles is often the first to leap into action, but not the
first to understand; here too it is the 'other' who has recognised
Jesus.

It may have been noticed that the disciple opposed to Peter in this
friendly rivalry is called sometimes 'the other disciple' (Jn 18:15;

20:2, 3, 4, 8), sometimes 'the disciple Jesus loved' (Jn 13:23; 19:26; 20:2; 21:7, 20). Some exegetes have suggested that the two different expressions must refer to two distinct people. But the similarity of the relationship to Peter inclines one to take it as one and the same person, and the different ways in which he is referred to as the result of different stages of composition. Besides, their identity is clearly indicated by the writer of 20:2, who has deliberately linked the two formulas, 'the other disciple, the one Jesus loved'. As for the person who is hidden behind this anonymity, a firm and ancient tradition identifies him with the apostle John himself, the master of the Johannine circle. This identification seems wholly plausible.

The linen bands and the head-cloth

This is the moment for us to discuss whether we can decide what the clothes were that Jesus was wrapped in. The synoptics mention only a shroud. John, when describing the burial by Nicodemus, speaks of linen bands or cloths, *othonia*, and here adds a *soudarion*, a cloth for the head. How can we reconcile these different data, and do they confirm or invalidate the celebrated shroud of Turin[1]?

Discussions of this subject are numerous and I cannot enter into details, but I would like to draw attention to the limitations of what can be proved by exegesis. Exegetes have tried to combine the data of John and those of the synoptics. Sometimes they have tried to make the shroud of the latter identical with the head-cloth of the former; but the word *soudarion* does not refer to a large shroud, but to a cloth which covers the head. Sometimes, in order to reconcile the four gospels, the following solution is proposed: the shroud of the synoptics was torn into strips and so became the linen bands of John. But this is very unlikely; if you want linen strips, you do not go and buy a large sheet and tear it up. Others draw attention to the fact that the Greek word *othonia* does not refer to linen bands but merely to pieces of cloth; it might thus be possible that John's cloths and the synoptic shroud were the same thing. And to this others add that the word *sindon* is badly translated: it does not necessarily mean a single piece of cloth like a shroud, but can mean several pieces. These would be the linen cloths of John.

[1] Cf. F.–M. Braun, *Le linceul de Turin et l'évangile de S. Jean. Étude de critique et d'exégèse*, Paris, 1940: J. Blinzler, *Das Turiner Grablinnen und die Wissenschaft*, Ettal, 1952.

After these vain attempts to reconcile all the data, yet other exegetes try to combine them all – shroud, linen-bands and head-cloth. According to them, Jesus was first wrapped in a large sheet, then linen-bands were wound round, and lastly his face was covered with the head-cloth. But this is to carry the desire to harmonise the data too far. Others think that it is impossible to reconcile John and the synoptics – the linen-bands and the shroud – at all. One has even come to the conclusion[1] that there were two burials; in the first, on the Friday evening, described by the synoptics, the body was not washed but rolled rapidly in a shroud; then, on the Saturday evening, the apostles came back, took the body, washed and wound it in the cloths described by John. The chief thing wrong with this hypothesis is that it is totally without foundation; there is nothing to show that there was a second burial on the Saturday evening, and a great deal against it. The only reason for putting it forward is that it helps to explain the Shroud of Turin. The Holy Shroud presupposes that the body was rolled in a single cloth without being washed, so that the blood and sweat produced the familiar imprint. If linen bands were used this impression could not have been made. But even the desire to safeguard the Holy Shroud cannot justify a theory which is inadmissible in itself, the theory of two successive burials.

For myself, I think we have to give up any idea of reconciling John and the synoptics. Neither of them set out to give us an exact representation of what happened. But perhaps John, once again, is the more worthy of belief. The synoptics do not mention the shroud as though it were a detail they had actually observed, but as part of the normal process of burying; so that their account is not be taken as possessing that kind of exactness from which we could draw scientific conclusions. If I had to choose I would prefer to follow John, while at the same time doubting whether his *othonia* were really linen-bands. This way of wrapping Egyptian mummies was hardly usual in Palestine, and it is possible that John only spoke in this way to suggest the bonds of death which Jesus broke (cf. Jn 11:44).

To sum up, the data supplied by the gospels, which are very simple but difficult to reconcile – and in the case of the synoptics somewhat

---

[1] Cf. W. BULST, 'Untersuchungen zum Begräbnis Christi' in *Münchener Theologische Zeitschrift*, III, 1952, pp. 244–55; and the refutation by J. BLINZLER, '*Zur Auslegung der Evangelienberichte über Jesu Begräbnis*', ibid., pp. 403–14.

artificial, since they are not writing as eye-witnesses – are not sufficiently precise to allow us to settle the debate over the Shroud. As an exegete, I prefer to opt out of the debate and leave it to historians or photographers or chemists to say what they can about this strange relic.

One last thing remains to be said about John's description and the way in which he makes it plain that the clothes are carefully arranged, the *othonia* in one place, separate from the *soudarion* which is put tidily on one side. Why is John so exact about this? Doubtless in order to show that there is no question of any ordinary robbery or theft, but instead that a divine hand – a non-human hand as Pascal might say – has passed by. Robbers, or the apostles themselves, would have handled the body hastily, the cloths would have been left scattered all over the place, as they were when mummies were stolen from Egyptian tombs. But here everything is well ordered, as though God, or his angels, had wanted to take the Lord away without upsetting anything.

The narrative of Luke: Peter at the tomb

Luke's narrative offers a curious parallel to John's, despite certain differences: *Peter, however, went running to the tomb. He bent down and saw the binding cloths but nothing else; he then went back home, amazed at what had happened* (Lk 24:12). This has features in common with John – Peter's visit to the tomb, the attitude of the apostle bending down, seeing the linen-bands lying there and then returning home. But there are differences too; Peter is alone, and nothing is said about the other disciple who runs faster, who does not go in but is the first to believe. In Luke, Peter goes away amazed, knowing only that the tomb is empty.

A certain doubt hangs over this verse of Luke's; it is not found in all the manuscripts. This disturbs the critics. Some believe that it is not by Luke at all, but has been added by a copyist who got his inspiration from John. It is a fact that Luke's verse 13 follows very well after verse 11 and this gives one the impression of an addition. According to other critics, this is not the case at all; on the contrary, Luke is John's source, and John has merely expanded this verse. However, it is still difficult to believe that John was able to draw his account and all the details it includes from such a brief verse of Luke's. And in fact Luke's text makes use both of Johannine words which he must have got from John, and at the same time Lucan

words which cannot be the work of a copyist but must be Luke's
own. From this we have to conclude that Luke knew, if not this very
passage of John, at least a tradition on which John also depends too.
Luke decided, perhaps later, to include it in his gospel and wrote this
verse for the purpose. Se we have in Luke and John two independent
but parallel traditions stemming from a common source which
recorded how Peter ran to the tomb and found it empty. Luke's
concise version will help us to recover the primitive form of this
source and to see how John has expanded it.

In Luke, Peter alone goes to the tomb. In actual fact, at Emmaus
the disciples are to say, 'Some of our friends went to the tomb and
found everything exactly as the women has reported' (Lk 24:24).
Luke, then, was aware that there were several disciples, but here he
only mentions Peter, and this suggests that the whole development
concerning the other disciple is an instance of John's usual way of
expanding. There is another important detail: Luke does not say
that Peter believed; he goes home surprised, as though he had not
understood. This could well be the primitive form of the tradition.
In this way, by comparing Luke and John, we arrive at what seems
to be the oldest tradition, older even than Mark's. According to this,
on which both Luke and John depend, Peter hears the news from
Mary of Magdala, goes to the tomb, finds it empty and is surprised,
but returns without seeing either Jesus or the angels. There is
nothing in this to disturb critics who are afraid of the supernatural
or the marvellous; it is precious for its very simplicity. I believe it
to be older even than the finding of the empty tomb as it is told by
the synoptics; and I shall now demonstrate this by looking at
John's passage concerning Mary of Magdala, and comparing it
with the synoptics.

The narrative of John: Mary of Magdala at the tomb

Meanwhile Mary stayed outside near the tomb, weeping (Jn 20:11).
John does not say where she has come from, nor what she has been
doing in the interval since she alerted Peter. We find her suddenly
at the tomb. The reader naturally assumes that she has come back
in the wake of Peter, waited politely at a little distance until the
apostles have looked at the tomb, and then, after their departure,
come closer. But this is all imagination: we have to recognise that
John says nothing of the kind and that the narrative here makes a

fresh start. This is another and different fragment, and the tradition tells us nothing about what preceded it; it is useless to try to combine it with the preceding passage. It stands by itself.

Then, still weeping, she stopped to look inside, and saw two angels in white sitting where the body of Jesus had been, one at the head, the other at the feet. They said, 'Woman, why are you weeping?' 'They have taken my Lord away' she replied 'and I don't know where they have put him.' As she said this she turned round . . . (Jn 20:11–14). This passage records an angelic manifestation (an angelophany) like that in the synoptics. But it is interesting to notice that here the angels serve no real purpose – rather like the angels on our altars – whereas in the synoptics they are used as messengers. Their question leads nowhere; and this suggests a doubt whether they are in their original position. The scene comes to life again when Jesus appears.

And saw Jesus standing there, though she did not recognise him (Jn 20:14). In all these appearances, Jesus does not reveal himself immediately, but only through a sign or a word which provokes an opening of the heart to faith.

Jesus said, 'Woman, why are you weeping? Who are you looking for?' Supposing him to be the gardener – the tomb is situated in a garden – *she said, 'Sir, if you have taken him away, tell me where you have put him, and I will go and remove him'* (Jn 20:15). Like Peter, the poor woman has no inkling yet of the resurrection; her heart is full of love but her faith has not yet been awakened – he isn't there, I want to find him even though he's dead, I want to see him wherever he is. Before such love and such anxiety, Jesus utters the word which is necessary to open her heart – her name.

Jesus said, 'Mary! 'She knew him then and said to him in Hebrew, 'Rabbuni!' – *which means Master* (Jn 20:16). This is a moving expression. The form 'Rabbuni' has been found in some Aramaic writings from Palestine dating from the first century and is certainly contemporary with the gospel.

Jesus said to her, ' Do not cling to me, because I have not yet ascended to the Father. But go and find the brothers, and tell them: I am ascending to my Father and your Father, to my God and your God.' (Jn 20:17). Jesus gives Mary a message as in the synoptics, but it is quite different; it has nothing to do with telling the apostles to go and find him in Galilee. Jesus gives to Mary, and so to them, an important theological lesson about his change of state. He is entering into glory, he is about to ascend to his Father – immediately, it seems; for in the evening he is to show himself to the apostles after ascending to his God. We can put it in this way: he will only come down again from his Father to show himself to the disciples. On leaving the tomb, his work – if we may use the expression – is to go to the Father, in glory. This is why he says, '*Do not cling to me*'. Mary had probably clutched his feet in the same gesture of affection she had used formerly. But it was no longer the moment for this; from now on, Jesus says, I belong to another world, you must let me alone; I am going to come back but first I have to ascend to my Father (in John's language, this means enter into the state of glory); I was flesh, I am becoming spirit.

When Jesus returns he will be wholly spiritualised, especially in the Eucharist. Here we should remind ourselves of those words from the discourse on the Bread of Life, 'Does this upset you? What if you should see the Son of Man ascend to where he was before?' (Jn 6:61), and this itself is to be read in the context where Jesus is speaking of the Bread that comes down from heaven and goes on to say, 'It is the spirit which gives life, the flesh has nothing to offer' (Jn 6:63). In the light of this parallel, it is plain that in the present passage Jesus is announcing the end of the material contacts of the preceding period. His state has changed, no one can take hold of him as they used to. But Mary is not to be afraid, he is coming back in a new, glorified, spiritualised state. In fact, of course, Jesus does come back to his own in the Eucharist and the other sacraments; we touch him again, but not in the same physical way that his contemporaries could during his earthly life. This then is the teaching, the doctrinal message that John puts into Jesus' mouth, and which Mary is to transmit to the apostles.

So Mary of Magdala went and told the disciples that she had seen the Lord and that he had said these things to her (Jn 20:18).

There is a striking parallel to this scene in Matthew. Matthew has just told us how the women set out, full of joy, to announce the news of the resurrection. *And there, coming to meet them, was Jesus. 'Greetings' he said, And the women came up to him and, falling down before him, clasped his feet. Then Jesus said to them, 'Do not be afraid; go and tell my brothers that they must leave for Galilee; they will see me there'* (Mt 28:9–10).

Everyone acknowledges that this short scene in Matthew is parallel to John's. There are certain differences; several women instead of Mary alone, and a much simpler message from Jesus, merely the repetition of the angels' message that they are to repair to Galilee. But one detail helps to explain John's account of the meeting with Mary: the women fall to the ground and clasp his feet; and this gesture justifies the 'Do not cling to me' uttered by Jesus to Mary.

The two accounts are complementary and critics agree in seeing them as two versions of the same appearance of Jesus to the holy women.

Comparison of the appearances to Mary

It remains for us to compare this appearance of Jesus to Mary with that of the angels. According to Mark, neither Peter nor John appears on the scene, nor does he record an appearance of Jesus to Mary. All Mark describes is the empty tomb and the angels who explain why it is empty. This is the essence of Mark's account, which is taken over by Matthew and Luke.

In John, on the other hand, it is Mary who finds the tomb empty, though she does not go in and only carries the news; the tomb is then visited by Peter and John, and lastly Jesus appears to Mary. When these narratives are compared in detail, it appears that John represents an older tradition, and this confirms a conclusion that we have already foreseen on other occasions: although it was composed later, John's gospel, in its earliest strata, preserves memories that are older even than those of the synoptics.

Luke demonstrates the historical validity of Peter and John's running to the tomb, by stripping it of details that overlay it in John. In Luke, it is perfectly plausible; it is simply and convincingly told and with no element of the marvellous: Peter, with one or perhaps several companions, found the tomb empty and went away bewildered. Our Easter faith begins from the objectively established and inescapable fact of the empty tomb. The fact is firmly established and John is a good witness. The appearance to Mary, too, is wholly probable; John's account is supported by Matthew, and although he has given it a theological content, that content fits the situation. On the other hand, John's account of the appearance of the angels to Mary seems to lack a proper foundation. I think, in fact, that we have here another piece of literary composition similar to that of the accounts of the burial. They both begin with a Johannine fragment totally independent of the synoptics, at the burial the lance-thrust, here the running to the tomb; they both end with a narrative which

resembles the synoptics while also showing Johannine characteristics, there the burial by Nicodemus, here the appearance to Mary;
and in between, each has a short passage which has been put in
under the direct influence of the synoptics, there Joseph of Arimathaea, here the appearance of the angels.

When we look closely at this appearance of angels recorded by
John (Jn 20:11–13), we can see that it is made up of reminiscences
taken either from the synoptics or from the immediate context in
John. It must have been done by someone who wanted to remind us
of the synoptic account, but the result is clumsy; the angels have
become mere ciphers; there are two angels (as in Luke), clothed in
white (as in all three synoptics), sitting (as in Mark) one at the head
and one at the feet. The angels say,' *Woman, why are you weeping?*"
(Jn 20:13), but this is exactly what Jesus is going to say in verse 15.
The composer of the passage has not looked very far afield, he is
working from the immediate context. Mary's reply is taken from
verse 2, '*They have taken my Lord away and I don't know where they
have put him*' (Jn 20:13). Then again, in the present text of John,
Mary turns round twice, and this is difficult to explain. Some exegetes have gone so far as to suggest that Mary is disturbed because
Jesus appears to her naked, in all the beauty of his risen body, a
suggestion which is wholly out of place! This duplication arises
from the fact that the text has been worked over; the two turnings
correspond to two different layers of composition.

The ending of Mark's gospel

From the comparison of Mark and John's narratives there emerges
a possible explanation of the strange way in which Mark ended his
gospel (Mk 16:8). Mark must have known the primitive tradition:
Mary of Magdala found the tomb empty (and nothing more) and
went to tell Peter. But Mark, having decided not to include the
appearance of Jesus, and wishing to announce the Easter miracle at
the end of his gospel, made up his mind to use the finding of the
empty tomb as his opportunity to proclaim the 'Easter kerygma'.
For this purpose, he introduces an angel – a classical technique in
the Bible – and puts the Easter kerygma into his mouth.

If we examine the angel's words in Mark we find the same proclamation of the Easter message that is continually on Peter's lips
in the Acts of the Apostles. Mark had conceived the whole scene as a

way of proclaiming the resurrection to those who already believe: the message of the resurrection was first heard at the empty tomb from the lips of an angel.

We can and must believe in the existence of the angelic world, but we are not obliged to admit that an angel actually appeared every time that the biblical narratives bring one on the scene. When an author wanted to express a message from God, a supernatural manifestation or a statement of faith, it was an accepted custom to put it into the mouth of an angel. We cannot do justice to the biblical writers unless we realise that this was their procedure.

It is my belief, then, that the primitive tradition is reflected better by Luke and best of all by John – Mary of Magdala, and Peter after her, saw the empty tomb and were astounded by it, no more. Then followed the appearances of Jesus which explained everything. The empty tomb was established without any angelic apparitions. This, I believe, was the first and most ancient form of the tradition. Mark is evidence for a second stage: having decided, for reasons of his own, against recording the appearances, he has to link the explanation to the finding of the empty tomb and so, by means of the angel, he announces straight away the fact of the resurrection.

Many 'independent' critics reject these narratives because of the artificial character of such angelic apparitions. The analysis which I have proposed should do away with their objections and restore a tradition about the discovery of the tomb which, despite its greater simplicity, preserves its full value. In this way, the discovery ceases to look like a late and suspect invention and becomes once more a firm and original fact, a primitive datum which, with the subsequent appearances, is fit to be the justification and the foundation of Christian faith in the resurrection of Jesus.

11. The Appearances of the Risen Jesus at Emmaus and in Jerusalem

THE APPEARANCE TO THE DISCIPLES AT EMMAUS

Mt	Mk
	16:12–13

¹³ That very same day, two of them were on their way
to a village called Emmaus, seven miles from Jerusalem,
¹⁴ and they were talking together about all that
had happened.
¹⁵ Now as they talked this over, Jesus himself came up
and walked by their side;
¹⁶ but something prevented them from recognising him.
¹⁷ He said to them, 'What matters are you discussing
as you walk along?' They stopped short, their
faces downcast.
¹⁸ Then one of them, called Cleopas, answered him,
'You must be the only person staying in Jerusalem
who does not know the things that have been
happening there these last few days'.
¹⁹ 'What things?' he asked. 'All about Jesus of
Nazareth' they answered 'who proved he was a
great prophet by the things he said and did in
the sight of God and of the whole people;
²⁰ and how our chief priest and our leaders
handed him over to be sentenced to death, and
had him crucified.
²¹ Our own hope had been that he would be the
one to set Israel free. And this is not all: two whole
days have gone by since it all happened;
²² and some women from our group have astounded
us: they went to the tomb in the early morning,
²³ and when they did not find the body, they came back to
tell us they had seen a vision of angels who declared he
was alive.
²⁴ Some of our friends went to the tomb and found
everything exactly as the women had reported, but of
him they saw nothing.'
²⁵ Then he said to them, 'You foolish men! So slow to
believe the full message of the prophets!
²⁶ Was it not ordained that the Christ should suffer and
so enter into his glory?'
²⁷ Then, starting with Moses and going through all the
prophets, he explained to them the passages throughout
the scriptures that were about himself.
²⁸ When they drew near to the village to which they were
going, he made as if to go on;
²⁹ but they pressed him to stay with them. 'It is nearly
evening' they said 'and the day is almost over.' So
he went in to stay with them.

Mt   Mk

APPEARANCE TO THE DISCIPLES IN JERUSALEM

Mt   Mk   Lk 24:36–43

6 ⁴⁷ When evening came . . .

                       ³⁶ They were still talking about
                       all this

⁴⁸ . . . he came towards them,
walking on the lake . . .

                       when he himself stood among
                       them,
                       and said to them, 'Peace be
                       with you!'
                       ³⁷ In a state of alarm and
                       fright,

⁴⁹ . . . they thought   they thought
it was a ghost . . .   they were seeing a ghost.
                       ³⁸ But he said,
⁵⁰ . . . they . . . were   'Why are you so agitated,
terrified . . .

                       and why are these doubts
                       rising in your hearts?
                       ³⁹ Look at my hands

Lk

³⁰ Now while he was with them at table, he took the
bread and said the blessing; then he broke it and
handed it to them.

³¹ And their eyes were opened and they recognised him;
but he had vanished from their sight.

³² Then they said to each other, 'Did not our hearts burn
within us as he talked to us on the road and explained
the scriptures to us?'

³³ They set out that instant and returned to Jerusalem.
There they found the Eleven assembled together with their
companions,

³⁴ who said to them, 'Yes, it is true. The Lord has risen
and has appeared to Simon.'

³⁵ Then they told their story of what had happened on
the road and how they had recognised him at the breaking
of bread.

Jn 20:19–20	Jn
¹⁹ In the evening of that same day, the first day of the week, the doors were closed in the room where the disciples were, for fear of the Jews.	20 ²⁶ Eight days later the disciples were in the house again and Thomas was with them.
Jesus came and stood among them.	The doors were closed, but Jesus came in and stood among them.
He said to them, 'Peace be with you',	'Peace be with you' he said.
²⁰ and (having said this)*	²⁷ Then he spoke to Thomas,
showed them his hands	'Put your finger here; look, here are my hands. Give me your hand;

Mt	Mk	Lk

		and feet;
'. . . it is I! Do not be afraid.'		yes, it is I indeed.
		Touch me and see for yourselves;
		a ghost has no flesh and bones
		as you can see I have.'
	16:14	
		⁴⁰ And as he said this
		he showed them his hands
		and feet.
		⁴¹ Their joy was so great
		that they still could not believe
		it,
		and they stood there dumb-
		founded;
		so he said to them,
		'Have you anything here to eat?'
		⁴² And they offered him a piece
		of grilled fish,
		⁴³ which he took and ate
		before their eyes.

APPEARANCE TO THE DISCIPLES INCLUDING THOMAS

Mt	Mk	Lk

Jn   Jn

and his side. | put it into my side.

                                     | Doubt no longer but believe.'

The disciples were filled with joy
when they saw the Lord,

                                     | 21 ⁵ Jesus called out,
                                     | 'Have you any food?'*

Jn 20:24-29

24 Thomas, called the Twin, who was one of the Twelve, was not
with them when Jesus came
    ²⁵ When the disciples said, 'We have seen the Lord', he answered,
'Unless I see the holes that the nails made in his hands and can
put my finger into the holes they made, and unless I can put
my hand into his side, I refuse to believe'.
    ²⁶ Eight days later the disciples were in the house again and Thomas
was with them. The doors were closed, but Jesus came in and
stood among them. 'Peace be with you' he said.
    ²⁷ Then he spoke to Thomas, 'Put your finger here; look, here
are my hands, Give me your hand; and put it into my side. Doubt
no longer but believe.'
    ²⁸ Thomas replied, 'My Lord and my God!'
    ²⁹ Jesus said to him, 'You believe because you can see me.
Happy are those who have not seen and yet believe.'

Luke's story of the disciples on the road to Emmaus has a beautiful poetic quality as well as being deeply spiritual and theological. But on reading it we come across certain historical and theological problems which we shall take in that order.

The historical basis of the appearance at Emmaus

There can be no doubt that this narrative is based on a historical reality, but Luke has not presented it as though it were an interview: it is a theological and liturgical composition. It is for us to uncover the author's intentions.

What is the setting of this event? It takes place *that very same day* (Lk 24:13), that is, on Easter Sunday. *Two of them were on their way* to Emmaus, probably two disciples. The expression 'two of them', however, seems odd after verse 12 which is concerned with Peter's visit to the tomb; it would follow more easily after verse 11, in which the women speak to the disciples but are not believed. It is possible that verse 12 is an addition, but if it is I believe it to have been made by Luke himself since it is in his style.

Two of them were on their way to a village called Emmaus, seven miles from Jerusalem (Lk 24:13). Here there are problems which cannot be evaded, to do with the distance and the site.

The name of the village is Ammaous. One Ammaous, well known to us through the history of the Maccabees, figures in the Bible, in Josephus and in the Mishna: this is an important and famous town, which became Nicopolis in the third century and was the birthplace of a Christian writer, Julius Africanus. It was situated quite certainly where the present-day Amwas now stands, near Latrun. There is nothing doubtful here. The details of the Seleucid campaign against the Maccabees, Gorgias' attack on the camp at Emmaus (1 M 4:1–25), all fit in very well with the topography of Amwas. But was this the only Ammaous? Is Luke perhaps referring to another place with the same name?

The name Ammaous is the Greek transcription of a Hebrew word which means a spring, or even 'warm spring'. And, in fact, there is another site in Palestine, near Jerusalem, which is called Ammaous in Josephus (*Wars*, VII, 217); this is the present-day Kolonieh on the road to Jaffa, a little before Abu-Gosh. Kolonieh, a village which was destroyed in the fighting in 1948, had taken the place of the ancient Mozah, which appears in the lists in the Book of Joshua (Jos 18:26). The Mishnah (*Sukkah* 4, 5) says that the inhabitants of Jerusalem used to go there to pick willow branches for the feast of Tabernacles; and the Talmuds[1] identify this Mozah with Kolonieh. The latter name derives from the fact that the Romans established a colony of veterans there after the war of 70 A.D.; the original inhabitants must have quitted the village at this point, leaving the site to the Romans, and installed themselves on the plateau which rises to the north, the present Khirbet Mizzeh, where fragments of Roman and Byzantine pottery are still to be seen. Mozah was sometimes written Mizeh, and Mizzeh is an Arabic formation which must derive from it.

Other places have also been suggested, such as Abu-Gosh or Qubeibeh, but it must be admitted that these sites have never been called Ammaous. If certain Arabs today use the name Amwas in speaking of Qubeibeh, this is a tradition which has been invented within the last fifty years.

The distance mentioned – in the Greek, 60 stadia – is another factor which needs examination. Some manuscripts read 160 stadia. A stadion is roughly equivalent to about 202 yards, 60 stadia to something over 7 miles, and 160 to around 18 miles. The first Ammaous is just about 18 miles away. True enough, the distance is shorter if you go direct via Abu-Gosh, but the Roman road, by which the miles were counted, took the Bethoron (Beit Our) route, of which one fork leads to Modin (Medieh), the other to Amwas. This road is a good 18 miles. Père Abel and Père Vincent, who opted for this Ammaous[2] near Latrun, now Amwas, believed that their case was borne out by the name and by the distance.

But the figure of 160 is open to question, the best manuscripts read 60, and this latter figure is supported by a certain unanimity of manuscript evidence coming from very different regions. According to Père Lagrange and several other critics, with whom I include myself, the figure 160 is a correction, which can easily be seen to go

---

[1] Babylonian Talmud, *Sukkah*, 45a; Palestinian Talmud, *Sukkah*, iv, 3, 54b.
[2] L. H. VINCENT and F. M. ABEL, *Emmaüs. Sa basilique et son histoire*, Paris, 1932.

back to Origen[1]. Origen, a widely read and highly critical scholar, came to Palestine in the third century, made enquiries and got to know of this Ammaous, whereas the other had doubtless fallen into oblivion; he therefore concluded that this must be the Emmaus of the gospel. Julius Africanus, a Christian whose place of origin it was, must have contributed to this identification. Firmly convinced of it, Origen did not hesitate to alter the manuscripts, changing the figure 60 to the apparently more suitable 160. This may seem surprising, but it is not the only instance of topographical variants in the gospels in which Origen had a hand: Bethabara, Gerasenes, to name two. At the outset of his career, in an interesting article, Père Lagrange collected these instances[2]. Origen, with the best intentions, used to alter the manuscripts to adapt them to a topography which he thought to be certainly correct. The manuscripts of Palestinian origin affected by Origen's corrections read 160 stadia, while the majority are unscathed and read 60; this makes it difficult to accept the identification with Amwas near Latrun.

A further question regarding the distance has to be answered – surely 160 stadia is too far for them to have gone and come back in one day? This objection, however, has no force, and here I am prepared to defend a theory which I do not myself support, and concede that it is possible to travel to Amwas and return the same day. Suppose that the disciples leave Jerusalem at eight in the morning and walk at a pace of three miles an hour; they would arrive at Amwas at two in the afternoon. There they have a meal, and about three o'clock they recognise the Lord. It is highly unlikely that they would then take a siesta, still less stay the night, before setting out for Jerusalem to carry the good news! Once they had seen the Lord, they would have started back again, hiring asses or other mounts if necessary. Leaving at three o'clock they could have been back in Jerusalem by nine in the evening, where they would find the disciples at the Upper Room. The length of the journey then is not the real difficulty, it is the figure given in the manuscripts which is more serious.

Where then is Emmaus? Qubeibeh is certainly 60 stadia away, but it was picked out for exactly that reason, and its tradition does not appear until the thirteenth or fourteenth century. Kolonieh, it is

[1] Cf. M.-J. LAGRANGE, Comm. Luc, 4th ed., pp. 617f.
[2] 'Origène, la critique textuelle et le tradition topographique', in Revue Biblique, IV, 1895, pp. 501–24; V, 1896, pp. 87–92 (this last part deals with Emmaus).

objected, is no more likely since it is only 30 stadia away. This is true, but there could be a slight confusion in the physical data here without offending against scriptural inerrancy. Luke did not belong to the country, he merely noted down the information he had gathered: they went to Emmaus, came back the same evening, 60 stadia. Later, using these notes for the writing of his gospel, he makes Emmaus 60 stadia away, forgetting that the figure referred to the double journey. This is a possible explanation. In general, critics adopt Kolonieh as the Emmaus of the gospels. There is no real evidence, but in a case like this we have to be content with probabilities[1].

The narrative of Luke

And they were talking together about all that had happened. Now as they talked this over, Jesus himself came up and walked by their side; but something prevented them from recognising him (Lk 24:14–16). It was the will of God that their eyes should be deprived of the ability to recognise their Master.

In the conclusion of Mark's gospel – which, though it stands in the canonical gospel, is apocryphal, i.e. not from Mark's own hand – we read: *After this, he shows himself under another form to two of them as they were on their way into the country* (Mk 16:12). Here Jesus takes on other features and changes his appearance, whereas in Luke it is the eyes of the disciples that are hindered from recognising him. Which is right? It hardly matters. But it is interesting to note that, in all these appearances, Jesus is not immediately recognised, there has to be a gesture on his part and a movement of faith and love on the disciples' for him to be recognised. It means that he belongs to a new world, one that differs from the world of normal experience, and that one can only approach him now by rising above oneself.

He said to them, 'What matters are you discussing as you walk along?' They stopped short, their faces downcast. Then one of them, called Cleopas, answered him . . . (Lk 24:17–18). The two disciples have not yet been named; here now is the name of one, Cleopas or Clopas. We do not know anything else about him, but his name is a

---

[1] The basilica of Amwas would confirm the topography of Julius Africanus and Origen if the latter itself were not suspect. But, in addition, several archaeologists doubt whether the basilica dates from the third century.

likely one; it is an abbreviation of Cleopatros and is not rare. He is not therefore necessarily identical with the Clopas mentioned by John as the husband of one of the women called Mary (Jn 19:25).

The name of the other disciple remains unknown. He is sometimes called Ammaon, which is merely derived from Emmaus. Some conmentators have suggested Luke himself, but this is not likely; Luke tell us in his prologue that he had to consult witnesses, so he must belong to another generation. Others have suggested Nathanael, but for no good reason. Further on, Luke mentions Simon (Lk 24:34), but this evidently refers to another appearance, distinct from that of Emmaus. A more attractive solution, in my opinion, is that the other disciple was Philip the deacon. This narrative belongs to a cycle of events which took place in the region to the west of Jerusalem; they are recorded principally in the Acts of the Apostles and concern the actions of Peter and Philip at Lydda, Jaffa, on the road to Gaza and at Caesarea. Luke probably received all this information from Philip, who lived at Caesarea, where the evangelist could have visited him often enough during the two years of Paul's captivity there (Ac 8:40; 21:8; 23: 31–5; 24:27; 27:1). It would be perfectly comprehensible in these circumstances if the Emmaus episode had been told him by Philip, who had been one of the participants. However, this is conjecture.

Then one of them, called Cleopas, answered him, 'You must be the only person staying in Jerusalem who does not know the things that have been happening there these last few days'. 'What things?' he asked them (Lk 24:18–19). And the disciples relate the recent events concerning Jesus, what he had done and how he had come to be executed. Then they go on: '*And some women from our group have astounded us: they went to the tomb in the early morning, and when they did not find the body, they came back to tell us they had seen a vision of angels who declared he was alive. Some of our friends went to the tomb and found everything exactly as the women had reported, but of him they saw nothing*' (Lk 24:22–4) This recalls in an abbreviated form what Luke has told us about the apparition of angels and Peter's visit to the tomb. It is worth drawing attention to the phrase 'some of our friends' since it shows that Peter was not alone as verse 12 might suggest. Jesus then replies and opens their hearts, '*You foolish men! So slow to believe the full message of the prophets! Was it not ordained that the Christ should suffer and so enter into his glory?*' (Lk 24:25–6). And he explains the scriptures to them.

When they drew near to the village to which they were going, he made as if to go on; but they pressed him to stay with them. 'It is nearly evening' they said 'and the day is almost over' (Lk 24:28–9). These phrases ought not to be taken absolutely literally; it is very characteristic of Eastern hospitality to ask guests to stay – 'Night is falling, you can start out again tomorrow' – even if it is no later than two in the afternoon.

Now while he was with them at table, he took the bread and said the blessing; then he broke it and handed it to them. And their eyes were opened and they recognised him; but he had vanished from their sight. Then they said to each other, 'Did not our hearts burn within us as he talked to us on the road and explained the scriptures to us?' They set out that instant – without wasting a minute – *and returned to Jerusalem. There they found the Eleven assembled together with their companions, who said to them, 'Yes, it is true. The Lord has risen and has appeared to Simon.'* The disciples from Emmaus do not even have time to open their mouths before the Eleven forestall them – the Lord is risen! *Then they told their story of what had happened on the road and how they had recognised him at the breaking of bread* (Lk 24:30–5). Some manuscripts put the phrase in verse 34, 'It is true. The Lord has risen and has appeared to Simon', into the mouth of the two disciples. Simon then becomes one of these two, whose names are Cleopas and Simon. However, from a critical point of view, the best reading, 'they said to them', refers to the Eleven, not to the two disciples. It is the disciples gathered in Jerusalem who welcome the two who return from Emmaus and interrupt them with the news that the Lord has appeared to Simon. Then the two are allowed to tell their story of the appearance at Emmaus.

The significance of the narrative[1]

What are the important points in this exquisite narrative? We have seen already, from the name Emmaus, the name Cleopas and the general plausibility of the story, that it is based on actual experience. Even if the exact location of Emmaus cannot be decided and the disciples are not otherwise known, we feel that a real memory underlies it and that it is not the creation of Luke, as is sometimes said. Later we shall have to explain how this appearance in Judaea

---

[1] Cf. J. DUPONT, 'Les pèlerins d'Emmaus (Luc, XXIV, 13–35)', in *Miscellanea Biblica B. Ubach*, Montserrat, 1954, pp. 349–74.

is to be reconciled with those in Galilee. Here, we need only give an account of this experience, which the enemies of the marvellous have tried to eliminate.

Renan tried to explain this 'so-called' appearance in a naturalistic way, by postulating a kind of day-dream of the disciples. As evening falls, the memory of earlier meals shared with Jesus bathes them in melancholy. 'Full of a tender sadness, they forget the stranger; it is Jesus they see holding the bread, breaking it and offering it to them. These memories possess them to such a point that they do not notice that their companion, who has to continue his journey, has slipped away. And when they issue from their dream . . .[1]' It is Renan who is dreaming, his implausible commentary explains nothing.

Some critics admit that Luke set out to report an experience that was both actual and marvellous, a manifestation of Jesus Christ. But they believe also that it can be shown to be unreal by being compared with other miraculous stories from antiquity in which the divinity manifested itself. In the Bible, God (or the Angel of Yahweh) manifests himself to Hagar in the desert or to Abraham near Hebron; in the pagan world, similar apparitions are reported in connection with cures at Epidaurus, and so on. As regards Hagar and Abraham, we believe in them as true manifestations of God, through whatever images they may be presented. As for the pagan epiphanies, they are of another kind altogether.

There are, in fact, not all that many ways in which to describe the appearance of a spiritual being. Here, the tone is concrete and plausible; it is not an angel from heaven or a phantom, it is a man who shows himself to them. Jesus appears in a wholly human form, so much so that they fail to recognise him and take him for a fellow wayfarer.

Finally, we must understand Luke's intention; he is not setting out to tell us of the miraculous apparition of a god, as the pagans did, but to explain, in a catechetical and liturgical way, how Jesus manifested himself. These two aspects indeed are the distinguishing features of the narrative.

Its catechetical aspect

In the way in which the disciples recall recent events and Jesus answers them, we can recognise the outline of the primitive catechesis

[1] E. RENAN, *Les Apôtres*, Paris, 1866, p. 20.

as it is recorded in the Acts of the Apostles. The discourses in that book transmit the preaching of the first years of the Church, preaching in which the essential facts were proclaimed – Jesus lived as a man approved by God, he performed miracles, wonders, healings, he did good; the Jews killed him, but God raised him from the dead, of this we are witnesses and scripture proves it. This is the broad outline of Peter's sermons at Pentecost, before the Sanhedrin and to the household of Cornelius, and of Paul's at Antioch in Pisidia. Luke knew this primitive preaching well and has reproduced it. When we compare it with the story of the disciples on the way to Emmaus, we can see that Luke has composed Jesus' conversation with the disciples in the light of this traditional catechesis. This is what Cleopas and his companion say: '*All about Jesus of Nazareth, who proved he was a great prophet by the things he said and did in the sight of God and of the whole people; and how our chief priests and our leaders handed him over to be sentenced to death, and had him crucified*' (Lk 24:19–20). In the Greek, and even in the translation, we find almost word for word the terms which will recur in Acts. The two books are by the same author; he has composed the catechesis in the Acts of the Apostles on the pattern of the primitive preaching, and also used it in order to present the conversation of the disciples with Jesus. Jesus' answer is explicable in the same way: '*You foolish men! So slow to believe the full message of the prophets! Was it not ordained that the Christ should suffer and so enter into his glory?*' Then, starting with Moses and going through all the prophets, he explained to them the passages throughout the scriptures that were about himself* (Lk 24:25–7). The argument from scripture is never absent from Peter's sermons and the primitive preaching. So, in order to describe a real conversation, but one of which there was no shorthand record and which had taken place perhaps thirty years earlier, Luke describes only what was probably said and uses the exact terms of the catechesis. He sets down, as a teacher and theologian, the first expression of that 'kerygma', that primitive preaching on which the Church is to be founded – Jesus lived, he died and rose again, and this fact is proved by the testimony of the apostles and by the scriptures.

Its liturgical atmosphere

Furthermore, Luke has set this narrative in a liturgical atmosphere. The encounter ends with the breaking of bread and it is by this sign that the disciples recognise Jesus. Is this breaking of bread the Eucharist? This has been discussed for a very long time, and the Fathers often questioned this interpretation. Is it possible that, on the very evening of Easter Sunday, before two anonymous disciples who could not have been present in the Upper Room, where there were only the apostles, Jesus celebrated the Eucharist he had instituted two days before? Could the disciples of the Emmaus road have understood? It would be difficult to accept this, and many exegetes have maintained that it could not have been the Eucharist.

However, Luke uses language which certainly recalls the Eucharist. *He took the bread and said the blessing; then he broke it and handed it to them* (Lk 24:30). These are the precise actions emphasised at the Last Supper (Mt 26:26 and parallels) and already noted down by the evangelists at the multiplication of loaves (Mt 14:19 and parallels); Acts too mentions the breaking of bread several times (Ac 2:42, 46; 20:7, 11; 27:35). Apparently Luke wants to suggest the Eucharist to us and teach us that it is in that action that Jesus is to be recognised. Not that, as is sometimes imagined, Jesus had a special way of breaking the bread – we have, instead, to think of it on a theological and liturgical level.

Luke wants us to learn that in the Eucharist we are sharing a meal with Jesus; he makes himself a fellow guest with men and gives them holy bread; in this, faith recognises and makes contact with Christ. The disciples of the Emmaus road whose eyes were not opened eventually recognised Jesus in the liturgical context in which Christians, through the Eucharist, recognise Christ. So, when Luke writes this scene, he is thinking of all those liturgical assemblies of the early Church that he knows so well and loves so much; his faith knows that Jesus is present at those meals when the brethren assemble to break the bread of the Eucharist. He is present as a stranger who is not at first recognised, but when the bread is broken and the Eucharist eaten the eyes of the brethren are opened and they know by their faith that he is there, they see him, they eat with him.

This is the deeper meaning that we should gather from Luke's story, which is far more important than the outward aspect of that story. Luke wants to teach us, through this real encounter between Jesus and the disciples on the way to Emmaus, that Christians experience the same encounter when they go to the Eucharist.

This interpretation is justified by the fact that it appears again in the works of Luke. Luke sees the idea of the risen Jesus eating with his disciples as of great importance. Already, earlier in his gospel, he has emphasised this several times: for example, where Matthew has, 'Did we not cast out demons in your name?', Luke in the parallel text adds, 'We once ate and drank in your company' (Lk 13:26), thus underlining the importance of this eating and drinking with the Lord.

Further on, Matthew wrote, 'You will yourselves sit on twelve thrones to judge the twelve tribes of Israel' (Mt 19:28), and Luke adds, 'You will eat and drink at my table in my kingdom' (Lk 22:30). Plainly Luke is thinking of the heavenly banquet of the Eucharist and of eternal life; according to the rabbis as well as the gospel, eternal life is a great feast, a simple human image which symbolises the joy of fellowship with God and which Jesus uses in several parables.

Luke is fond of this theme, and this is why, in the post-resurrection appearances, he insists more than the others on the meals which Jesus shared with his disciples. We shall see further on that Jesus eats in the presence of his disciples that very evening in the Upper Room; Luke notes this fact partly to prove his body is real, but also because this communion with Jesus represents the encounter of faith at the Eucharist. The same concern appears at the beginning of the Acts, 'When he had been at table with them, he had told them . . .' (Ac 1:4) and in Peter's sermon to Cornelius, 'We are those witnesses – we have eaten and drunk with him after his resurrection from the dead' (Ac 10:41). It is Luke's own insistence on this theme which justifies our pointing out here how he has set out to teach us about the encounter with the Lord at the Eucharist.

I would go further. I think that narratives like this were conceived and composed in the atmosphere of the first liturgical assemblies. It is not only the detail at the end, but the whole way in which it is arranged, that suggests a plan based on the structure of the eucharistic assembly: first the readings, which recall the preparing of the way in scripture and then what Jesus himself did – the epistle and gospel; then the meal, to which the Lord comes and at which he is eaten. In a sort of forepart of the Mass, the Emmaus disciples have the scriptures explained to them in a discussion with Jesus; they are like catechumens receiving their first instructions and becoming open to faith. Then, when their hearts have been prepared by this preliminary catechesis, they join in the breaking of bread, the Lord makes himself present, and their eyes are opened. They make a spiritual communion, since they have encountered the Lord.

Already, in narrating the institution of the Eucharist, it seems as if Luke has added certain passages which are found elsewhere in Mark and Matthew, to make a kind of discourse suitable for a liturgical assembly. The dispute over precedence which rises among the disciples (Lk 22:24–7) and which is so startling at such a moment, must surely originally have been caused by the request of the sons of Zebedee (Mt 20:24–7). Luke will have inserted it here because its message – that the greatest must be the one who serves – is so suitable for the eucharistic celebration. In the assemblies of the first brethren, the apostles and the deacons gave themselves up to serving at table, looking after the poor, and distributing the bread, first the food for a normal meal and then the Eucharist; and they liked to recall the Lord's words about the equality of all and the service of the lesser by the greater. Luke follows this up with the saying about the twelve thrones from which the apostles are to judge the twelve tribes of Israel (Lk 22:28–30), thus providing a reminder of the ecclesiastical rank of the apostles in this liturgical setting. The passages concerning imminent tribulations, Peter's role in strengthening the faith of the rest, and the two swords (Lk 22:35–8), fall into place well enough in these first liturgical suppers of the brethren, in which they found encouragement for the struggle for the kingdom of God.

In the Acts of the Apostles we read, 'They remained faithful to the teaching of the apostles, to the brotherhood, to the breaking of bread and to the prayers'. This sounds very like the programme for a liturgical vigil. The vigils began with the recitation of the gospel, recollection of memories of the Lord and his instructions, communal prayers and the singing of psalms; then, when the right atmosphere had been established, when their souls were ready and their hearts on fire, the Lord's words were said again, the actions performed that he had performed – and he was there, they ate with him, they were present at the eschatological feast. It is good for us to get back behind the gospel narratives to the primitive communion-meals of our brothers, since they are the basis of our liturgy and of the present-day Mass. It is very possible that many passages in the gospels were conceived in this liturgical atmosphere, an atmosphere of living and friendly encounters rather than that of an author sitting at his desk. We must imagine the brethren saying to the elders, 'Tell us about Jesus, what he said, what he did', and then Peter or another disciple would speak about the Lord's miracles and sayings and discourses. In this way, little by little, the gospel tradition crystallised in a liturgical framework. And this, too, justifies the current renewal of the liturgy, since it should be the normal framework of Christian teaching; the proclamation of the Word is best situated in the sacramental encounter with the Lord. Of this, the Emmaus episode is an excellent example. It is a splendid specimen of primitive catechesis in a liturgical setting, and of the encounter with the Lord in the Eucharist.

The appearance to Peter

At the end of Luke's narrative we learn that *the Lord . . . has appeared to Simon* (Lk 24:34). It is certainly Simon Peter who is meant. In his first epistle to the Corinthians Paul repeats a tradition concerning the appearances, 'Christ died for our sins, in accordance with the scriptures . . . he appeared to Cephas' (1 Co 15:3–5). Both texts tell us that Cephas, Simon Peter, saw the Lord, and perhaps was the first to do so. This is very probable, but it is odd that we know nothing more about it. It must, of course, be distinguished from the appearance on the shore of the lake, since that takes place later and Peter is not alone.

However, this dearth of information ought not to be too much of a surprise. We can scarcely doubt that Jesus appeared to his mother, and yet nothing is said about it; it is, as it were, a lesson in humility and renunciation. God willed to let our curiosity go hungry. The gospel says nothing about the appearance to Mary that all Christian piety assumes came first, and makes only a dry statement about the second, to the leading apostle, whereas it goes into detail about the one to the two unknown disciples. God teaches us in a mysterious way. Later, we shall be told of the appearance on the shore of the lake and the words of encouragement to Peter, but here all we have is this brief note of an appearance to Peter, perhaps even before the disciples saw him on the way to Emmaus.

The apostles in the Upper Room: Luke's narrative

The disciples are gathered, probably in the Upper Room, on the evening of Easter Sunday, and are talking among themselves about the appearance to Simon and that at Emmaus. *They were still talking about all this when he himself stood among them and said to them, 'Peace be with you!' In a state of alarm and fright, they thought they*

*were seeing a ghost. But he said, 'Why are you so agitated, and why
are these doubts rising in your hearts? Look at my hands and feet;
yes, it is I indeed. Touch me and see for yourselves; a ghost has no
flesh and bones as you can see I have.' And as he said this he showed
them his hands and feet. Their joy was so great that they could not
believe it . . .* (Lk 24:36–41). This psychological note is very characteristic of Luke. It is because they are so full of joy that they are
unwilling to believe; at Gethsemane, it was because they were so
sorrowful that they went to sleep. Luke makes excuses for people,
and incidentally gives us a lesson in fraternal correction – that we
should look for possible excuses for our brother.

*And they stood there dumbfounded; so he said to them, 'Have you
anything here to eat?' And they offered him a piece of grilled fish,
which he took and ate before their eyes* (Lk 24:41–3). We shall examine
later the verses which follow this and which record the command to
preach throughout the world. Here Luke is reporting a recognition-
appearance.

It is possible to distinguish between two kinds of appearance of
the risen Jesus – appearances concerned with recognition and those
concerned with the mission. In the first, it is a question of recognising
Jesus, of understanding and believing that it is he; in the second, he
sends the disciples out to conquer the world, to go forth and preach.
We must first examine the recognition-appearances. We have already
studied one, that to Mary of Magdala; after an initial mistake, she
recognises Jesus and learns that he is in a new state, 'Do not cling
to me, I am going to my Father', which means, it is indeed I but I am
in the state of glory. Similarly at Emmaus, he walks for a long time
beside the disciples without their recognising him, then the breaking
of bread opens their eyes. Basically the same scene is played out
again in the Upper Room that evening. Jesus shows himself but the
apostles do not recognise him. They are plunged in fear and alarm
and think they are seeing a ghost, until Jesus proves that it is indeed
himself by showing them his hands and feet and eating in their
presence.

John's narrative

John's narrative is very similar, except for certain complementary
details. *In the evening of that same day, the first day of the week, the
doors were closed in the room where the disciples were, for fear of the*

*Jews. Jesus came and stood among them. He said, 'Peace be with you',
and showed them his hands and his side. The disciples were filled with
joy when they saw the Lord* (Jn 20:19–20). The verses which follow
these (Jn 20:21–3) are drawn from mission-appearances and will be
studied in the next chapter.

After that, John relates another recognition-appearance, this time
concerning Thomas, who had been absent on the previous occasion
and had refused to believe what the other apostles told him, *'Unless
I see the holes that the nails made in his hands and can put my finger
into the holes they made, and unless I can put my hand into his side,
I refuse to believe'* (Jn 20:25). Jesus humours his intransigence.

Eight days later, Jesus shows himself again. Notice the interval
of eight days; it is now the following Sunday and it was especially on
Sunday that the Eucharist was celebrated – another indication of the
liturgical setting of these narratives. On the following Sunday, then,
Jesus gives Thomas the proof he was hoping for, *'Put your finger here;
look, here are my hands. Give me your hand; put it into my side. Doubt
no longer but believe'* (Jn 20:27). And Thomas has at last to recognise
his Master.

Comparison of the narratives of John and Luke

John's narrative is so similar to Luke's that it is open to us to en-
quire whether the manuscripts have not assimilated one to the other.
Luke's expressions, *he said to them, 'Peace be with you'* (Lk 24:36)
and *he showed them his hands and his feet* (Lk 24:40) are found
almost identically in John. These verses are, in fact, missing from
certain manuscripts and it has been suggested by critics that they
were added later, following John. It is difficult to decide. Personally,
I would prefer to believe that Luke himself knew and used the
Johannine tradition, which in its earliest stages could well antedate
Luke. This would perhaps be borne out by the fact that Luke has
not borrowed uncritically but has made small and intelligent changes;
for example, John mentions the hands and the side, Luke the hands
and the feet; this is because John has described the side wounded by
the lance-thrust, and Luke has not, and Luke therefore omits it
here, and draws attention instead to the wounded feet.

In fact the two narratives reveal slightly different tendencies, but
they have in common a theological interest in proving the resurrection in a physical manner and demonstrating that the risen Jesus

is not a ghost but a real being. They are evidently intended to answer
the objections of Jews or Greeks, who accused the apostles of believing in subjective impressions or fantasies. In reply to these
objections the narratives assert that the disciples were entirely
convinced of the resurrection of Jesus even though at first they
doubted it.

This apologetic interest does not diminish the historicity of the
facts; on the contrary, it presupposes it, otherwise the facts would
prove nothing. The material proofs of the reality of the resurrection
are the miraculous entry, the wounds on the body and, in Luke only.
the eating.

In John, as in Luke, Jesus enters the Upper Room in a miraculous
way. This is clear enough in John, *the doors were closed.* Luke does
not mention the closed doors; it sounds as though Jesus enters
unobserved, suddenly. Why does he present it like this? It may be
that he thought that this detail would reinforce the theory that Jesus
was a ghost, *they thought they were seeing a ghost* (Lk 24:37).
To prevent unintelligent readers making this mistake, he avoids
stressing the closed doors. However this may be, it is plain that for
Luke, as for John, Jesus is no longer subject to the laws of this world;
he enters as he pleases, without worrying about human obstacles.

Then Jesus shows his wounds. Here again, we notice a difference
between the two gospels. According to John, Jesus wishes to prove
his identity; it is the same body as before the resurrection, the same
wounds that he had before. The disciples recognise him, and 'were
filled with joy when they saw the Lord' (Jn 20:20). Luke, on the other
hand, emphasises the fact that Jesus has a real body. 'Touch me and
see for yourselves; a ghost has no flesh and bones as you can see I
have' (Lk 24:39). Here the stress is not on the fact that Jesus is the
same person, but on the fact that he has a real body of flesh and bone
that can be touched. At bottom the idea is the same, but there is a
different shade of meaning, identity in John, physical reality in Luke.

This is why Luke adds the eating; Jesus eats some grilled fish in
the presence of his disciples. By this Luke does not mean that glorified
bodies need food; only that Jesus accommodates himself to their
understanding and gives his disciples a proof that he can eat and
therefore is not a mere phantom but a man. In his appearances,
Jesus adapts himself to men; to prove that he is truly flesh and blood,
even if this flesh and blood belong to a new order, he lends himself to
this manifestation of the life of the senses. Besides, we must not

forget that Luke likes to show us Jesus eating with the disciples (see pp. 279f). In John, Jesus does not eat during this appearance, and, on the shore of the lake, he will give them fish cooked over charcoal and make them eat but without eating himself. The reason that Luke records this detail is, of course, that the Eucharist recalls meals shared with the Lord.

The second appearance in the Upper Room

Only John reports this second appearance in the presence of Thomas, and he does so with a high degree of realism. He brings home vividly the physical reality of Christ's body, into whose wounds Thomas can put his finger. We are not told that the other disciples made this gesture during the first appearance; they were sufficiently discreet to be content with seeing, whereas Thomas finds greater difficulty in surrendering. As all the Fathers of the Church declare, his unbelief won for us an argument that sustains our faith; he had the benefit of an experience that we cannot enjoy but on which our faith can rest.

Thomas makes reparation for his unbelief with the words, '*My Lord and my God!*' (Jn 20:28). Could Thomas have uttered this phrase just as it stands? The apostles understood the divinity of Jesus in its fullest sense only after Pentecost. Even in his lifetime, of course, they had a feeling that he was of divine rank, the Son of the Father, but there is a difference between this conviction of the heart and the clear formulation of it by the intelligence.

It was wholly abnormal for a Jew to call a man God or the Son of God. Before the first Christians could achieve this affirmation, they had to reflect on the scriptures and on the texts in the Old Testament concerning the Son of Man, the Servant, the Messiah, the Logos, the Word and the Spirit, which prepared the way for it. Only little by little did they come to a clear formulation of what they had obscurely felt. It needed time to transpose this great mystery into human language. We must therefore distinguish that deep faith, which is very old, preceding even the resurrection and springing into new life very soon after it, from its intellectual formulation, which took longer to come to fruition. Against this background, the expression, 'My Lord and my God', sounds slightly anachronistic and we are quite justified in asking whether Thomas could have uttered it in that form.

There is, in addition, another anachronism in the text. John makes Jesus say, '*You believe because you can see me. Happy are those who have not seen and yet believe*' (Jn 20:29). In the second sentence both verbs are in the past, and, as they stand, are inexplicable if spoken by Jesus. It sounds like a later saying, 'Happy are those who did not see him in those days, and yet have believed.' Jesus himself would in fact have said, 'Happy are those who are going to believe without having seen' – as Père Mollat's translation makes him say. There would be no difficulty at all if this is what the text read; but the future is less well supported and the past is to be preferred. It must be a later formulation, dating from thirty to forty years after the actual events, when the eye-witnesses had disappeared and the first Christians regretted that they had not seen Jesus.

However, even if this phrase and the preceding one, 'My Lord and my God', are late as regards their wording, they are no less of great value. Thomas made a real act of faith, he recognised the Lord. And in reply to him, Jesus praised the faith of those who believe without having seen.

These are recognition-appearances, encounters in which Jesus manifests himself. Their catechetical and liturgical elements are nourishment for our own Christian way of life, and in our liturgical encounters with the Lord we are not less favoured than the disciples at Emmaus or in the Upper Room at Jerusalem; Jesus comes to our table, he breaks the bread, our eyes are opened and we eat with him.

12. The Appearance by the Lake of Tiberias

THE FIRST CONCLUSION OF THE FOURTH GOSPEL

Mt   Mk   Lk

THE SECOND CONCLUSION OF THE FOURTH GOSPEL

APPEARANCE BY THE SIDE OF THE LAKE TIBERIAS

Mt   Mk   Lk

5 [5a] 'Master,' Simon replied,
we worked hard
all night long and caught nothing . . .

[1] . . . he was standing one day
by the Lake
of Gennesaret . . .

[4] When he had finished speaking

Jn 20:30-1

[30] There were many other signs that Jesus worked and the disciples saw, but they are not recorded in this book.
[31] These are recorded so that you may believe that Jesus is the Christ, the Son of God, and that believing this you may have life through his name.

Jn 21:24-5

[24] This disciple is the one who vouches for these things and has written them down, and we know that his testimony is true.
[25] There were many other things that Jesus did; if all were written down, the world itself, I suppose, would not hold all the books that would have to be written.

Jn 21:1-14

[1] Later on, Jesus showed himself again to the disciples. It was by the Sea of Tiberias, and it happened like this:
[2] Simon Peter, Thomas called the Twin, Nathanael from Cana in Galilee, the sons of Zebedee and two more of his disciples were together.
[3] Simon Peter said, 'I'm going fishing'. They replied, 'We'll come with you'. They went out and got into the boat

but caught nothing that night.

[4] It was light by now
and there stood Jesus
on the shore,

though the disciples did not realise that it was Jesus.
[5] Jesus called out, 'Have you any food,* friends?' And when they answered, 'No',

Mt	Mk	Lk

he said to Simon,
'Put out into deep water
and pay out your nets
for a catch'.
⁵ᵇ ' . . . but if you say so,
I will pay out the nets.'
⁶ᵃ When they had done this, they netted
such a huge number of fish . . .

⁷ So they signalled to their companions
in the other boat
to come and help them;
when these came,
they filled the two boats
to sinking point.

⁶ᵇ . . . their nets began to tear, . . .

THE REHABILITATION OF PETER AND ANNOUNCEMENT OF HIS MARTYRDOM

⁶ he said,

'Throw the net out to starboard
and you'll find something'.

So they dropped the net,
and there were so many fish
that they could not haul it in.
    ⁷ The disciple Jesus loved said to Peter, 'It
is the Lord.' At these words 'It is the
Lord', Simon Peter, who had practically
nothing on, wrapped his cloak round him
and jumped into the water.
    ⁸ The other disciples

came on in the boat
towing the net and the fish;

they were only about a hundred yards
from land.
    ⁹ As soon as they came ashore they saw that
there was some bread there, and a
charcoal fire with fish cooking on it.
    ¹⁰ Jesus said, 'Bring some of the fish
you have just caught'.
    ¹¹ Simon Peter went aboard and dragged
the net to the shore, full of big fish,
one hundred and fifty-three of them;
and in spite of there being so many
the net was not broken.
    ¹² Jesus said to them, 'Come and have
breakfast'. None of the disciples was
bold enough to ask, 'Who are you?';
they knew quite well it was the Lord.
    ¹³ Jesus then stepped forward, took the bread and
gave it to them, and the same with the fish.
    ¹⁴ This was the third time that Jesus showed himself
to the disciples after rising from the dead.

Jn 21:15–19

¹⁵ After the meal Jesus said to Simon Peter,

Mt   Mk   Lk

THE DESTINY OF THE DISCIPLE JESUS LOVED

Jn

'Simon son of John, do you love me more than
these others do?' He answered, 'Yes Lord,
you know I love you'. Jesus said to him,
'Feed my lambs'.
    ¹⁶ A second time he said to him, 'Simon son
of John, do you love me?' He replied, 'Yes
Lord, you know I love you'. Jesus said
to him, 'Look after my sheep'.
    ¹⁷ Then he said to him a third time,
'Simon son of John, do you love me?' Peter
was upset that he asked him the third time,
'Do you love me?' and said, 'Lord,
you know everything; you know I
love you'. Jesus said to him, 'Feed
my sheep'.
    ¹⁸ 'I tell you most solemnly, when you were
young, you put on your own belt and walked
where you liked; but when you grow old
you will stretch out your hands, and
somebody else will put a belt round
you and take you where you would rather
not go.'
    ¹⁹ In these words he indicated the kind of
death by which Peter would give glory to
God. After this he said, 'Follow me'.

Jn 21:20–23

    ²⁰ Peter turned and saw the disciple Jesus
loved following them – the one who had leaned
on his breast at the supper and had said
to him, 'Lord, who is it that will betray you?'
    ²¹ Seeing him, Peter said to Jesus, 'What about
him, Lord?'
    ²² Jesus answered, 'If I want him to stay
behind till I come, what does it matter to
you? You are to follow me.'
    ²³ The rumour then went out among the
brothers that this disciple would not die.
Yet Jesus had not said to Peter, 'He will
not die', but, 'If I want him to stay
behind till I come (,what is that to
you?).'

The appearance of Jesus on the lakeside is recorded in chapter 21 of John's gospel. This chapter raises a problem, since it has the look of an appendix; this is due to its style on the one hand and on the other to the conclusions which precede (Jn 20:30–1) and follow it (Jn 21:24–5).

Critics who have analysed this chapter observe that sometimes the style is wholly Johannine and sometimes it betrays the work of another hand. Père Boismard has devoted a detailed study to this subject[1] and comes to the conclusion that there are plainly Johannine elements in it fused with non-Johannine, and so intimately fused that it is impossible to distinguish different fragments that could be separated from one another. It seems as though a Johannine ground has been taken up and re-worked by someone else; Père Boismard thinks that it can be established that this second writer closely resembles Luke. This conclusion is novel enough and may seem paradoxical, but it is not all that surprising. Luke was a writer of note, a charitable man and much appreciated by the first Christians. It is not improbable that when he passed through a community, for example the group dependent on John, the disciples would have asked his help in composing this or that passage. This might well be the origin of the Lucanisms that are believed to be discernible in the fourth gospel.

The conclusions of John's gospel

Chapter 21 has another peculiarity; it ends with a formal conclusion, although chapter 20 already has one.

After the second appearance in Jerusalem, in Thomas' presence, we read: *There were many other signs that Jesus worked and the disciples saw, but they are not recorded in this book. These are recorded so that you may believe that Jesus is the Christ, the Son of God, and that believing this you may have life through his name* (Jn 20:30–1).

[1] 'Le chapitre xxi de saint Jean. Essai de critique littéraire', in *Revue Biblique*, LIV, 1947, pp. 473–501.

It looks as though the gospel was meant to end there, but then it goes on: *Later on, Jesus showed himself again* . . . (Jn 21:1).

Chapter 21 seems to pick the story up again, and then to add its own conclusion, or rather two conclusions. *This disciple is the one who vouches for these things and has written them down, and we know that his testimony is true.* (Jn 21:24). This sentence is intended to confirm what has just been said about Jesus' words concerning John's destiny. It recalls the verse concerning the lance-thrust (Jn 19:34–5) in which we feel we are listening to a group of disciples – 'This is the evidence of one who saw it, trustworthy evidence, and he knows he speaks the truth' – a kind of collective guarantee of the testimony. Similarly here, it sounds as though the group of disciples of John is signing and authenticating the testimony of its master.

The conclusion continues: *There were many other things that Jesus did; if all were written down, the world itself, I suppose, would not hold all the books that would have to be written* (Jn 21:25). This verse, in its turn, recalls the first conclusion in chapter 20, though it is by no means identical; what they have in common is that both let us know that everything has not been recorded. But in the first case (Jn 20:30), the tone is more theological; the choice has been made with a view to providing support for the disciples' faith. The second conclusion (Jn 21:25) uses a rhetorical formula and is not afraid to exaggerate; if one were to write down everything that Jesus had done, the world would not be large enough to hold it.[1]

The authenticity of verse 25 has been questioned by critics. Canon Vaganay published an article in which he proved from internal evidence that verse 25 does not belong to what precedes it and could have been added.[2] Some months later this conjecture was confirmed by ultra-violet ray photographs.[3] The British Museum having

---

[1] This formula is well known in Greek and Latin literature (cf. O. Weinreich, *Antike Heilungswunder*, Giessen, 1909, pp. 199–201). Such exaggerations are to be found even among the rabbis – 'If all the skies were parchment, all the trees pens and all the seas ink, it still would not be enough to put down in writing the wisdom I have learnt from my Master; and yet I have taken from the wisdom of the sages only as much as a fly carries off from the ocean into which it has fallen' (*Sopherim* 16, 8). The formula in verse 25 therefore comes from a background of secular rhetoric of which we have other examples.

[2] 'La finale du quatrième évangile' in *Revue Biblique*, XLV, 1936, pp. 512–28.

[3] Modern scientific processes are of great value in helping us to read old manuscripts and decipher writing that is almost effaced. Thus the manuscripts from the Judaean desert are often very badly deteriorated through the flaking or mildewing of the pages, so that the ink has become almost illegible and the eye can no longer decipher it. Infra-red photography brings out many details that the naked eye cannot distinguish.

acquired the Codex Sinaiticus[1], it became possible to photograph the last page of John's gospel and establish that there was an earlier state of the manuscript in which chapter 21 stopped at verse 24. Originally there had been a *coronis* to mark the end of the text, and the words 'Gospel according to Saint John'. Later, the scribe scraped these out, wrote in verse 25, and added the *coronis* and 'gospel according to Saint John' lower down[2]. This correction can be attributed to the same scribe who wrote the first text, since the writing is in the same hand. Verse 25 must have been missing from the text he first copied, he then discovered it in another manuscript, became concerned about its omission and added it in. This is a good example of the way a scientific technique can confirm a skilful conjecture.

The fact that there are two conclusions to John's gospel suggests that originally it ended with chapter 20; a little later, it seemed a good idea to add chapter 21 and finish with another conclusion. But this last chapter is no less interesting for all that, and is from a Johannine source.

It divides into three parts: the miraculous draught of fish and the appearance of Jesus on the lakeside; the passage concerning the primacy of Peter; and the dialogue about the deaths of Peter and the other disciple.

The appearance of Jesus on the lakeside

Later on, Jesus showed himself again to the disciples. It was by the Sea of Tiberias, and it happened like this: Simon Peter, Thomas called the Twin, Nathanael from Cana in Galilee, the sons of Zebedee and two more of his disciples were together (Jn 21:1–2). It is not the whole apostolic college that is gathered together, but only certain apostles who, it seems, have returned to Galilee after the resurrection and gone to work again. A problem arises from this which we will deal with a little further on (p. 302).

---

[1] Codex Sinaiticus is of great value since it dates from the end of the fourth century. It was found at the monastery of Sinai and bought for very little by Tischendorf who presented it to the emperor of Russia, whereupon the manuscript went to St Petersburg. After the First World War it was bought by the British Museum from the Soviet government. As soon as it arrived in England it was studied with the help of every modern technique. In this way palaeography helps the study of the Bible.

[2] Cf. H. J. M. MILNE and T. C. SKEAT, *Scribes and Correctors of the Codex Sinaiticus*, British Museum, 1938, p. 12 and fig. 3.

Simon Peter said, 'I'm going fishing'. They replied, 'We'll come with you'. They went out and got into the boat but caught nothing that night. It was light by now and there stood Jesus on the shore, though the disciples did not realise that it was Jesus (Jn 21:3–4). Once again the disciples fail to recognise Jesus. In all these appearances there has to be a gesture, an approach by Jesus and a movement of faith on the part of the disciples for him to be recognised. Here it is through a miracle that Jesus makes himself known.

Jesus called out, 'Have you any food, friends?' And when they answered, 'No', he said, 'Throw the net out to starboard and you'll find something'. So they dropped the net, and there were so many fish that they could not haul it in (Jn 21:5–6). This is the sign that is to open the eyes of the disciples. And then, as on other occasions in the fourth gospel, it is not Peter but the 'disciple Jesus loved' who understands; seemingly he is endowed with greater spiritual insight – at least that is what the evangelist wants to convey to us (see above p. 252).

The disciple Jesus loved said to Peter, 'It is the Lord'. At these words 'It is the Lord', Simon Peter, who had practically nothing on, wrapped his cloak round him and jumped into the water (Jn 21:7). If the other disciple takes precedence in spiritual insight, Peter is always first to react instinctively from the heart and leap into action. The other disciples stay in the boat and wait for their arrival at the shore. In actual fact they are not far off it, only about a hundred yards, and the net has to be drawn in; if everyone had set off to swim the fish would have been lost. So they consent to staying behind and bringing in the fish.

As soon as they came ashore they saw that there was some bread there, and a charcoal fire with fish cooking on it. Jesus said, 'Bring some of the fish you have just caught'. Simon Peter went aboard and dragged the net to the shore, full of big fish, one hundred and fifty -three of them; and in spite of there being so many the net was not broken (Jn 21:9–11). Why 153 fish? No one really knows, though it is plain that the number is meant to convey some symbolism[1]. Like all the authors of his period, John likes symbolic numbers. Here we suspect some kind of more or less Pythagorean calculation to which we no longer have the key. At any rate, there are a lot of fish, and this is the miracle as the result of which the apostles recognise Jesus.

---

[1] It has been pointed out that 153 is the sum of the first seventeen numbers, $153 = 1 + 2 + 3 \ldots + 17$.

Jesus said to them, 'Come and have breakfast'. None of the disciples was bold enough to ask, 'Who are you?'; they knew quite well it was the Lord (Jn 21:12). The apostles are overawed and do not dare to speak – they know it is the Lord, but they did not recognise him! It is and is not he; Jesus belongs to a new world and they sense something mysterious. Jesus restores their confidence.

Jesus then stepped forward, took the bread and gave it to them, and the same with the fish (Jn 21:13). In this way Jesus reveals himself, but he does not eat. Luke would certainly have shown us Jesus sharing the meal; not so John. Notice the nature of the sign; the instrument of recognition is a miracle of food given to the disciples. Our minds are led to the idea of spiritual nourishment, as earlier over the manna and the multiplication of the loaves. In the last analysis, what Jesus gives his disciples is life.

The miraculous draught of fish

We must break off here, since it is impossible to avoid the problem of the relationship between this episode in John and that recounted by Luke in chapter 5 of his gospel. Luke's scene does not take place after the resurrection but long before, when Jesus is starting his ministry in Galilee. After the baptism and the temptation, Jesus comes back to Nazareth, where he speaks in the synagogue, then he goes to Capernaum where he heals a demoniac, as well as Simon's mother-in-law and many others; subsequently he leaves Capernaum, and it is at this point that Luke reports the calling of the first four disciples, which in his version is accompanied by a miraculous haul of fish.

In Mark and Matthew, the call is told very simply: Jesus passes along the lake where some fishermen are casting their nets; 'Follow me,' he tells them, 'and I will make you fishers of men' (Mt 4:18–19); Mk 1:16–17). And they follow him, one pair leaving their nets, the other their boat and their father.

Luke's narrative retains some elements of the passage in Mark and Matthew, but it also includes the miraculous haul of fish that we come across again in John.

Now he was standing one day by the Lake of Gennesaret, with the crowd pressing round him listening to the word of God, when he caught sight of two boats close to the bank. The fishermen had gone out of them and were washing their nets. This opening is similar to Mark and

Matthew. *He got into one of the boats – it was Simon's – and asked him to put out a little from the shore. Then he sat down and taught the crowds from the boats.* When he had finished speaking he said to Simon, 'Put out into deep water and pay out your nets for a catch'. ' 'Master,' Simon replied 'We worked hard all night long and caught nothing, but if you say so, I will pay out the nets' (Lk 5:1–5). As in John, the fishermen have worked all night in vain; and Simon obeys. *And when they had done this they netted such a huge number of fish that their nets began to tear* (Lk 5:6). John remarks that the net did not break, but the idea behind it is the same; there were so many fish that the net was in danger.

So they signalled to their companions in the other boat to come and help them; when these came, they filled the two boats to sinking point. When Simon Peter saw this he fell at the knees of Jesus saying, Leave me, Lord; I am a sinful man' (Lk 5:7–8). Peter is overcome, so too are James and John, the sons of Zebedee; these are the same persons as in Mark and Matthew. *But Jesus said to Simon, 'Do not be afraid; from now on it is men you will catch'* (Lk 5:10).

This narrative of Luke's is surprising, combining as it does the call of the first four disciples from Mark and Matthew with the miraculous haul recorded in John. Plainly something can happen twice, and there may have been two miraculous hauls. However, anyone who is familiar with the practices of the evangelists and the way in which traditions get fused and re-worked may well ask whether this is not one and the same tradition which has been expressed in two different ways, the same story of a miraculous haul, but placed by Luke at the beginning of the ministry and by John after the resurrection. Many scholars, including Catholics, have asked just this question.

There are two possible answers to it. Either John is right in placing it after the resurrection and Luke has anticipated it in order to associate it with the call of the disciples: or, alternatively, Luke is right to put it at the outset of Jesus' ministry, and it is John or his tradition that has moved it to after the resurrection. Both opinions are strenuously defended and it is very difficult to take sides.

Personally, I am tempted to believe that Luke is right and that the miraculous draught of fish took place during Jesus' earthly life; in the Johannine tradition it has been combined with a post-resurrection appearance. This opinion is difficult to justify in detail; I would, however, draw attention to the fact that this miracle, if it takes place in Jesus' lifetime, fits very well into a sequence of signs that John himself has marshalled in his gospel to prepare for the revelation of the glory of Christ. Moreover, it is difficult to understand the disciples' returning to work, in Galilee, after the resurrection. They had surely left their nets behind long ago to follow the Lord; they may have hesitated for a moment, but once they had seen the risen Jesus in Jerusalem and believed in him, they had only one thing to do – set out on the worldwide task of preaching which Jesus had laid upon them. Is this the moment to go back to Galilee to take up fishing again? The Fathers raised the question how Peter and the rest of them, having left their boats, could return to their jobs after the resurrection. Certainly it is possible to explain it, but it is much easier to understand if John has recorded as happening after the resurrection something which in fact took place earlier.

If this solution is admitted, all that is necessary is to take out the episode of the net and the miraculous draught and transfer it to the time of Jesus' earthly ministry, with Luke; everything else can stay – the appearance on the lakeside after the resurrection, and its consequences. This affects the balance between the appearances in Judaea and those in Galilee, a question which will be studied later. The difficulty had to be at least mentioned, but, although its solution remains problematical, it is not of the first importance. What is more important is to learn that Jesus manifests himself on the shore of the lake and feeds his disciples; then he speaks, addressing himself to Peter.

The primacy of Peter

After the meal, Jesus said to Simon Peter, 'Simon son of John, do you love me more than these others do?' He answered, ' Yes Lord, you know I love you'. Jesus said to him, 'Feed my lambs'. A second time he said to him, 'Simon son of John, do you love me?' He replied, ' Yes Lord, you know I love you'. Jesus said to him, 'Look after my sheep'. Then he said to him a third time, 'Simon son of John, do you love me?' Peter was upset that he asked him the third time, 'Do you love me?' and said, 'Lord, you know everything; you know I love you'; Jesus said to him, 'Feed my sheep' (Jn 21:15–17). What strikes one at once in this beautiful narrative is the number three – three questions, three replies. Certain slight variations in the terms are also noticeable, 'lamb' and 'sheep', as well as the difference, which can hardly be expressed in English, but which exists in Greek, between 'love' rendered by the verb *philein* and by the verb *agapan*. These two Greek words correspond perhaps to 'have an affection for' and 'love'; some, perhaps oversubtle, exegetes have seen in this a delicate shade of meaning; thus Mgr Cassian Besobrasoff, a Russian Orthodox bishop, suggests that it is used to convey a sense of anticlimax – Jesus, unable to wring out of Peter an assurance of 'the love of a disciple' contents himself with asking for a 'merely human and personal attachment'[1]. This suggestion is without foundation: the changes in wording, *philein* and *agapan*, lambs and sheep, are stylistic and have no theological significance. There is instead a sense of rising to a climax; Peter has to make affirmation on affirmation, since his master appears to doubt him, until the third time he is quite upset – but Lord, you know everything, you know I love you and yet you make me say so three times!

That Jesus asks him three times is plainly to reverse the three denials. The majority of critics are agreed on this point. But following what was said earlier (p. 71) about Peter's denials, can we say that there were three, or only two, or even only one? The answer is that in the present state of the text there are three. Chapter 21 of the fourth gospel therefore presupposes that the synoptics already existed in more or less their final form. In demanding this reparation from Peter, Jesus intends to re-establish Peter in his office of pastor, make him compensate for his failure, and give him back his rank of leader in the presence of the disciples.

This text is important for the primacy of Peter, and I want to recall two other texts of the gospel which, with it, make up the theological evidence on this matter. Too often the discussion is confined to the text in Matthew: '*You are the Christ, the Son of the living God*' . . . '*You are Peter and on this rock I will build my Church. And the gates of the underworld can never hold out against it.*' (Mt 16:15–19). This text is of the first importance and must never be underestimated. Beyond all doubt, Peter is praised for his faith and chosen to be the rock, the foundation which is to uphold the building which is the Church and assure its power and stability. But this is not the only text which establishes the primacy of Peter; and this is

[1] Saint Pierre et l'Église dans le Nouveau Testament. Le problème de primauté', in *Istina*, 1955, pp. 261–304, esp. p. 297f; cf. my refutation, ibid., p. 329 (*Exégèse et Théologie*, II, p. 278).

fortunate since, on closer inspection, it establishes his primacy over the Church rather than over the rest of the apostles.

If we had this text alone, it would be possible to say, as Protestants often do, that Peter is the spokesman of the rest, and that he is addressed as representing the whole group of apostles. Jesus questions them all, and, since all cannot reply, Peter, as the eldest and worthiest, replies, 'You are the Christ', but they all speak through him. When Jesus says, 'You are Peter and on this rock . . .' this means – according to the Protestant interpretation – that *the apostolic group* is to be made the foundation of the Church. Peter is not clearly distinguished from the other apostles. This is important for the problem of the primacy as it is posed today.

Our separated brethren have no difficulty in admitting that the Pope, or the bishops, or the ecumenical patriarchs, have jurisdiction over the faithful. What is at stake is whether the Pope of Rome has jurisdiction over the other bishops throughout the world. In general the orthodox reply that the Pope has a primacy of honour and nothing more; Rome is a venerable and very ancient see, founded by Peter, and we are prepared to grant the Pope a precedence of honour, but as regards power and jurisdiction he is no more than the equal of the patriarchs of Constantinople or Moscow. This is the fundamental point under debate, and it is not easy, using the Matthew passage alone, to show that Peter alone was chosen, and that it was not the apostolic college that was chosen in his person.

It is for this reason that I draw attention to the two other texts which complement the confession at Caesarea, that in John 21 and another very valuable one in Luke: '*Simon, Simon! Satan, you must know, has got his wish to sift you all like wheat; but I have prayed for you, Simon, that your faith may not fail, and once you have recovered, you in your turn must strengthen your brothers*' (Lk 22:31-2). After the Last Supper, Jesus is speaking to Simon and the other apostles who are present in the Upper Room – 'Satan is going to try you, you apostles' – Jesus is thinking of the apostolic group, not Christians in general – 'you will be badly shaken, but I have prayed that your faith, Peter, will not fail, and when you have recovered, when you have regained your faith or at least your confidence, you are to strengthen your brothers.' Who are these brothers if not the other apostles? Jesus charges Peter with the duty of strengthening the other apostles in the faith, he sets him at their head in the realm of faith. Peter receives what can be called a primacy or an authority

over the other apostles. Similarly, on the level of succeeding gen-
erations, the Pope, the successor of Peter, has a mission in faith
towards the other bishops. He is not their equal; in the magisterium
of the Church's faith he has a special rank, he is the head of the
apostolic college; he is not merely the first in honour, he is the head
of the episcopal body.

Of course the dignity and greatness of the college of bishops
must be maintained. It would be a mistake to see the person of the
Pope as the one and only authority; the role of the bishops assembled
together is brought out clearly by a Council. The sovereign authority
in the Church is the college of bishops, which meets, debates, decides
and makes laws. But this college of bishops, which is the successor
of the apostolic college, since the bishops are the successors of the
apostles, has a head in the person of the bishop of Rome, the
successor of Peter, just as the apostolic college has a head in the
person of Peter. And just as Peter had a mission of faith towards the
other apostles, so too the bishop of Rome, as Pope, has a duty in
faith towards the rest of the bishops. This text of Luke is therefore
very important as a complement to the episode at Caesarea (Mt
16:15-19).

I think that John's text (Jn 21:15-17) also can be explained in
the same sense, though less clearly. When Jesus says, 'Do you love
me more than these others do?', 'these others' refers to the others
present, Thomas, Nathanael and the sons of Zebedee, that is,
apostles or disciples. Jesus asks Peter to show that he loves Jesus
more than the other apostles do, and it is because Peter declares that
he does that he receives his investiture: 'Feed my lambs, look after
my sheep'. From that moment, the lambs and sheep represent not
only Christian people in general, but also, and most of all, the other
apostles.

These two texts (Jn 21:15-17 and Lk 22:31-2) are therefore very
valuable; they complement the Caesarea confession (Mt 16:15-19)
and teach us that the Pope, Peter's successor, is not the equal
merely of the bishops, not the first merely in honour, but that he
received a ministry and an authority from Christ which sets him
above the rest of the bishops. This is founded on the scriptures and
is to be maintained in the face of all interpretations that contradict it.

Another question then arises which concerns history and goes
beyond the limits of the scriptures. It is objected that these texts
may be valid for Peter; but can it be proved that they are valid for

Peter's successors, that Jesus willed that Peter should have successors at all? Jesus addresses himself to Peter; where are these successors? We have to admit that in the text Jesus does not say 'you and your successors'. But surely it is taken for granted. Jesus is not speaking only for Peter's ears, for Peter is going to die soon, as Jesus shortly announces (Jn 21:19): Jesus is founding a Church which is to exist for a long time, and he prays for those who are to believe on hearing the apostles (Jn 17:20); he foresees the ages to come. When Jesus mentions the rock which is to uphold the Church he is thinking of the future. So that function which Peter receives, and that which the apostles receive, will have to pass on to others who succeed them. This is not literally stated in the gospels, but the implication is perceived by common sense; to refuse to see it is to shut one's eyes, if not to the evidence, at any rate to the normal course of history.

A last detail will demonstrate how Peter or his successor is the vicar of Christ. In these different texts Peter is given titles which are in the first place titles of Christ. In Matthew's passage he is called the 'Rock', but in the rest of the New Testament it is Jesus who is the rock. We recall the rock from which the Hebrew people drank in the desert (1 Co 10:4), and certain texts of the psalms and of Isaiah: sometimes it is the stone which the builders have rejected and which has become the corner-stone, sometimes the stone of offence over which one stumbles, sometimes a foundation stone. The texts of Isaiah and the psalms, which use the stone as an eschatological symbol, have been used in the New Testament (Mt 21:42; Rm 9:33; 1 P 2:6–8) and applied to Jesus to signify that he himself is the foundation stone. Paul can say that the foundation of the Church, the rock, is Christ (1 Co 3:11; Ep 2:20). There is no contradiction here, however; Christ is the rock, but Peter is also the rock because he represents Christ, Peter is the rock by virtue of being the vicar of Christ.

The same goes for the title of Shepherd. Jesus is the first shepherd, as the prophecies of Ezekiel and Zechariah apply to him, and as he himself says, 'I am the good shepherd' (Jn 10:11). But when, here, he says, 'Feed my lambs, look after my sheep', he is communicating this title to his vicar – 'You will be the shepherd in my place'. Jesus himself is going away, he must have a successor, so he hands over to Peter; after Peter, others will take his place, who in their turn will be the heirs, the vicars of the one and only shepherd (1 P 5:2–4).

We read also in Matthew's account of the episode at Caesarea that Peter is to receive the 'keys of the kingdom'. Now it is Jesus who carries the keys of the house of David (Rv 2:7); the Book of Revelation applies to him a text from Isaiah where this is said of the master of the palace in Jerusalem (Is 22:22). It is a piece of semitic symbolism: the master of the palace carries the keys – not little modern keys that can be put in the pocket, but ancient wooden keys with great iron tongues, such as can still be seen in the old monasteries of Egypt. The key is the badge of his office, the master of the palace carried a large key on his shoulder. The Book of Revelation says that Jesus carries the keys of the kingdom, the keys of the house of David: Peter, as his vicar, is to receive them in his turn.

This transference of the attributes of Jesus to his vicar is full of meaning – rock, shepherd, key-bearer; Peter is established as the successor to Jesus, though of course on the human level. Peter is not the Saviour, he is the administrator of the house of God, the Church, but as such he is placed above his fellow servants.

Those texts could also be quoted in which Jesus speaks of the steward to whom his master confides the charge of the other servants during his own absence (Mt 24:45–51). This steward is often regarded as a symbol of Peter: the apostles and disciples are the servants who look after the Church; since they must have a head, Peter is put in charge of the other disciples, even before he is put in charge of the people of Christ. In the Christian Church, the Pope is put in charge even of the body of bishops; he is the one and only head, even though he is their brother in the priesthood. In this way monarchy and democracy are reconciled – there is monarchy, because there is a head, the vicar of Christ, but there is democracy too because that head serves the others in charity and works with them at the bidding of the Holy Spirit.

The deaths of Peter and the other disciple

The last section of this passage concerns Peter's death. *'I tell you most solemnly, when you were young, you put on your own belt and walked where you liked; but when you grow old you will stretch out your hands, and somebody else will put a belt round you and take you where you would rather not go.' In these words he indicated the kind of death by which Peter would give glory to God.* (Jn 21:18–19).

Everyone recognises in this Peter's martyrdom, but one cannot go further than that. Tradition tells us he was crucified, even that he was crucified upside down; this may be true, but the gospel does not tell us. In the text Jesus makes a clear announcement of Peter's martyrdom; he will be bound despite his own wishes and led where he does not want to go, that is, to execution, as all the Fathers interpret it.

It is important to notice that these words follow immediately on Peter's consecration to the primacy. God's privileges must be paid for. Peter receives a most eminent and lofty charge, that of governing the Church in Jesus' name, but it is to end in martyrdom. Similarly, when Jesus, at Caesarea Philippi, had drawn from the apostles their declaration that he was the Messiah, he added immediately, 'Say nothing about this, the Son of Man has to be crucified'. Again, after the transfiguration, when he had shown his glory to his three intimate disciples, he said as they came down the mountain, 'Tell no one until I have risen from the dead, for the Son of Man must . . .' In God's providence there is always the other side of the coin: a mission gifted with exceptional graces is counterbalanced by great suffering. So too here, Peter cannot be promoted to the dignity of Pastor of the Church without immediately being told that it is to be counterbalanced by the grievous death of a martyr. It is a lesson we should all remember: it is possible to be eager for God's favours and charisms, but it must be kept in mind that God does not give them by themselves – they are accompanied by the cross.

On hearing this, *Peter turned and saw the disciple Jesus loved following them – the one who had leaned on his breast at the supper and had said to him, 'Lord, who is it that will betray you?'* (Jn 21:20). We are reminded here that the disciple in question had an even closer relationship with the Lord than Peter had.

Seeing him, Peter – a little too curious – *said to Jesus, 'What about him, Lord?'* (Jn 21:21). I accept what is to happen to me, says Peter, but what about him, is he to be a martyr too, or will you spare him? You did not choose him as head of the Church, he is younger, what have you in store for him? Peter is speaking affectionately, intrigued by the destiny of his young companion.

Jesus answered, 'If I want him to stay behind till I come, what does it matter to you? You are to follow me' (Jn 21:22). Peter is put in his place. It is a way of saying: mind your own business, you have your destiny, do your job until your martyrdom without worrying about the fate of others. The reply itself is evasive, 'If I want him to stay behind . . .' Jesus does not say that he is to stay behind until he comes, but certain people have understood it in this sense.

The rumour then went out among the brothers that this disciple would not die (Jn 21:23). John's disciples must have been happy to be able to repeat this remark; their master was not going to die. But John nevertheless died, at a great age we are told. St Jerome says[1] that at Ephesus, in his extreme old age, he used ceaselessly to repeat, 'Little children, love one another.' And when his hearers complained that it was monotonous, he answered, 'My children, it is the Lord's commandment; if you do this, it is enough.' His death was a shock for his disciples: had not Jesus said he was not to die? And it is to remove this small stumbling-block, this point of uncertainty, that the disciples here bring out the exact meaning: *Yet Jesus had not said to Peter, 'He will not die', but, 'If I want him to stay behind till I come, what is that to you?'* (Jn 21:23). This reflection in fact bears only on the disquiet that existed in certain communities, it does not tell us any great truth concerning the universal Church. It concerns a particular church, perhaps that of Ephesus.

The passage ends with an act of homage to the vanished master. *This disciple is the one who vouches for these things and has written them down, and we know that his testimony is true* (Jn 21:24). This has the additional interest that it presumes that John died at a great age; if he had died young, or if he had been martyred, as is sometimes said, there would be no value in the story; it is because he lived a long time that the rumour that he would not die became so widespread. The tradition receives confirmation from this, unless two Johns have got confused in it . . .

The appearance to Peter

Is it possible that this appearance on the lakeside recorded in John is the same as the appearance to Simon mentioned by Luke (Lk 24:34)? When the disciples arrive in Jerusalem from Emmaus, before they can open their mouths to describe the appearance with which they have been favoured, they are told by the apostles that the Lord has appeared to Simon. Clearly Simon Peter is meant, but where did it happen? Are we to think of the appearance related by John?

---

[1] *Comm. Gal.*, bk. 3, ch. 6 (MIGNE, Patrol. Latina, XXVI, 433c).

To identify them as the same seems unsatisfactory for two reasons. First, Simon is not alone, Jesus appears to six or seven disciples, and it is not Peter who recognises him first but 'the disciple Jesus loved'. Secondly, the appearance takes place some time after the resurrection and in Galilee, whereas in Luke the words addressed to the disciples on their return from Emmaus presuppose that the appearance to Peter has taken place on Easter Sunday itself and in Judea. It therefore cannot be the same appearance. Once again we have to resign ourselves and admit that we have no detailed record of it. It remains an enigma, like the appearance to Mary, probable yet unrecorded.

However, the fact of the appearance to Peter is solidly established. Paul writes to the Corinthians: *I taught you what I had been taught myself, namely that Christ died for our sins, in accordance with the scriptures; that he was buried; and that he was raised to life on the third day, in accordance with the scriptures; that he appeared first to Cephas and secondly to the Twelve. Next he appeared to more than five hundred of the brothers at the same time, most of whom are still alive, though some have died; then he appeared to James, and then to all the apostles; and last of all he appeared to me too; it was as though I was born when no one expected it* (1 Co 15:3-8). Peter heads this list of appearances, which everyone acknowledges to be very ancient. It confirms Luke's allusion to an appearance to Peter very shortly after the resurrection.

Why is this appearance not told us in detail? Some commentators think it was deliberately suppressed. There was, they say, a rivalry between different schools of disciples bordering on jealousy, in particular between those of Peter and those of James. James, bishop of Jerusalem and brother of the Lord, played an important role in the church of Jerusalem; he was the leader of the Judaeo-Christian movement that was still close to Judaism. An apocryphal writing, The Gospel according to the Hebrews, recounts an appearance of Jesus to James[1]. There was therefore a circle of disciples who gave precedence to the appearance to James, while others insisted on the appearance to Peter, and yet others, as we have seen, were more attached to John. Some exegetes wonder whether Paul's text (1 Co 15:3-8) is not the result of combining different lists of appearances, one to Peter and the Eleven, the other to James and the apostles,

---

[1] According to this work, James had made a vow not to eat until he had seen the Lord. His prayer was heard, Jesus appeared to him and made him eat.

which have the look of rival lists forming a doublet. They then go on to suggest that in certain circles this rivalry has brought it about that the appearance to Peter is passed over in silence in order that the appearance to James may stand out in greater relief. Perhaps the gospel of Mark originally ended with an appearance to Peter, which has subsequently been suppressed.

Theories like these are of necessity highly conjectural, and there is no doubt that it is better to resign oneself to remaining in a state of ignorance. Here I have only tried to bring out the indisputable fact of an appearance to Peter and its importance[1].

The gospels do not tell us everything, and what they do say is somewhat disorganised. We have a handful of traditions which have been collected; it may not be everything, but it is enough. Thanks to these sometimes contradictory fragments we have a number of proofs which converge and confirm one another when they come into contact. Jesus appeared here, there, everywhere, and printed himself on the faith of his believers. We have to forgo any knowledge of the personal details or the chronology of these appearances, but we are given enough for us to realise how Jesus made himself known, the liturgical atmosphere in which he did so, and the manner in which he sent his disciples on their mission.

The gospels are not interested in people in a modern fashion; they work on the level of salvation, on God's level. For individuals come and go; but the gospel gives us the essentials. Here the essential is Jesus' appearance on the lakeside and the rich vein of teaching about Peter's primacy, a primacy acknowledged and confirmed over the rest of the apostles and the Church.

---

[1] OSCAR CULLMANN, *Peter, Disciple–Apostle–Martyr*, London, 1953, pp. 56–65, is convinced that Peter was the recipient of the first appearance of the risen Jesus, and that this confirmed his authority in the eyes of the other brothers.

13. The Universal Mission

THE MISSION OF THE APOSTLES

Mt	Mk	Lk

18 [18] I tell you solemnly,
whatever you bind on earth
shall be considered bound in heaven;
whatever you loose on earth
shall be considered loosed in heaven.'

THE UNIVERSAL MISSION OF THE APOSTLES

Mt	Mk	Lk 24:44-9

[44] Then he told them, 'This is what I
meant when I said, while I was still
with you, that everything written
about me in the Law of Moses, in the
Prophets and in the Psalms, has to
be fulfilled'.
[45] He then opened their minds to
understand the scriptures,
[46] and he said to them, 'So you see
how it is written that the Christ
would suffer and on the third day
rise from the dead,
[47] and that, in his name, repentance
for the forgiveness of sins would be
preached to all nations,
beginning from Jerusalem.

Jn 20:21–3   **Jn**

²¹ And he said to them again,
'Peace be with you.
As the Father sent me,   17 ¹⁸ 'As you sent me
                                          into the world,
so I am sending you.'   I have sent them
                                          into the world,'

After saying this
he breathed on them and said,
'Receive the Holy Spirit.

²³ For those whose sins you forgive,
they are forgiven;
for those whose sins you retain,
they are retained.'

Lk

⁴⁸ You are witnesses to this.

⁴⁹ And now I am sending down to you
what the Father has promised.

Stay in the city then,
until you are clothed
with the power from on high.'

APPEARANCE ON A MOUNTAIN IN GALILEE: UNIVERSAL MISSION

Mt 28:16–20   Mk

¹⁶ Meanwhile the eleven disciples set out for Galilee,
to the mountain where Jesus had arranged to
meet them.
¹⁷ When they saw him they fell down before him,
though some hesitated.
¹⁸ Jesus came up and spoke to them. He
said, 'All authority in heaven and on earth
has been given to me.
¹⁹ Go, therefore, make disciples of all the
nations; baptise them in the name of the
Father and of the Son and of the Holy
Spirit,
²⁰ and teach them to observe all the commands
I gave you. And know that I am
with you always; yes, to the end of time.'

Ac

1 ^{8b} ' . . . and then you will be my
witnesses not only in Jerusalem but
throughout Judaea and Samaria,
and indeed to the ends of the earth'.
⁴ When he had been at table with
them, he had told them not to leave
Jerusalem,
but to wait there
for what the Father had
    promised . . .
What you have heard me speak
    about'.

^{8a} 'But you will receive
power when the Holy Spirit
comes to you,'

Lk   Jn

APPENDIX TO MARK: UNIVERSAL MISSION

Mt   Mk 16:9–20

⁹ Having risen in the morning on the first day of the week,
he appeared first
to Mary of Magdala
from whom he had cast out seven devils.

¹⁰ She then went
to those who had been his companions,
and who were mourning and in tears,
and told them.
¹¹ But they did not believe her
when they heard her say
that he was alive
and that she had seen him.
¹² After this,
he showed himself
under another form
to two of them
as they were on their way
into the country.

¹³ These went back

and told the others,

who did not believe them either.
¹⁴ Lastly he showed himself to the Eleven themselves while they were at table. He reproached them for
their incredulity and obstinacy, because they had refused to
believe those who had seen him after he had risen.
¹⁵ And he said to them, 'Go out to the whole world;
proclaim the Good News to all creation.
¹⁶ He who believes and is baptised will be saved, he who
does not believe will be condemned.
¹⁷ These are the signs that will be associated with believers:
in my name they will cast out devils; they will have the
gift of tongues;
¹⁸ they will pick up snakes in their hands, and be unharmed
should they drink deadly poison; they will lay their hands
on the sick, who will recover.'
¹⁹ And so the Lord Jesus, after he had spoken to them,
was taken up into heaven: there *at the right hand of God
he took his place*,
²⁰ while they, going out, preached everywhere, the Lord
working with them and confirming the word by the signs
that accompanied it.

Lk	Jn
8 ² . . . Mary, surnamed the Magdalene, from whom seven demons had gone out	20 ¹⁸ So Mary of Magdala
	went
	and told the disciples
1	
	that she had seen the Lord . . .
24 ³ That very same day,	

two of them
were on their way
to a village
called Emmaus, . . .
³³ They set out that instant
and returned to Jerusalem . . .
³⁵ Then they told their story
of what had happened on the road . . .

     24:36–43   20:19–20

    24:51

THE ASCENSION

Mt   Mk   Lk 24: 5–53

⁵⁰ Then he took them out as far as
the outskirts of Bethany, and
lifting up his hands he blessed them.
Now as he blessed them,

he withdrew from them
and was carried up to heaven.

⁵² They worshipped him

and then went back to Jerusalem
full of joy;
⁵³ and they were continually in the
Temple praising God.

Ac   Jn

1 ⁹ As he said this

he was lifted up
while they looked on,
and a cloud took him
from their sight.
¹⁰ They were still staring
into the sky . . .

¹² So from the Mount of Olives . . .
they went back to Jerusalem . . .

In the mission appearances, Jesus encounters the whole group of the apostles and sends them out to conquer the world. Each of the four gospels has its own way of presenting this mission.

The narrative of John

On the evening of Easter Sunday, Jesus appears to the apostles. He shows them his hands and his side and says, 'Peace be with you'. Then he goes on, '*As the Father sent me, so I am sending you.*' *After saying this he breathed on them and said, 'Receive the Holy Spirit. For those whose sins you forgive, they are forgiven; for those whose sins you retain, they are retained.*' (Jn 20:21–3).

'As the Father sent me, so I am sending you' – this is the mission. The saying recalls several others: that Christ is delegated by the Father, and the apostles by Christ, is one of the themes of John's gospel. We must remember this phrase, since it defines our own apostolic mission: all of us, priests, religious and layfolk, who feel that we have been sent out by God to conquer the world, to extend the Church and bring mankind, our brothers, back to God, have been sent not by a mere human organisation – the Pope and the Church – but by Christ and through Christ by God himself. These are the links that make possible a profound theology of mission.

A missionary is an envoy of, one sent by, God. God sent his Son, the Son sends his disciples, and the disciples or their successors continue to send others. This is a great truth, for thus the mission is placed in a trinitarian framework – Father, Son and also Holy Spirit, since it is at this very moment that Jesus says to his apostles, 'Receive the Holy Spirit.' We are by grace called to know the Father as the Son knows him, and to love the Father and the Son as the Spirit does. This inward life, which is a programme for holiness, is accompanied by an outward life which is also of a trinitarian nature, since it is the Trinity, Spirit, Son and Father, which sends us out on our mission.

In the Bible, the Trinity is revealed to us first and foremost under this aspect of sending and mission, and not in terms of the ineffable relationship between the three persons themselves, of which theology tries to plumb the depths. In scripture the Word is revealed because God sends it to men to enlighten them and print his image on them. The Spirit is revealed as the breath that God sends into his creature to animate it, raise it and make it live. Thus, in the Bible, the Trinity is revealed to us under its aspect of something which is sent to us by God.

Our mission today exists in the same trinitarian framework, and we shall always derive benefit from remembering that we are envoys of the Holy Trinity. It is not a question only of those who are called by the actual name of missionary and go off to far-distant lands, but of any apostle, even in the suburbs of our cities. Every Christian must be a missionary, but he is not alone; the whole Church is with him, and behind the Church is the Trinity.

After this main point, there is another feature to be noticed in John – the giving of the Holy Spirit for the forgiving of sins. According to Luke, the Spirit is to come later, after Jesus has ascended to his Father; it is then that he will send his Spirit, on the day of Pentecost, and it is at Pentecost that the Church keeps the solemn festival of the giving of the Spirit.

How does it come about that, according to John, the Holy Spirit is given to the apostles on the very evening of Easter Day? This is really a false problem since there is no opposition between the Holy Spirit of John who pardons sins and the Holy Spirit of Luke who presides over the universal proclamation. They are two different aspects of the same infinitely rich reality, which is the breath, the power, of God.

John emphasises the inward and sanctifying aspect of the Spirit, who in fulfilment of the promises of the prophets comes to purify the soul of the sinner, to restore him to innocence and give him that justice, that life with God which is the life of Grace. It is the Spirit promised by Ezekiel (36:25-7), a promise renewed by Jesus in his discourse after the Supper, the Spirit who comes to the inward soul of every Christian to enlighten him, to remind him of the words of God, and to purify him by pardoning his sins.

Luke, on the other hand, in the story of Pentecost, is talking about the Spirit under his 'charismatic' aspect. It is the Spirit that God gives the faithful for the welfare of the Church as a whole, not now for inner holiness, but for outward action and the spreading of the gospel. The Acts of the Apostles and the epistles mention these gifts of the Spirit: – prophecy, apostolate, evangelisation, the gift of tongues, the gift of healing, leadership, etc., all the aptitudes that God grants his faithful to permit them to play their part within the body of the Church and to build up his kingdom. This is the aspect under which the Spirit is given at Pentecost, according to the narrative in the Acts, and that book goes on to show us the spreading of the gospel throughout the world, a narrative in which we see the Spirit come down upon the faithful and express itself, as at Pentecost, in marvellous gifts, the gift of speaking in tongues and with religious fervour, the gift of performing miracles such as the cures carried out by Peter and Paul. The Acts of the Apostles has even been called the gospel of the Holy Spirit. When Jesus has ascended to his Father, the Spirit continues his work, inspiring every Christian and giving him courage, power, and energy for the apostolate. He is the one who builds the Church and spreads it throughout the world.

These two aspects of the Holy Spirit are not opposed but complementary: on the one hand the Spirit sanctifies the inward heart of the individual, on the other his power causes the body of the Church to grow. So we should be wrong to use too material terms, to delimit in too human a fashion the profound reality of the Holy Spirit, and to set ourselves false problems like this one – when was the Holy Spirit given to the apostles, Easter evening or Ascension Day? He was given on both those days and on plenty of others as well.

This problem crops up again in the distinction between baptism and confirmation. Baptism confers the Holy Spirit as a sanctifying power, an inward force which animates the Christian with the Spirit of Christ and makes him live like Christ. Confirmation is the new Pentecost applied to each individual Christian and gives him the Spirit in such a way as to make an adult of him: he is to live no longer for himself alone like a child, but is to have a mission in the Church – even without being a priest or belonging to a religious order – the mission that every Christian has of working for the kingdom of God. Nor does the Spirit came only once, he has to come constantly, and we often say, 'Veni Sancte Spiritus'. This unique, ineffable and divine reality – his power, energy and light – descends on us under different aspects and at different times. Each of these descents of the Spirit must be welcomed; they are not to be opposed to one another but to be seen as mutually complementary; the more often they come, the more they should be welcomed.

One last thing remains to be noticed: the gift of forgiving sins links up with a saying that Jesus has already uttered during his life on earth; he has already promised this gift twice. Once, at Peter's confession at Caesarea, Jesus says, '*I will give you the keys of the kingdom of heaven: whatever you bind on earth shall be considered bound in heaven; whatever you loose on earth shall be considered loosed in heaven'* (Mt 16:19). In this context, it is a question of a power which is wider than that of forgiving sins, it is a power of decision. The expression 'binding and loosing', well known among the rabbis, refers not only to sins but to plenty of other matters. It includes both teaching and jurisdiction: asserting a doctrine or denying a heresy is 'binding and loosing'; to allow a custom, make a law, forbid something, is also 'binding and loosing'. It is in this general sense that Peter receives the power of the keys at Caesarea, a power not only to forgive sins but to make decisions about them. And it is on this that the Pope's power of jurisdiction is based, and that of the Church with him.

There is another occasion on which Jesus promises this gift, and (as the context indicates) with a more precise intention. Jesus is addressing all the apostles – not only Peter – on the subject of sins and faults within the community and of fraternal correction, and he adds, *'I tell you solemnly, whatever you bind on earth shall be considered bound in heaven; whatever you loose on earth shall be considered loosed in heaven'* (Mt 18:18). Through the apostles, Jesus is speaking to all bishops and all priests ordained by the bishops, who receive the power to forgive sins, and in this context, which is particularly concerned with sin, he uses the same expression 'binding and loosing'.

The same gift is presented here in John. After his resurrection, Christ fulfils the promise he has made during his life on earth. It could be described as the institution of the sacrament of penance in its final formulation.

In this passage, then (Jn 20:21-3), John offers us a profoundly trinitarian view of the Church's mission, and then shows us the action of the Spirit, who, through his inward gift and the power of forgiving sins, is going to guide the missionaries in their work.

The narrative of Luke

Like each of the synoptics, Luke adds new features which complete the portrait of the missionary.

Then he told them, 'This is what I meant when I said, while I was still with you, that everything written about me in the Law of Moses, in the Prophets and in the Psalms, has to be fulfilled'. He then opened their minds to understand the scriptures, and he said to them, 'So you see how it is written that the Christ would suffer and on the third day rise from the dead, and that, in his name, repentance for the forgiveness of sins would be preached to all the nations, beginning from Jerusalem.

You are witnesses to this. And now I am sending down to you what the Father has promised. Stay in the city then, until you are clothed with the power from on high' (Lk 24:44–9). This discourse of Christ's contains a definite echo of what Luke is to write in the Acts, which itself is a summary of the primitive catechesis. It is an outline of the apostolic witness, of the preaching which was the soul of the first mission of the apostles and which must continue to be the programme of mission for us in our own day.

Our task now is to distinguish the various elements that are presented here. They form a kind of ideal programme of mission, viz., the apostolic witness, the argument from scripture, the goal (which is repentance and the forgiveness of sins), and the objective (all nations of the earth).

The apostolic witness

The missionary's two instruments are witness and scripture. The apostle is by definition a witness; this is very clear in the Acts, where it is the quality above all required of apostles. When Judas has defected and the Eleven want to replace him, Peter says that they must choose someone who knew Jesus, lived with him and saw his resurrection – someone therefore who can bear witness (Ac 1:21–2). Matthias and Joseph Barsabbas are proposed and the lot falls to Matthias.

In his speeches, Peter, after announcing the fact of the death and resurrection of Christ, never fails to go on: and we are witnesses, we saw him, we lived with him, we ate and drank with him (Ac 2:32; 3:15; 5:32; 10:39–42; 13:31).

The main function of the missionary, to the end of time, is to be a witness, that is to say, to give, through the whole of his personal life, assurance that he has seen what he is reporting to others, that he is not speaking lightly, not offering teaching in which he does not himself believe. He is the surety for what he says. This might be thought difficult for those who have not lived through the events of the gospel. There are no longer any witnesses in one of the senses in which that word can be applied to the apostles. But the witness, even of the apostles, had much more to do with their faith than with the experience of the senses. True, they had seen Christ, but how many others had seen him too? The Jews of Jerusalem and of Galilee, Caiaphas, Pilate, all these saw him, lived alongside him, but they are not witnesses, because they had no faith, they had not surrendered

their lives, they had not that spiritual sight which goes beyond the
outward evidence of the senses – the appearance of Jesus as man, the
suffering on the cross – and penetrates to the underlying reality of the
saviour who rises from the dead to give life to the world. Real witnesses are those who have seen by faith.

The apostles are witnesses because they believe; the post-resurrection appearances show this. At the first glance, they do not
recognise Jesus, their physical eyes see nothing, they take him for the
gardener or a simple traveller; it is when they believe and their hearts
are opened that they become witnesses and the subjects of a spiritual
experience. On this level, we are their equals, since we too are able
to believe. We do not see the Lord with the physical eyes of the
body as they did; but by God's gift, the inward gift of faith, we see
with the same spiritual sight as they did. Humanly speaking, our
faith rests on their witness, on the word of the Church and on those
who have lived before us, but in the final analysis, as we know well,
our faith rests on the inward word of God.

Theological faith does not depend essentially on this or that
human word, on this or that argument proposed to it, it rests on the
veritas divina, on the word of God that resounds in our hearts and
makes us believe. This is why faith is a theological, a supernatural
virtue, a gift of grace which we are meant to use, but which can also
be lost through our own fault. This grace by-passes human experience; it exists in us, even though we have not had the experience
of the first witnesses. Just as much as the apostles, we can and must
be witnesses, we have to bring to our mission the living personal
faith of those who have encountered Christ. Peter and the apostles
encountered him on the roads of Galilee and Jerusalem, then in his
risen appearances; Paul on the road to Damascus. Each of us has
to have encountered him, not perhaps in a vision like that of the
Damascus road, but in the depths of spiritual experience. Each of us
who has been called to the Christian life, once our minds and hearts
have been roused to fervour, know that we have encountered Christ.
Please God it may not be a single and unique encounter, but that our
life may be one long meeting with Christ in faith. Only on these
conditions will our witness have any value in the eyes of the world.
Those we are speaking to will be quite easily able to tell whether
we are reciting something we have learnt by heart, like a street
vendor trying to dispose of his wares without really believing in
them himself. If we are only vendors, no one will believe us. But if

others feel that we live by what we preach, that we have encountered the object of our faith, that our whole life is given over to the Father, the Son and the Holy Spirit, then we shall be really effective witnesses and we shall be believed.

What the scriptures teach

Personal witness is not enough; to it there must be added, as Christ tells us, the scriptures, that is, the teaching of the Church, especially as enshrined in the Bible. Jesus here alludes to all the scriptures, the Old Testament with Moses, the prophets and the psalms, and the New, which is implicit in the understanding which Christians have of the Old. The New Testament, in fact, is nothing else but the experience of Christ as lived through by the first Christians and interpreted by them in the light of the Old; this new scripture completes and crowns the Old.

The scriptures, which had foretold Christ, and which relate his life – a message of faith – are the great argument that is to be used to convert the world. That is how Peter and Paul preached. In the Acts, each time that Peter preaches he quotes texts from the psalms or the prophets, he proves that Christ had to rise, that the Messiah could not remain dead, that his sufferings were prefigured in the Servant of Isaiah, etc. Paul does much the same: after listening to him, the Jews go and examine the scriptures to see if all these things had really been foretold (Ac 17:11).

So it should be for us too. We no longer live in the same Jewish atmosphere, and for this reason we have a tendency not to value the arguments from scriptures in the same way, and to content ourselves instead with theological conclusions deduced by others from the scriptures. What happens in the end is that all that the faithful get is a rather desiccated theological digest, made up of formulas taken from a nineteenth-century catechism. Today, especially, we feel that such teaching has got altogether too far from the original word of God. It is impossible to be content with the formulas of an out-of-date catechism. I am perfectly ready to believe that such a work contains the teaching of the Church, but surely it is better to go back to the real sources, the profounder teaching of the Church and its origins in scripture?

A return to the scriptures is taking place at this moment; it is something to be thankful for, since it responds to a deep desire of the soul. If in our generation people have this liking for scripture, it is because the jolts of contemporary life have brought a return to essential values. The limitations that nineteenth-century conventionality imposed on the mind have gone, and now in religion as in everything else there is a need to find the springs of life again. They were looking for the true, the 'existential' (as they say) as opposed to the 'essentialism' which plays about with abstract ideas and with concepts that those brought up on the catechism cannot understand. They want to return to living, concrete realities, for it is those ways that God spoke. This recall to the real has led all hearts back to the scriptures, since in them they find the flowering of God's action among men, and hear how he has spoken to us in a human, historical manner. Their minds are sick of shreds of doctrine withered like specimens in a book of plants; they are, as it were, turning to the open country to pick fresh flowers, and to the holy scriptures to discover a new understanding of their faith in them.

We must continue to drink from this spring, but equally we have to continue to work at it. The scriptures are not an enclosed garden; they are land which you have to know how to work to make it produce. You have to know how to avoid illusions, but anyone who discovers the inexhaustible riches of the word of God is well rewarded. Reading the Bible is not just an amusement, an occupation for a retreat, or a kind of 'spiritual reading' somewhat better than others; it is what can and must nourish our apostolate and the depths of our life. Christ tells us as much here, in this text of Luke: when our faith and our witness have been well nourished from the sources of the divine word, we shall be equipped and enabled to bring that faith to others.

The aim of the mission

Luke tells us also the aim of this mission: the apostle who comes with a faith nourished on the scriptures should win repentance and the forgiveness of sins. We find this in all the speeches in the Acts. Peter or Paul, once they have witnessed to the Passion and the resurrection and explained the scriptures, end with this conclusion: 'My brothers, be converted, repent, receive baptism and you will be forgiven' (Ac 2:38; 3:19; 5:31; 10:43; 13:38). This is the end that we must always have in view since it reaches the very foundations of life. The Christian mission will have no effect if it does not succeed in winning back men's hearts and revolutionising their lives. If it succeeds only in making Christian teaching better known and more interesting, it has achieved only a partial aim. For the result to be real, the word of God – the seed, as Jesus called it – must take root in the earth; the teaching which is given, the witness which is brought, must have a real impact on lives and souls, and they must be made to feel the need to change. Conversion and repentance are the *metanoia* demanded by the apostles in all their preaching. We must be inspired by the same desire, whoever it may be that we are speaking to, but we also have to learn to be gentle and circumspect, since souls are not to be treated with violence. Our human action alone cannot convert the heart, only God can bring it to take the final step. But our role as apostles, missionaries, witnesses, is to present a message of such urgency that the other person is brought to face the question and see the need to change. When our prayers, and perhaps our self-sacrifice, are added to this, and our whole spiritual life too, the grace of God will do its work. We must not be like one of those preachers of a new philosophical doctrine which tickles the ear, mentioned by St Paul (2 Tm 4:3). We have to stir men's hearts and change their lives.

The universality of the mission

Luke uses the following expression – '*All the nations, beginning from Jerusalem*' (Lk 24:47; cf. Ac 1:8). This has a very Lucan ring. In his works Jerusalem occupies a privileged position. His gospel begins in Jerusalem, in the Temple, with the vision of Zechariah, the father of the Baptist; again, the gospel of the Infancy ends in the Jerusalem Temple. When the infant Jesus is presented there, the aged Simeon hints at the programme of worldwide evangelisation and Mary is told about the coming sufferings and crisis within the chosen people. Jesus then goes to Galilee, and from there he comes back to Jerusalem; this last journey is recorded by all four gospels, but only Luke at the end of the narrative has Jesus tell them, '*Stay in the city then, until you are clothed with the power from on high*' (Lk 24:49). The last verse of his gospel reads, '*And they were continually in the Temple praising God*' (Lk 24:53).

After putting the Temple at the beginning and the end of his gospel, Luke gives it the same importance in the Acts of the Apostles. It is at Jerusalem that Jesus leaves his apostles and ascends into heaven; Pentecost, the first sermons, the first cures, all take place in the neighbourhood of the Temple. The Temple is, as it were, the cradle of the new-born Church; Christianity issues from the very centre of Judaism.

Luke is deeply conscious of the connection between the Old and the New Testaments, between the Jewish Temple chosen by God for centuries and the new worldwide expansion. There is a profound truth here that I want to develop with the help of Matthew.

The narrative of Matthew

Matthew says, *Meanwhile the eleven disciples set out for Galilee, to the mountain where Jesus had arranged to meet them* (Mt 28:16). This meeting place had been announced when they were walking to Gethsemane, and then again later by the angels at the empty tomb. But the mountain was not mentioned.

What mountain is it? I am certainly not able to point it out, and I doubt whether Matthew himself could have done so. The mountain is somewhat theological – not that it did not exist, but that we have to remember that for the Bible a mountain is a place where man raises himself towards God. Even in pagan religions the human mind felt the reality of this. It is enough to recall some of the heights on which sanctuaries were built: Carmel, where a votive offering has been found carrying a dedication to the god Carmel – possibly the very Baal with whose priests Elijah was in conflict; or, in Syria, Jebel Akra, Mt Cassius, where the ancients built a temple in honour of Baal Safon. In every country in the world, mountains are places where the human spirit feels itself close to the divine.

In the gospel, Jesus makes use of this law of human psychology: he climbs the mountain to call his disciples to him, to separate himself from the crowds and propound his spiritual teaching. So Matthew has got into the habit of conceiving the 'mountain' as a privileged place, and he hardly troubles to identify it. There is no really high mountain in Galilee; the Jebel Jermak, the highest in Palestine, rises to about 4,000 ft. Near the lake there are some small hills, among them the 'Mount of the Beatitudes' which, again, cannot be precisely identified. Here the same atmosphere prevails: to gather his people for a final meeting, Jesus summons them to a mountain in Galilee. It is useless to ask for greater precision.

What is important is that Matthew, alone besides John (Jn 21:1), tells us of an appearance in Galilee. Let us remind ourselves of the problem: Jesus had said, 'After my resurrection I shall go before you to Galilee' (Mk 14:28), and the angel had recalled these instructions (Mk 16:7). But Luke does not mention an appearance in Galilee and has even changed Mark's phrase to make the angel say, 'Remember what he told you when he was still in Galilee' (Lk 24:6). Even John, in chapter 20, records no Galilee appearance; everything happens in Jerusalem, on Easter Day and eight days later. Chapter 21, in which John does describe an appearance in Galilee, raises another problem, since we have been led to ask whether the miraculous haul of fish took place after the resurrection, or befroe it as Luke has placed it.

But Matthew is precise upon this point. To speak the truth, we have not yet succeeded, and perhaps, for lack of sufficient documentary evidence we shall never succeed in working out how the different appearances are related one to another. When did the disciples go back to Galilee? Before or after the appearances in Judaea? Most probably after, since according to Luke and John it is on the very day of the resurrection that Jesus appears at Emmaus and in Jerusalem. Forty days later they are again in Jerusalem for the ascension. Did they go back to Galilee in the meantime, and then return to Jerusalem? We may surmise that they did, but the texts are not exact enough to allow us to reconstruct a calendar of their movements.

It would be fitting that Jesus should have wished to manifest himself also in the place where the gospel saw the light, that is in Galilee; but we can say no more than that. Just as we have had to forgo detailed accounts of certain appearances which are only briefly mentioned, such as that to Peter, so here, too, we must learn to control our curiosity. God tells us what he wants us to know; we must learn to be silent and acknowledge our ignorance.

When they saw him they fell down before him, though some hesitated (Mt 28:17). This is surprising. How can it be that anyone still doubted at this moment? For this reason some commentators translate it differently, *those who had hesitated.* Matthew is alluding to previous hesitations; now they hesitate no longer, they fall down before him.

In my opinion this translation is incorrect; it does not respect the Greek. I prefer the meaning given by the first translation, 'though some hesitated'. Does this mean that now, at the last moment, after other appearances, they still hesitate? It is to be noticed that Matthew has not recorded any other appearance to the disciples. Each gospel follows its own line of thought. The last thing of the kind Matthew included was a brief account of the appearance to the women as they left the tomb; he described no appearances to the disciples in Judaea, at Emmaus or in Jerusalem. But he does know that, at the time of these appearances, not everyone believed; and this fact is important, for the disbelief with which they began in a way reinforces the value of their later conviction and faith. So, since he has not recorded any other appearance, Matthew includes this detail here. In this one appearance that he relates, he makes a kind of synthesis in which he gives a brief indication of everything, including the hesitations. In reality these hesitations belong to earlier appearances, but in the economy of Matthew's narrative it looks as if they still exist at the final meeting with Jesus.

Jesus came up and spoke to them. He said, 'All authority in heaven and on earth has been given to me' (Mt 28:18). This sentence seems to presuppose that Christ is in heaven, that he has taken possession of his throne. He is Christ the King, in the glory of his Father, and his power is universal. This appearance therefore suggests that Jesus has already ascended to heaven, and raises a problem to which we shall have to return later, to do with the ascension. The deepest meaning of the ascension is Jesus' entry into glory, and in this sense it took place on Easter Day itself, at the moment of the resurrection. We cannot admit an interval in Christ's own glorification, as though there had been a kind of intermediate state in which he had issued living from the tomb but was not yet glorified. This is inadmissible on theological grounds, and is shown to be false by texts such as this one. Jesus ascended to his Father immediately after his resurrection, as the text of John indicates (Jn 20:17). We shall see later why there is also an ascension on the Mount of Olives, but this latter is not Jesus' first entry into glory. Christ is in glory from the moment that he issues from death, from the very instant that the Holy Spirit gives life back to his being. Here, the text is perfectly clear: Jesus comes from that glory to reveal himself and tell them, 'I have all power.'

'Go, therefore, make disciples of all the nations' (Mt 28:19). I have translated as well as I can Matthew's expression, 'Render disciples to all the nations.' This is sometimes given as 'Teach all nations', but the Greek is more precise, 'Make disciples of all the nations', let all nations become disciples.

Here we run up against a fundamental problem. Jesus is sending his disciples out to conquer all the nations; Luke says the same, 'Proclaim to all nations'. But we know that during his earthly life Jesus did not preach to pagans, and in fact refused to do so. Thus, he told the apostles to go and preach, but to leave the pagans and the Samaritans alone (Mt 10:5). Jesus himself, when he was travelling in the neighbourhood of Tyre and Sidon, having left Palestine and its unruly crowds in order to teach his apostles, still did not preach to the foreign crowds. When a Syro-Phoenician woman asked him to heal her daughter, he answered, 'I was sent only to the lost sheep of the House of Israel' (Mt 15:24). This reply seems harsh; the poor woman continues to entreat him, 'Even the dogs eat the scraps . . .', Jesus cannot resist; he makes, so to speak, an exception and heals the child. Since Jesus was not willing to preach to the pagans how is it that he is now sending his apostles out to the pagan nations? What has happened to bring about this change of attitude?

The explanation is as follows[1]. During his life on earth, Jesus worked deliberately to bring about God's original plan. This design, announced by the prophets, was the salvation of the pagans *through Israel*. The whole Bible illustrates this plan of salvation. God chooses a people and applies himself to converting them; when he has converted and saved them, he will give them the Messiah in order to draw all humanity to this salvation in their wake; then the light will shine throughout the world. This doctrine is set out especially in the Book of Isaiah (see, for example, Is 2:1-5). Jesus tried loyally to apply this programme, to preach to his own people and shape Israel, leaving till later the universal dimension of salvation. But at this point man's free will intervened; God's plan was checked, for the people, speaking through its leaders, rejected his salvation. The plan however succeeded because a small minority, the 'remnant', consented. Nevertheless, in cold fact, the people of God, following their leaders, first in Palestine, then throughout the Diaspora, said no. Instead of accepting the light which was to shine out from Jerusalem over the world, Israel rejected it, and in that very city put her Messiah to death. Israel blocked God's plan, and God, who is all-knowing and all-powerful, allowed this to happen out of respect for human freedom. God knew that it would be so, yet man acted with full liberty.

Faced with this rejection, God and his Christ modified their plan: salvation would not now come to the nations through Israel, but directly. After the resurrection, Jesus deliberately changes his instructions and sends his apostles out on a worldwide mission – 'Go and preach to all nations'. In addition we should note, because it is important, that a nucleus of Israel did listen to the Word, to such good effect that after all it was Israel who gave the light to the world. The apostles who are going out to preach, and the whole primitive Church with them, are converted Israelites. In the communities where

[1] Cf. J. JEREMIAS, *Jesus' Promise to the Nations* (S.C.M. Press, 1958).

Paul preaches, he is to find small groups of Israelites who will accept
the Word. God's original plan is therefore to be carried out by them,
and it is through Judaism, through the Jewish scriptures, that the
pagans of Asia Minor, Rome and Greece come to know the gospel.

The refusal of the Messiah by the bulk of Israel hastened the
mission to the pagans and, so to speak, forced God's plan to take a
short cut. Look again at Paul's preaching in the Acts of the Apostles.
He begins by preaching to the Jews in their synagogues and says,
'We had to proclaim the word of God to you first, but since you have
rejected it, since you do not think yourselves worthy of eternal life,
we must turn to the pagans' (Ac 13:46). Even then, when he does
go to the pagans, it is not without a sideways glance, still apostolic,
at the Jews, as he states very clearly in the epistle to the Romans:
'I have been sent to the pagans as their apostle, and I am proud of
being sent, but the purpose of it is to make my own people envious
of you, and in this way save some of them' (Rm 11:13-14). When the
Jews see the pagans being converted, they will be converted in their
turn: Paul hoped that it would happen quickly, but it was not to be.
Yet the divine plan remains. Perhaps Israel will one day return
as a whole, when she at last understands that the Christian Church
and Christian salvation really fulfil her own ideal and her own
religion, when she decides to rid herself of a certain pharisaic legalism
which still has a hold on her people despite the liberation wrought by
Jesus Christ. The day when the Jews can get outside this absorption
in themselves and understand that the whole substance of their
faith is contained and developed in the Christian religion, when they
see the pagan world converted to the true God, they themselves, in a
kind of holy envy, will return. God's plan is wonderful, mysterious,
says St Paul (Rm 11:25, 33), but it will certainly be accomplished
in the course of the centuries. We are only little children and we
live only for a few minutes; God's designs are wholly beyond us.

So the worldwide mission entrusted to the apostles by the risen
Jesus unfolds according to a quite deliberate plan of God and his
Christ. In the gospel, Jesus often announced the summons to the
pagans through Israel's mediation; thus, after a cure, he said, 'Many
will come from east and west to take their places with Abraham and
Isaac and Jacob at the feast in the kingdom of heaven' (Mt 8:11).
Jesus always desired the salvation of the whole world, although he
was following the plan laid down by God.

Nevertheless, we must recognise that it was difficult for the first

Christians fully to understand this plan of salvation. Peter and James were Jews, and though they understood that the pagans were receiving the call, it took them longer to realise that they could be dispensed from the Mosaic law. We can see this in the Acts of the Apostles, particularly in the debates at the council of Jerusalem: according to some, 'Unless you have yourselves circumcised in the tradition of Moses you cannot be saved' (Ac 15:1). To which Peter's reply is, 'It would only provoke God's anger now, surely, if you imposed on the disciples the very burden that neither we nor our ancestors were strong enough to support?' (Ac 15:10). After a long discussion, and with the help of the Holy Spirit, it was decided that they should not bind pagan converts to observe the Mosaic law. This was not achieved without a struggle. Paul did a great deal to make this truth understood, and played his part in freeing salvation from those limitations which were preventing it from becoming universal. Once again, a clear statement of Jesus was only fully grasped and understood after much groping and with the help of the Holy Spirit.

Matthew continues, *'Baptise them in the name of the Father and of the Son and of the Holy Spirit'* (Mt 28:19). In actual fact, the apostles have been baptising since their original mission; moral conversion and forgiveness of sins are effected through baptism.

A problem is raised here by the formula, 'in the name of the Father and of the Son and of the Holy Spirit'. It is sometimes asked whether Jesus uttered it in that form at that moment, since it does not appear again in the Acts, where baptism is performed in the name of Christ. Some theologians, for example St Thomas,[1] admit that at the beginning the baptismal formula could have been only Christological and not trinitarian. The formula transcribed here by Matthew could correspond to liturgical usage in his time, that is about A.D. 70–80. Matthew must have recorded it spontaneously in the form into which it had developed. There is nothing in this to upset us. Something similar can be observed in the case of the sacramental words of the Eucharist, where the formulas recorded by the evangelists differ slightly according to the liturgical usage of the time; the churches then, just as they do now, used formulas which were different on the surface but identical in substance.

Thus Matthew would have written down the baptismal words in the formula used in his day. But we are not to conclude from this that Jesus did not reveal the Holy Trinity, or that the rite of baptism

[1] *Summa*, III, 66, 6, ad 1.

does not originate from him. 'The Father, the Son and the Spirit' is an expression which summarises his whole teaching, in saying after saying – 'My Father sends me', 'I come from my Father', 'I will give you my Spirit', and so on. If we question the literary form of the formula, it does not mean that we are casting doubt on Christ's revelation of the Trinity. The formula therefore may very well be slightly anachronistic and reflect ecclesiastical custom of the time.

Jesus goes on, ' . . . *and teach them to observe all the commands I gave you.*' (Mt 28:20). It is not enough to believe, not enough to repent and be baptised, it is necessary also to observe the commandments. One's whole life must follow one's faith. It is all very well to overturn the human heart and bring about the change in the convert's life; but the convert must also be given to understand that a whole new life is opening up in front of him that has to be led day by day. After the enthusiasm of conversion and the enlightenment of baptism there follows the ordinary life of every day with all its difficulties, in which the Christian ideal demands that we fulfil day after day what we have promised to God, and that we live that divine life which asks so many sacrifices of our human nature. Jesus demands of us baptism, conversion, enthusiasm inspired by the Spirit, yes – but he also demands the fulfilment of his commandments. This is often made clear by John: He who loves me is he who observes what I have commanded; he who does not observe what I have commanded does not love me. True love is that which day after day obeys.

'*And know that I am with you always; yes, to the end of time*' (Mt 28:20). These words put into another form what we have already seen in John with regard to mission by the Trinity. Christ, with his Father and his Spirit, takes possession of the missionary and is not going to abandon him for one instant. A missionary works for Christ and in his name; he must always remember this and guard against the folly of supposing that it is himself who speaks, himself who succeeds – he can do nothing unless he represents humbly the whole Trinity by whom he has been sent.

The narrative of Mark

The ending of the second gospel was not written by Mark himself, but it is a canonical text and is of interest for its own sake. It summarises the appearance to Mary of Magdala, the encounter with the disciples at Emmaus and the appearance to the Eleven in which Jesus reproached them for their unbelief (Mk 16:9–14).

Jesus then says, '*Go out to the whole world; proclaim the Good News to all creation* – here is the worldwide mission – *He who believes and is baptised will be saved; he who does not believe will be condemned*' (Mk 16:15–16). We can only understand this antithesis when we realise that it is a case of Semitic parallelism: it is a mistake to think that anyone who does not have explicit Christian faith and who has not been baptised will be condemned. We are not, as some people do, to cast into hell all who have not been baptised. It is possible to believe in Christ without knowing him, or with an imperfect knowledge, while at the same time living for God and for means of God's salvation with a loyal heart. In this case it is a question of implicit faith, like that of the men of the Old Testament, who believed in Christ, also without knowing him, and who were saved by him.

Baptism of desire applies to those loyal people who live for God, and who serve him as well as they can whether as Jews, Moslems, pagans or whatever they may be. If they are upright before God and do their best with the grace at their disposal, they are saved. We must not fall into the trap of imagining hell as very crowded. Myself I believe it to be sparsely inhabited, because the mercy of God is so great – and man's stupidity so great too – that a great deal of intelligence, will-power and obstinacy is needed to arrive at a state where one makes hell one's firm and final choice. Certain theologians think that at the end of our lives, after what appears to be death, there is an instant in which we go from one world to the other, in which we realise that this world is departing from us, and that we have to take sides for or against God; this is when the final choice is made, and God's grace is there urging us to choose well. If anyone then succeeds, because of a whole lifetime of sin and hatred, in saying 'No' to God, God on his part cannot do the impossible, but continues to respect the freedom even of him who wills damnation for himself. It is difficult to arrive at such a point; many cannot do it; even after a life of passion and debauchery, they utter from their hearts the saving cry, 'My God, have mercy on my madness'.

Hell is not a punishment decreed by God, as though God were some sort of inspector on the look-out for delinquents – 'You missed Mass one Sunday, you're damned'. Unfortunately there are people who do conceive hell in this way; and this is why others refuse to believe in its existence. God cannot inflict terrible punishments for trifling offences, he does not chase his creatures like that! This is to misunderstand the judgment of God. In this judgment it is not

God who punishes, but man who punishes himself in God's despite. The damned are those who in spite of all God's efforts succeed in rejecting him, in choosing against him; then, when the play is over, they understand their madness and rend themselves for ever – 'Fool that I was, I chose wrong'. The damned torture themselves – God has done everything he can to save them.

Indulgence, however, must not be taken too far. There are those who think that at the end of time there is to be a general amnesty[1]. It would be nice if there were, but this seems to me to be contrary to the faith. Following Christ, the Church teaches that since man is free the possibility exists of everlasting torment. Freedom and punishment go together. But this does not oblige us to believe that hell is crowded. The phrase, 'He who does not believe will be condemned', must be taken in its widest sense.

'*These are the signs that will be associated with believers: in my name they will cast out devils; they will have the gift of tongues; they will pick up snakes in their hands, and be unharmed should they drink deadly poison; they will lay their hands on the sick, who will recover*' (Mk 16:17–18). It is not difficult to recognise here the signs which are recorded in the gospel or in the Acts of the Apostles. The power *to cast out devils* has already been granted to the apostles by Jesus, in the gospel; and exorcisms also occur in Acts too (Ac 16:18). They will have *the gift of tongues:* This is the glossolalia which was experienced at Pentecost, and also when the Holy Spirit came down on Cornelius and a group of converts (Ac 10:44–6; 19:6). The announcement that *they will pick up snakes* reminds us of the story of Paul in Malta; Paul picks up a torpid viper in a bundle of sticks and the viper bites him without doing him any harm (Ac 28:3–5). Jesus had already told his disciples, 'I have given you power to tread underfoot serpents and scorpions . . . nothing shall ever hurt you' (Lk 10:19). *Drinking deadly poison without harm* is not mentioned in the gospel, but the first Christians told just such a story about Justus Barsabbas. Lastly, *the imposition of hands on the sick* is found both in the gospel and in the Acts of the Apostles.

It may be objected that Christians today do not perform marvels like these; does the same go for their mission? But in fact these concrete signs, described from a particular point of view at a particular epoch, are not to be expected of the present-day missionary, in what-

---

[1] Cf. W. MICHAELIS, *Versöhnung des Alls. Die frohe Botschaft von der Gnade Gottes*, Berne, 1950, and my review in *Exégèse et Théologie*, II, pp. 172–77.

ever country he is working. They were necessary at a time when paganism was very widespread and Christianity in its infancy; they are no longer necessary today.

The apostles were moved by a force from God that multiplied their powers tenfold, even in human affairs, and this force enabled them to accomplish things that man cannot do alone. In our personal, or in our community, lives, such signs exist but under another form. The various religious orders have had heroic beginnings, they were founded against every human possibility, in the face of resistance by political powers, in poverty. The work has risen out of nothing – the money arrived but no one knew from where – because God was behind it. Men and women have had a wholly unexpected success in their personal lives, for example the Curé d'Ars and others not naturally gifted, whose supernatural effectiveness and influence have far surpassed the simple means at their disposal. These are the real signs of the missionary. There is no need for poisons and serpents; the power of the Word of God in the Church, in the missionary, in the Christian, is the only sign to be desired. It is not for us to work miracles, but there is wisdom and prudence in relying on the power of God, and marching ahead without being faint-hearted.

The Ascension[1]

This last act of Jesus is recorded by Luke and Mark. *And lifting up his hands he blessed them. Now as he blessed them, he withdrew from them and was carried up to heaven* (Lk 24:50–1). Mark says, *And so the Lord Jesus, after he had spoken to them, was taken up into heaven: there at the right hand of God he took his place* (Mk 16:19).

According to Luke this event takes place on the evening of Easter Sunday. There is no interval in Luke's account; the disciples leave for Emmaus and return, Jesus appears in the Upper Room, shows them his hands, eats with them, speaks to them and charges them with their mission, then he leads them out towards Bethany and ascends into heaven. Everything happens on Easter Day; there is no indication that any of the action takes place later. In Acts, however, the Ascension is said to take place forty days later (Ac 1:3). Mark gives no precise date. Which are we to choose?

The earliest Christian theologians place the ascension of the Lord on Easter Day itself. Theologically this is the only possible solution.

[1] Cf. P. BENOIT, 'Ascension', in *Revue Biblique*, LVI, 1949, pp. 161–203; reprinted in *Exégèse et Théologie*, I, pp. 363–411.

Jesus does not wait in a cave in Jerusalem for the door of heaven to be opened. From the very instant that he issues from death, he enters into Life. What are we to make, then, of the ascension on the Mount of Olives? It is the final departure. Jesus who has ascended into heaven chooses to come down again – these are very clumsy expressions, God's world is not a world like ours, it has other dimensions – for a period of appearances. He lives in another world, but reveals himself still from time to time in this one in order to give proof that he is living, and to instruct and encourage his faithful. Luke mentions a period of forty days, a figure which seems perfectly plausible.

After this space of time, on the Mount of Olives along the Bethany road, Jesus leaves his disciples and makes it plain that he is leaving them for good. Luke does not set out to describe an emotional scene, nor, like the apocryphal writings, to paint a stormy picture of Jesus ascending in the midst of prostrated angels. He remains very discreet, only underlining two or three features, taken from the Old Testament, which signify the entrance into glory, into the world of God. Cloud (Ac 1:9) is the vehicle necessary for the ascent to heaven; God rides the clouds and comes down, according to the psalms (Ps 104:3); the witnesses in the Book of Revelation go up on a cloud (Rv 11:12); according to Paul (1 Th 4:17) those who are still alive at the Parousia will be carried up on clouds. Luke therefore says that Jesus goes up on a cloud, to show that he is going from earth to heaven. The two angels are there (Ac 1:10–11) to give a theological explanation of the scene – he has gone, he is no longer among you, he will come back at the end of time. The physical details of the scene are of minimal importance, Luke is not giving us a journalist's account but a piece of theological teaching: Jesus has left his apostles for ever, in the sense of those physical appearances at the Church's birth. He has disappeared from their eyes and is not to return until the Parousia. This is what we are meant to understand by the ascension at the Mount of Olives, though we know that the real ascension, in its deepest sense of the entrance into glory, took place immediately after the resurrection.

The last sentence of Luke's gospel is one which we might take as a programme for our lives. *They worshipped him and then went back to Jerusalem full of joy; and they were continually in the Temple praising God* (Lk 24:52-3). After meditating on these pages of the gospel, we should, like the apostles, give ceaseless and joyful praise to God in his Temple, in his Church and in our souls.